PSYCHOLOGY LIBRARY EDITIONS: COGNITIVE SCIENCE

Volume 20

MEMORY

MEMORY

Phenomena, Experiment, and Theory

ALAN J. PARKIN

Routledge
Taylor & Francis Group

LONDON AND NEW YORK

First published in 1993 by Blackwell Publishers Ltd.
Reprinted in 1999 by Psychology Press Ltd.

This edition first published in 2017
by Routledge
2 Park Square, Milton Park, Abingdon, Oxon OX14 4RN

and by Routledge
711 Third Avenue, New York, NY 10017

Routledge is an imprint of the Taylor & Francis Group, an informa business

British Library Cataloguing in Publication Data
A catalogue record for this book is available from the British Library

ISBN: 978-1-138-19163-1 (Set)
ISBN: 978-1-315-54401-4 (Set) (ebk)
ISBN: 978-1-138-63915-7 (Volume 20) (hbk)
ISBN: 978-1-315-63735-8 (Volume 20) (ebk)

Publisher's Note
The publisher has gone to great lengths to ensure the quality of this reprint but points out that some imperfections in the original copies may be apparent.

Disclaimer
The publisher has made every effort to trace copyright holders and would welcome correspondence from those they have been unable to trace.

Memory

Phenomena, Experiment, and Theory

Alan J. Parkin

Psychology Press
a member of the Taylor & Francis group

First published 1993, reprinted 1993 and 1995 by Blackwell Publishers Ltd

Reprinted 1999 by Psychology Press, a member of the Taylor & Francis group

Psychology Press Ltd, Publishers
27 Church Road
Hove
East Susssex, BN3 2FA
UK

British Library Cataloguing in Publication Data
A CIP catalogue record for this book is available from the British Library

ISBN 0-86377-632-9 (pbk)

Printed and bound in the UK by MPG Books Ltd, Bodmin, Cornwall

Contents

For Frances

Preface

In 1987 I published a book called Memory and Amnesia. Part of the book was an overview of basic research issues in human memory. I have subsequently discovered that those opening chapters have been used quite a lot for introductory teaching, and this has prompted me to write this more extensive text, which is aimed primarily at more advanced undergraduates and postgraduates. Inevitably my book covers material dealt with elsewhere, but I have gone to some lengths to include topics which are typically given less coverage. In particular I have laid some emphasis on what one might term the 'Toronto school' that is, the work of theorists such Craik, Schacter, and Tulving – as well as providing accounts of memory development and aging – areas usually avoided by textbooks on memory. Also, as a reflection of my own interests, I have included a substantial amount of neuropsychological material.

I would like to thank John Gardiner, Jane Oakhill, and Josef Perner for their comments on parts of this book, as well as the many students whose comments over the years have helped shape my approach to the subject. I would also like to thank Ann Doidge, Yumi Hanstock, and Sylvia Turner for help with production. I am also most grateful to Jean van Altena for her detailed and extremely helpful copy-editing. Finally, my deepest thanks to Frances Aldrich, not only for suggesting the cover illustration, but for putting up with my preoccupations while writing this.

I hope those who read this book will experience some of the enjoyment and fascination with human memory that has sustained my interest in the subject for the last twenty years.

Alan Parkin
Brighton, September 1992

1

The Present and the Past

To remember is to live.

Martin Buber

In 1953 a young man was admitted to a Montreal neurological clinic for what was later described as 'frankly experimental' brain surgery. The man, who has become known to the scientific world as HM, was suffering from intractable epileptic seizures, and it was agreed that the only remaining option for treatment was to remove the regions of the brain where the seizures arose. The operation involved **temporal lobectomy,** in which parts of both the left and the right temporal lobe were surgically excised. In one important way the operation was a success, because HM's epileptic seizures were now controllable by drugs; but the operation also had a dramatic and wholly unexpected side-effect – HM became **amnesic.**

HM is still alive at the time of writing, but remembers little of the personal or public events that have occurred during the last 40 years (see Ogden and Corkin, 1991; Parkin, in press). Immediately after his operation HM lived with his parents, but his father died in 1967, and his mother in 1977. HM has lived in a nursing home since 1980, but in 1986 he thought that he was still living with his mother, and he was unsure about whether his father was still alive or not. He has learned only a handful of new words, and prominent public events like the Vietnam War or the Watergate scandal mean little to him. It is not without reason that HM says: 'Every day is alone, whatever enjoyment I've had, whatever sorrow I've had.'

At first sight 'amnesia' (literal meaning: without memory) seems an appropriate characterization of HM's condition, but further observation suggests that it may be inaccurate. For HM can still speak and understand language, and he has retained the various skills he acquired before his illness. He also has reasonable recall of events that happened in his early life, but less recall for the years immediately before his operation. Another indication that HM has preserved some memory function is that he is **conscious**.

Memory and Consciousness

For most of us memory is what allows us to recall things from the past – events that happened hours, days, or months ago. Few us of would concede, without some reflection, that being conscious is, itself, an act of memory. Consider hearing the sentence 'The sun, made hazy by the thin cloud, shone on the tin roof.' You perceive it as a whole, part of what you regard as the **present** moment. Yet, when we examine what must have happened in order for you to understand the sentence, we find that you must have stored the first part of the sentence, dealt with the relative clause, and then linked it with the final clause. This is a process that occurs across time, so the system underlying conscious awareness must itself depend on some form of memory.

The idea that conscious experience requires memory is not new. In his *Principles of Psychology* William James (1890) called the memory system supporting consciousness **primary memory**, to distinguish it from **secondary memory**, which comprises our permanent record of the past. James suggested that primary memory be thought of as 'the rearward portion of the present space of time', rather than the 'genuine past'. An important corollary of primary memory was that its contents were highly accessible and that it required little effort to retrieve them. By contrast, retrieving the contents of secondary memory required a deliberate, effortful act.

William James was the most prominent psychologist of his time, and was read widely during the latter years of the nineteenth century and the first half of the twentieth. However, his ideas about memory did not start to influence experimental psychology until the 1960s. This extraordinary delay can be attributed to the direct influence of **behaviourism** (which we will consider in more detail in chapter 6). The behaviourists believed in a purely objective approach to the explanation of behaviour, and they rejected any theoretical concepts that embodied subjective elements. The concept of consciousness, which was critical to James's account of primary memory, is purely subjective, so it is perhaps not surprising that the behaviourists showed little interest in James's important insight into human memory.

Experimental Method in the Study of Human Memory

Before considering any experimental research into human memory, we need to examine the rationale underlying the various techniques used. The dominant approach to human memory research stems from the tradition established by Hermann Ebbinghaus (1885). Ebbinghaus took the view that human memory could not be investigated rigorously unless every effort were made to exclude the influence of extraneous factors on the outcome of experiments. He realized that a major contaminating factor could be the prior knowledge that subjects bring to an experiment. Subjects might exhibit different amounts of remembering simply because they knew differing amounts about the material they were required to learn before the experiment started.

To solve this problem, Ebbinghaus suggested the use of nonsense syllables as **target** stimuli in memory experiments. These would be unknown to the subjects, and thus any differences in the memory for these items under different conditions would represent a genuine property of the memory system. Ebbinghaus conducted most of his research on himself. His basic technique involved repetition of a list of nonsense syllables until he could recall it perfectly. In one classic experiment he examined his rate of forgetting by examining how easily he could relearn a list after different time intervals. Figure 1.1 shows the amount of savings in relearning after different retention intervals. At first, forgetting is rather rapid, but after about 8 hours further forgetting occurs at a relatively slow rate.

The methodological approach developed by Ebbinghaus still dominates experimental work on memory (e.g. Young, 1985), but not all psychologists are convinced that this is the right course. Their objection is that the use of nonsense syllables and other meaningless stimuli to investigate memory lacks any **ecological validity**; for human beings do not, in real life, ever have to learn nonsense, so theories derived from experiments using this method have little or no value.

An alternative approach, first put forward by Bartlett (1932), is that

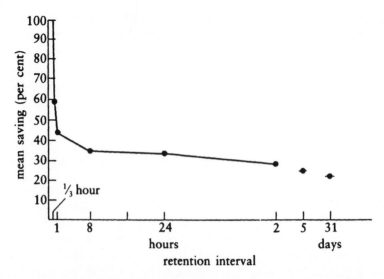

Fig. 1.1. Forgetting rate, as measured by Ebbinghaus. From Baddeley, 1976, p. 8. Reproduced with the permission of Harper and Row Publishers.

human memory can be properly understood only by getting subjects to learn and recall material that means something to them. The problem with this approach is that it introduces many of the extraneous factors that Ebbinghaus tried to avoid. A very striking example of how the recall of 'real' memories can mislead is provided by the unique case of John Dean.

John Dean was an aide to Richard Nixon at the time of the Watergate scandal, and was party to many conversations relating to the infamous cover-up. Dean produced extensive accounts of conversations with the President and his aides, and his facility for recalling details was so impressive that some reporters dubbed him 'the human tape recorder'. Unknown to Dean at the time, the conversations he was describing were being secretly recorded, thereby providing a basis on which his apparently amazing memory could be evaluated.

Neisser (1982) examined the relationship between Dean's testimony and the recordings. Far from being accurate, Dean's testimony was found to contain many inaccuracies; but it would be unfair to describe it as dishonest. Rather, it seems to have been based on what Neisser termed 'repisodes' – statements that are essentially correct but are not a literal account of any one event. Furthermore, Dean added an egocentric flavour to these accounts so as to enhance his apparent role in the affair.

The case of John Dean is extreme, but it illustrates the ability of human subjects to distort and bias the retrieval of memories that are meaningful to them. There are certainly occasions when the study of bias and distortion in memory are of major importance (e.g. inaccuracies due to racism); but, when it comes to producing experimental evaluations of theories, the control offered by the Ebbinghaus tradition is still favoured by most investigators.

Although nonsense syllables are not used very often now, experimenters still rely heavily on techniques involving the learning of 'meaningless' material, such as lists of unrelated words. There are a number of reasons for this. First, current human memory research derives from the behaviourist tradition, in which control of stimulus variables was an absolute principle. Second, this kind of experimentation lends itself more easily to the development of theories. Later we will see how certain theories of memory are tied very closely to the use of verbal stimuli as memory items. However, research into more meaningful aspects of memory is also carried out. There is, for example, active research into autobiographical memory – the way people organize and retrieve information about their personal past (Conway, 1990).

Primary and Secondary Memory Revisited

Waugh and Norman (1965) were impressed with James's idea that remembering from primary memory was a virtually effortless experience, and set out to investigate this using the **probe digit task**. This involved the subject listening to a sequence of 16 digits which was then followed by a probe digit. The subject's task was to name the digit that occurred after the probe. Thus in the sequence *5824972537196435* 6 the correct answer is 4.

Figure 1.2 shows that as the number of items occurring after the probe digit increased, performance on the probe task became poorer, declining at a steeper rate with five or fewer intervening items. The much better performance when only a few items intervened between the probe and the target was attributed to the items still being in primary memory and thus very easy to recall. The change in the gradient was taken as indicating the transition from primary to secondary memory, and its occurrence at the five-item point provided the first empirical demonstration of separate primary and secondary memories and the first estimate of primary memory capacity.

An important feature of the probe digit task is that it prevents subjects from engaging in **rehearsal**. This term describes the natural human

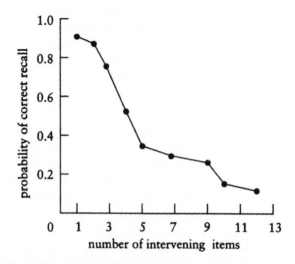

Fig. 1.2. Performance on the probe digit task. Adapted by Gregg (1986) from Waugh and Norman (1965), p. 91. Reproduced with the permission of Routledge.

tendency to repeat information when trying to remember it. Waugh and Norman assumed that the amount of rehearsal an item received directly influenced the probability of its entering long-term store. Preventing rehearsal enabled them to examine two competing theories of why information was lost from primary memory. They distinguished between a time-based **decay** process in which new memory traces deteriorated with time and a **displacement** process in which the contents of primary memory were retained until displaced by new information. To distinguish these theories, they examined performance on the probe digit task at different rates of presentation. Because rehearsal was prevented, they could assume that items passed into memory in an orderly fashion and that any failure to remember items could not be attributed to the recycling of earlier items due to rehearsal. They found that variations in presentation rate still produced results similar to those shown in figure 1.2. This supported the displacement theory, because if decay were responsible for forgetting, the effect of intervening items should have been more pronounced at slower presentation times.

Testing HM's Primary Memory

Wicklegren (1968) became interested in HM, and, in particular, was curious to know how HM performed on a task assumed to require only primary memory. He employed a similar but easier version of the probe digit task used by Waugh and Norman. Following an auditory signal, HM was shown a sequence of eight digits followed by a single test digit. His task was to decide whether or not the digit had been in the list. His performance was very accurate, and varied little as a function of the test digit's position in the list, thus suggesting that his primary memory function was normal.

Further evidence of normal primary memory in HM can be found by looking at his ability to do the **digit span task**. This task measures the ability to repeat a random series of numbers in the correct order immediately after seeing or hearing them. This task is widely assumed to measure our span of awareness, and normal subjects behave very consistently on the task, scoring an average of seven plus or minus two (Miller, 1956). HM's digit span has varied a little over the years, but when last evaluated, it was seven, thus indicating normal primary memory.

HM's case is not unique, and psychologists have studied many other patients with amnesia. Figure 1.3a shows the performance of a range of different amnesic patients on verbal and non-verbal memory span tasks, and, in every case, their performance is well within the normal range. This stands in marked contrast to their extremely poor ability on tests requiring the retention of information over longer periods of time (figure 1.3b). With evidence like this, there can be little doubt that what we have so far called primary memory exists independently of the secondary memory that allows us to retain information over longer periods of time.

The Importance of Neuropsychology

Already in this chapter we have twice referred to data from a brain-damaged subject as evidence for a particular theory about the organization of normal memory. Before drawing on this type of evidence any further, it might be wise to look at the logic underlying the use of this sort of evidence. K. Craik (1943) writes: 'In any well-made machine one is ignorant of the working of most of the parts – the better they work the less we are conscious of them ... it is only a fault which draws attention to the existence of a mechanism at all.'

This quotation appears at the beginning of Ellis and Young's influential book *Human Cognitive Neuropsychology* (1988), and it neatly summarizes the rationale for what has become known as 'cognitive neuropsychology'. Basically, cognitive neuropsychology assumes that the

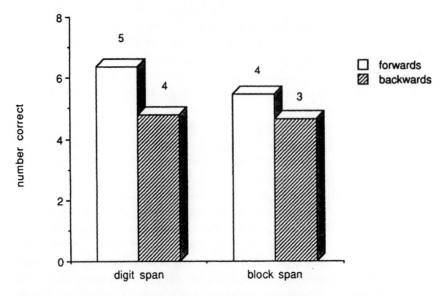

Fig. 1.3a. Performance of amnesic patients on digit span and block span tests. Block span is a non-verbal equivalent of digit span. Forward span requires the subject to reproduce items in the same order as the experimenter. Backward span requires the subject to reproduce them in reverse order. The numbers indicate the minimum score within the normal range.

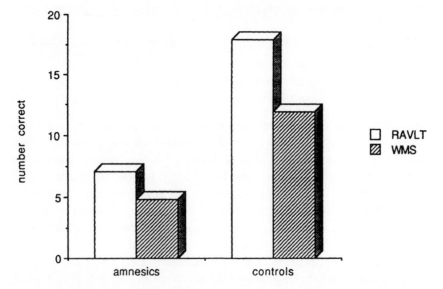

Fig. 1.3b. Performance of amnesic patients and controls on two tests of longer-term retention, *The Rey Auditory Verbal Learning Test* (RAVLT) and *The Wechsler Memory Scale* (WMS). Adapted from Corkin et al. (1985), pp. 26–7. Reproduced with permission.

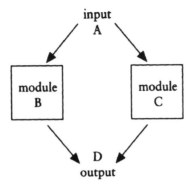

Fig. 1.4. Hypothetical modular system in which the input A can give rise to the output D via processing by either of two intervening modules.

various components of cognition, including memory, are spatially distributed within the brain and that, furthermore, each of these mental functions is **modular**. A modular system is one in which several components interact to perform a function, but each component, or **module**, is functionally autonomous – i.e. it can continue to operate if other modules cease to work for any reason. When the brain is damaged, either by accident or by illness (so-called natural experiments), it is assumed that modules may become dissociated from each other in a meaningful way and thereby reveal something about the underlying organization of the system.

Consider the hypothetical case illustrated in figure 1.4. Here an input A can give rise to an output D via two modules, B and C. It is assumed that these two modules achieve the output in different ways, but under normal circumstances it is not possible to observe the independent operation of these two modules, and so their separate existence is not proved. However, if we were to observe two brain-damaged patients producing output D, but in different ways, we would have evidence that two processes were involved, and by analysing the patients' behaviour in detail, we might gain an insight into how each of the modules works.

When the pattern of behaviour consistent with B intact and C inactive and vice versa is observed, we have what is known as a **double dissociation**, which indicates that a particular function has two components, each of which can operate independently of the other. When we observe a dissociation of one kind only – i.e. evidence that B is intact and C inactive but *not* vice versa – we have a **one-way dissociation**.

Double dissociations constitute a more compelling basis for arguing that a system comprises several functionally independent modules, but one-way dissociations, if observed frequently, are also considered good evidence for modularity. The evidence from patients like HM is one such case, for preserved primary memory in the presence of impaired secondary memory is regularly observed in amnesic subjects, which provides a strong argument for separate memory systems – despite the fact that secondary memory without primary memory cannot be observed because a patient in this condition would be unconscious.

Data from neuropsychological studies also provide test cases for psychological theories, in that if a theory cannot explain why a patient's behaviour has broken down in a particular way, then the theory must be wrong. Within neuropsychology, however, there is some debate as to whether just one instance of a brain-damaged subject behaving inconsistently with a theory is sufficient to reject the theory. Some argue that neuropsychological data from one subject is insufficient to rule out a sampling error, whereas others take the opposite view by claiming that only individual neuropsychological cases are valid evidence. We will not debate this issue further here, except to note that the neuropsychological patients described in the pages that follow all have deficits that have been observed in several different patients.

The 'Multistore' Model of Memory

The 1960s saw a massive growth in the use of computers and increased public awareness of how computers worked. Computers are essentially large databases that are operated on by a central processing unit. This unit represents the 'workspace' of the computer – the place where new information is inputted, existing information retrieved, and decisions involving the database executed. Psychologists were quick to see a similarity between this arrangement and James' model of memory, with primary memory resembling the central processing unit and secondary memory representing the database. This led directly to Atkinson and Shiffrin's (1968) **multistore model**, which can be seen, conceptually, as an extension of the concept of primary and secondary memory as developed by Waugh and Norman (see figure 1.5).

The model depicts memory as entailing the flow of information between three interrelated **stores**. New information first enters the **sensory store**. This is an extremely transient storage system which retains information about the pattern of sensory stimulation. Sensory storage of visual information is known as **iconic memory**, and its discovery arose from experiments by Sperling (1960). Subjects were presented with visual

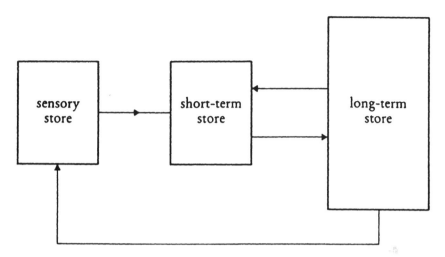

Fig. 1.5. The multistore model of memory. Adapted from Atkinson and Shiffrin (1968), p. 93.

arrays comprising three rows of four random letters for very brief periods (e.g. 50 milliseconds). In the **whole report** condition, subjects had to report as many letters as possible; typically, they reported only four or five letters correctly. In the **partial report** condition, a tone occurred after the display had terminated, indicating which of the three rows should be reported. Performance in the partial report condition was almost perfect, provided the delay between the end of the display and the tone did not exceed 500 milliseconds.

The fact that subjects could report the content of any row accurately suggests that they had more information about the array available than was indicated by performance in the whole report condition. This **partial report advantage** was attributed to the operation of iconic memory, and the disappearance of this advantage at intervals greater than half a second indicated that storage in this memory system was extremely short-lived. Although evidence such as this indicates the existence of iconic memory, its function is less clear. Some people have argued that it serves no function, whereas others have suggested that it is essential for the early stages of visual analysis.

The auditory equivalent of iconic memory is **echoic memory.** The need for a store of this kind is evident from the nature of the various sounds we recognize. Phonemes in speech, for example, are often identifiable only from the combination of perceptual cues that occur at different points in time. Many types of evidence point to the existence of this store, but a particularly clear example is provided by Howell and Darwin (1977). They measured subjects' response times in judging whether two sounds were the same phoneme. On some trials the two phonemes were acoustically identical, but on others there were slight acoustic differences. Same judgements were found to be faster for phonemes that were acoustically similar, but only when the interval between the two phonemes was less than 800 milliseconds. This finding indicates that subjects are able to retain information about the detailed perceptual qualities of the stimulus but, as in the case of iconic memory, the memories formed are of very short duration.

Information in sensory store then passes into **short-term store (STS)**. This is analogous to primary memory in that it represents the locus of conscious mental activity. The activities of STS are represented as various **control processes** which can be brought to bear on information in response to specific requirements. These control processes also determine the contents of STS, in that the information currently being processed can be displaced by new information appropriate to the task currently being undertaken. Atkinson and Shiffrin stressed the importance of rehearsal in the transfer of information from STS to permanent storage, a structure which they termed **long-term store (LTS)**. In addition, they acknowledged the importance of **encoding** as a factor in memory functioning. Any memory system must store information in terms of some form of code. Just as a telephone system transforms your voice into an electromagnetic wave and then back into speech at the other end, human memory must convert information into a code and then convert this code back into a record of the information when remembering is required. Understanding encoding is therefore crucial to our explanation of how memory operates.

Encoding Differences

Investigations of encoding in human memory led to the view that STS and LTS might be distinguished by the type of code they used. As we noted earlier, memory researchers commonly use words as stimuli. One reason for this is that words have three distinct **encoding dimensions** – i.e. types of information that could serve as a basis for a code:

Orthographic – the pattern of letters comprising the word
Phonological – the sound of the word
Semantic – the meaning of the word

A number of studies suggested that STS used phonological coding. Conrad (1964) investigated the ability of people to repeat back, in the correct order, visually presented sequences of letters that, phonologically, were either confusable (e.g. CTVG) or non-confusable (e.g. XVSL). He found that phonologically confusable strings were more difficult to remember, even when potential confounding influences of visual similarity were controlled for. This effect, known as the **phonological confusability effect**, suggests that a phonological code is the basis on which subjects remember words in an immediate memory task.

Conrad's findings were extended by Baddeley (1966a), who showed that phonological confusability effects also occurred when subjects had to repeat back immediately sequences of similar-sounding words (e.g. 'mad', 'map', 'man'), as compared with unrelated sequences (e.g. 'pen', 'dog', 'sky'). However, confusability effects did not occur when semantically related word strings (e.g. 'huge', 'great', 'big') were used. In a subsequent experiment Baddeley (1966b) examined the effects of phonological and semantic confusability on delayed recall, and found the reverse result: namely, that phonological confusability had no effect on recall, whereas semantically confusable word strings were recalled more poorly than unrelated word strings.

These findings led to the view that STS and LTS might be distinguished in terms of encoding differences, with STS being based on a phonological code, and LTS on a semantic code. Although consistent with the data, this theory could not possibly be correct. For if true, it predicts that we will not immediately understand anything we see, including this sentence. Presumably this is not the case. Added to this, much of the information that enters STS cannot be readily translated into a phonological code, yet we are still able to remember it. Consider the human face. People are very good at recognizing pictures of unfamiliar people even if they have previously been shown a photograph of them for only a few seconds. This is nowhere near enough time to describe the face verbally, and even if it were, there is good evidence that the description is irrelevant to subsequent recognition performance (Chance and Goldstein, 1976).

We are thus led to reject the idea that STS could be based solely on phonological coding. It must make use of semantic coding as well, thereby rendering it indistinguishable from long-term store as regards coding. At this point you may be wondering why I have raised the issue of encoding differences at all, since, as a means of differentiating STS and LTS, the idea seems fatally flawed. The reason is that the phonological confusability effect turns out to be of considerable interest for other reasons, which we will turn to in chapter 6.

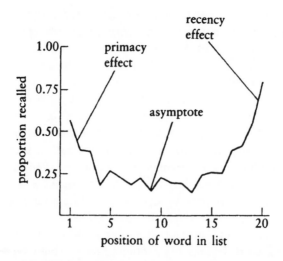

Fig. 1.6. Typical finding of a free recall experiment, showing the three components of the serial position curve. Adapted from Glanzer and Cunitz, 1966, p. 354. Reproduced with the permission of Academic Press.

The Serial Position Curve

The most systematic body of evidence favouring the idea of STS and LTS comes from experiments using the **free recall task**. This technique involves the serial presentation of items, usually words, for about two seconds each. After the last item, the subject is asked to recall the items in any order. The subject's recall is then plotted as a function of each item's position in the list. The resulting **serial position curve** has a characteristic shape (see figure 1.5), and can be divided into three portions: **recency** refers to the high level of recall found for the last few items in the list; **primacy** to enhanced recall of the first few items; and the **asymptote** describes the low performance in the middle of the curve. A number of theorists (e.g. Glanzer and Cunitz, 1966) proposed that recency reflected the 'effortless' output of STS, whereas recall of items from earlier in the list took place from LTS.

   These serial position effects were not sufficient to support the STS/LTS dichotomy, however. One could argue, for example, that more recent items were more strongly represented and that this is why they were remembered more easily. In order to prove that the recency portion of the serial position curve arises from a different store from that responsible for recall over the rest of the curve, it is necessary to demonstrate **functional double dissociation**. If different parts of the curve

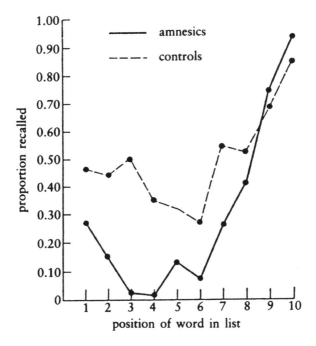

Fig. 1.8. Serial position curves of amnesic and control subjects. Adapted from Baddeley and Warrington, 1970, p. 179. Reproduced with the permission of Academic Press.

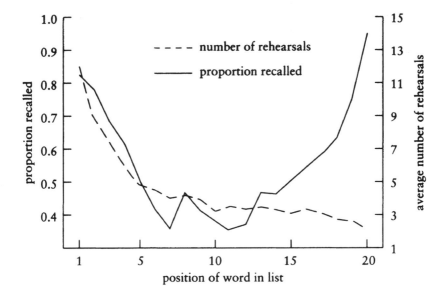

Fig. 1.9. The relationship between the serial position curve and the number of times each word was rehearsed. Adapted from Rundus, 1971, p. 66. Reproduced with the permission of Academic Press.

serial position curve there is a positive relationship between the two variables: the more an item was rehearsed, the better it was remembered. In the recency portion, however, no such relationship was found.

Rundus's result fitted nicely with the STS/LTS idea. The positive relationship between rehearsal and recall in the earlier parts of the list supported the view that transfer to LTS depended critically on the conscious recycling of information. Furthermore, the reason for the primacy effect appeared to be that items early on the list received more rehearsal. The absence of any correlation between rehearsal and recall of the most recent items was because these had not had sufficient time to be incorporated in the rehearsal process and depended entirely on STS for their recall.

Although rehearsal provides a good account of how we perform in the free recall task, its broader significance is questionable. Subjectively, rehearsal does not appear to play a very important role in everyday remembering. Hopefully, you are retaining quite a lot of information about human memory from reading this book, but I would be surprised if you were actively rehearsing it. Also, as we have already noted, much of what we remember is not easily verbalized. Finally, the concept of rehearsal places too great an emphasis on the role of intentionality in learning. In the next chapter we will see that retention is often very good even when we do not intend to remember. Rehearsal is therefore best seen as a specific learning strategy that can be applied to the learning of verbal information, rather than as a fundamental process governing transfer from STS to LTS.

Negative Recency
Interpretation of recency effects in terms of the STS/LTS distinction gained support from a further phenomenon known as **negative recency**. F. I. M. Craik (1970) gave subjects a series of trials, each involving the free recall of a list of words, and typical serial position curves were generated. When the experiment was over, the subjects were given a final surprise recall test in which they were asked to remember as many words as possible from all the lists. The striking feature of the result was that words from the last few positions in the lists – i.e. words that had shown recency effects in immediate free recall – now had a level of recall that was significantly *lower* than words formerly in the asymptote portion of the curve. This result was explained by arguing that, following immediate free recall, subjects failed to rehearse recent items because they did not know about the unexpected memory test at the end of the experiment. As a result, these items had little chance of transfer to LTS and were therefore difficult to recall at that later stage.

Problems with Interpreting the Serial Position Curve

A central assumption about STS is that it has a limited capacity. It should therefore be possible to devise some means of measuring exactly what that capacity is. The experiments we have considered so far have led us to conclude that the recency effect in immediate free recall constitutes output from STS. It is therefore a simple step to argue that if we can gain a reliable estimate of the size of the recency effect, we will have estimated the capacity of STS itself. This was attempted by Glanzer and Razell (1974), who, on the basis of 21 free recall experiments, concluded that the average size of the recency effect was 2.2 words. However, this neat conclusion was undermined by further experiments carried out by the same researchers. First, they tested free recall using proverbs (e.g. 'A stitch in time saves nine') rather than words as stimuli, and found that the recency effect was 2.2 proverbs. Next, they used unfamiliar sentences as stimuli, and found a recency effect of 1.5 sentences.

Glanzer and Razell's findings demonstrate that the size of the recency effect cannot be measured in simple word units. For the amount of information contributing to the recency effect varies, depending on the nature of the information being remembered. This finding illustrates a fundamental problem in attempting to measure human memory capacity. Artificial storage systems, such as floppy discs, compact discs, and magnetic tapes, have measurable fixed capacities, because information is fed into them in the form of basic units (so-called bytes of information). In order to measure the capacity of human memory, we would first need some similar method for reducing information to be remembered to basic units. This may be possible in the future, but at present our lack of a basic unit for measuring the size of different pieces of information put into memory precludes any attempt to measure memory capacity accurately.

Other recent evidence has also led to a revision of the earlier view of the serial position curve's theoretical significance. In our original account it was proposed that the recency effect is abolished by distraction because it displaces, or in some other way interferes with, the representation of late items in STS. This account makes a strong prediction about the relationship between distraction and memory. Extrapolating from the findings of Glanzer and Cunitz (1966), it predicts that any distraction lasting 15 seconds or more will abolish the recency effect.

Using a technique first described by Bjork and Whitten (1974), Hitch, Rejman, and Turner (1980) examined the nature of the serial position effects found with immediate free recall, delayed free recall, and under conditions of **continuous distraction**. In the last condition each item was

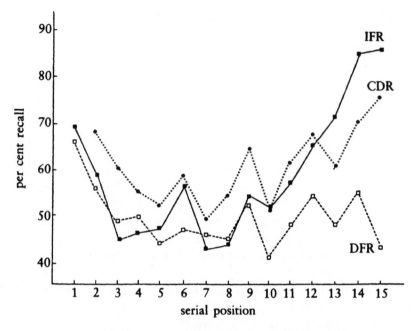

Fig. 1.10. Recency effects for immediate free recall (IFR), delayed free recall (DFR), and recall under conditions of continuous distraction (CDR). From Baddeley, 1986. Reproduced with the permission of Oxford University Press.

separated by a period of distraction lasting 12 seconds, and, following the last item, a further distraction lasting 20 seconds was introduced. Figure 1.10 shows the results. Immediate free recall generated a typical serial position curve, and no recency effect was found in delayed free recall. A surprising finding, however, was a significant recency effect in the continuous distraction condition, even though the final item was followed by a period of distraction long enough to remove the recency effect in delayed free recall.

One way of viewing the above results which would allow us to maintain our STS account of recency in immediate free recall is to see the recency effect in the continuous distractor condition as having a different origin. However, this would violate an important principle of scientific explanation. In experimental psychology, like any other science, the principle of **parsimony** (sometimes known as Occam's razor) is valid. If two or more phenomena can be covered by a single explanation, this is to be preferred to an account in which those phenomena are explained in different ways.

It has been proposed (e.g. Glenberg et al., 1980) that the pattern of recency effects obtained in the three different conditions shown in figure 1.10 can be accounted for by a single function in which probability of recall obeys a function calculated by the following ratio:

$$probability \ of \ recall = \frac{presentation \ interval \ between \ items}{time \ elapsed \ between \ presentation \ of \ item \ and \ start \ of \ recall}$$

According to this **constant ratio rule**, the critical factor determining recall ability is not the amount of distraction that occurs between item presentation and test, as might be the case with a simple displacement account of STS. Instead, recall of terminal items will be greater when the presentation interval between items and the time elapsing before recall are of similar magnitude. Test conditions which meet this requirement generate recency effects regardless of the size of time interval used (see Baddeley, 1986, for a more detailed discussion of this point).

Significance of the Constant Ratio Rule

Producing a formula that predicts the shape of recency effects obtained under various conditions does not, in itself, explain anything. All it does is to specify the conditions needed to demonstrate recency in the laboratory. However, it does strengthen our conviction that a single theory might account for both types of recency effect. At present we have little idea about what the common mechanism underlying recency effects might be. One possibility is that recency effects are attributable to a retrieval process known as **scanning** (Craik and Jacoby, 1976). This can thought of as a 'looking back' process in which the contents of the immediate past are made available in some automatic effortless fashion and the task of the retrieval mechanism is to discriminate the target information from any other information that may be present. Recency effects arise because, as information sinks further back in time, it becomes less discriminable from other information, rather in the same way that a line of telegraph poles gradually merge as they become further away. The constant ratio rule may reflect the fact that this scanning process is more efficient if target information is located at regular intervals, as is the case when the retention interval and the inter-item intervals are the same length.

Scanning can be contrasted with the **reconstructive** processes needed to retrieve information that is further back in time. Reconstructive processes form the basis on which we retrieve most information, and we will consider these processes more thoroughly in chapter 4. For the moment we simply note that retrieval via reconstruction involves the effortful interaction between information currently in consciousness and that stored in memory.

Current Status of the STS/LTS Dichotomy

The last section has moved us away from a **structural** view of STS and LTS to a more **process**-oriented approach, in which short-term and long-term storage phenomena are attributed to differences in the mechanisms used to retrieve information, depending on how long it has been stored in memory. One might argue, however, that the concept of scanning is just an alternative way of describing a short-term storage system of limited capacity. After all, both ideas centre on the notion that a chunk of the immediate past can be brought back to mind in a different, less effortful, way than things that happened longer ago. The difference between the structuralist and the process accounts is that the latter assumes a flexibility in the extent to which either retrieval strategy is applied. A process account can therefore accommodate the demonstration of recency effects occurring across different time spans by proposing that the extent to which scanning can be utilized depends partly on the exact relation between items of target information and the background from which they must be discriminated. By contrast, the structural view has difficulty accounting for recency effects occurring across different time spans.

STS and LTS from a Biological Perspective

The account given above has been primarily concerned with the psychological evidence for short- and long-term memory stores. But memory is also a biological process; so we should look at biological evidence for different memory stores. Most persuasive, perhaps, is the evidence provided by amnesic patients like HM, in whom short-term storage functions appear normal, but long-term storage seems completely absent. We can, however, identify other biological evidence.

At a physical level we can define a memory trace as some permanent alteration of the brain substrate in order to represent some aspect of a past experience. Many differing views about the biological nature of memory traces have been put forward. In the Middle Ages memories were thought to be stored in the cerebro-spinal fluid of the ventricles.

Descartes rightly considered that it was the solid substance of the brain that contained memory, but he wrongly located it in the pineal gland. Much later, when the nucleic acids (RNA and DNA) were discovered, a number of scientists proposed that RNA, with its modifiable ability to store information, might be the basis on which memories were stored.

Subsequent research investigating the RNA theory of memory provides a somewhat bizarre, if entertaining, episode in the history of physiological psychology (see Squire, 1987). The outcome, however, was that although RNA activity is an essential correlate of memory formation (not surprising since RNA controls all enzymatic activity), it could not possibly be the substrate of memory.

With the idea of memory molecules laid to rest, scientists quickly realized that the biological substrate of memory must lie in some permanent alteration to neurons themselves. The brain contains an enormous number of neurons, and each of these interacts with others by means of **synapses**. These are chemical bridges whereby one neuron can either inhibit or stimulate another. Patterns of inhibition and stimulation of this nature can be used as a basis for storing information. Although the exact manner by which neurons are modified in order to form new permanent memories has not been fully explained, it is agreed that the process by which this occurs, known as **consolidation**, is time-based. Hebb (1949) formulated an influential theory concerning this relationship between brain physiology and memory. He suggested that initial presentation of a stimulus led to the activation of groups of neurons, which he termed 'cell assemblies'. The activity of these cell assemblies maintained a representation of the stimulus long enough to allow the formation of a permanent long-term trace. But if consolidation is time-based, it is logical to ask how long the process takes. Hebb himself envisaged a process lasting around 30 minutes, but evidence from studies of disrupted memory suggests that the transition from active to passive storage normally occurs much more rapidly than this.

Neuropharmacology offers a relatively new and important means of investigating human memory (e.g. Warburton and Rusted, 1991). The neural pathways underlying all brain function depend on neurotransmitters, by which nervous impulses are transmitted across synapses. The exact involvement of different pathways in memory can be explored by employing neuropharmacological agents which either inhibit or facilitate the activity of particular neurotransmitters. Drugs that inhibit activity are called **antagonists**, those that facilitate it **agonists**.

The so-called **cholinergic blockade** technique involves administration of a drug know as **scopolamine (hyoscine)**, an antagonist of **acetylcholine**, a neurotransmitter known to be essential for consolidation. Figure 1.10

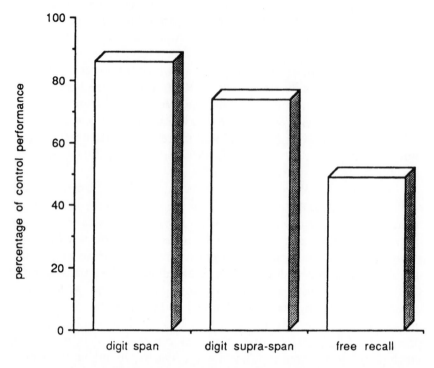

Fig. 1.11. The performance of subjects under the influence of scopolamine in comparison with control subjects on three tests of memory. Data from Drachman and Sahakian, 1979, p. 354.

shows the effect of scopolamine on subjects' ability to perform two types of memory task. The span task requires subjects to reproduce information immediately after it has been presented, and, presumably, on these tasks, subjects make maximal use of active, short-term storage. The recall task involves learning a list of words and recalling them after a 60-second period of distraction. As can be seen, scopolamine has no major effect on memory span, but severely impairs recall after 60 seconds. This finding shows that active storage is having little influence on memory after only 60 seconds.

Active storage thus appears to be short-lived. But it would be wrong to conclude that the act of consolidation is fully executed within a minute or so. Many theorists hold the view that consolidation is a multiphase process, in which an initial fixation is established quite rapidly and is followed by subsequent, 'elaborative' consolidation in which the new memory trace becomes more fully integrated with pre-existing memories, memories to which a simple list recall task may not be sensitive. The length of time over which this additional consolidation occurs might be measured in minutes, hours, or even years! (Squire, 1987).

It has not been possible, therefore, to provide any kind of mapping between the physiological correlates of memory storage and the different stages of memory formation identified in psychological theories such as the modal model. In particular, it is not possible to equate the period of active storage with our concept of STS and consolidated memories with LTS. From this perspective, the ability of the amnesic patient to show normal recency in free recall but not over longer time periods arises because the mechanisms controlling the recency-based retrieval strategy are independent of the processes controlling the memory substrate on which that retrieval strategy operates.

Overview

Psychological theories of memory make a fundamental distinction between the memory processes underlying conscious mental activity (STS) and those responsible for longer-term memory (LTS). Evidence for this dichotomy comes from the study of amnesic patients and from experiments on normal subjects. Initially, experiments attempted to specify STS and LTS in structural terms, using data from techniques such as the serial position curve. However, this approach proved problematic, and was replaced by a more process-oriented view according to which recently formed memories are retrieved in a different way from those formed further back in time. The biological evidence still compels us to accept a distinction between short- and long-term memory storage, but this does not map directly on to the same concepts when applied in the psychological domain.

2

Structure or Process?

We soon forget what we have not deeply thought about.

Marcel Proust

In chapter 1 we concluded that, despite clear biological evidence for short- and long-term storage systems, attempts to develop a structural account of memory ran into difficulties. Furthermore, it was suggested that memory might be better understood in terms of the operation of different processes: that more recent information might be accessible via a different form of retrieval process than that operating for more distant memories. The distinction between scanning and reconstructive retrieval was, in fact, one aspect of an alternative approach to memory known as **levels of processing (LOP)** (Craik and Lockhart, 1972).

Levels of Processing

The basic premise underlying LOP is that advances in understanding memory can be achieved by examining the relationship between the type of encoding processes undertaken during learning and the pattern of subsequent retention. Craik and Lockhart did not reject the STS/LTS distinction, but argued that it failed to reveal anything new about human memory. However, the distinction between STS and LTS is upheld, in modified form, in their own account of memory.

Craik and Lockhart's proposal was that processing of a stimulus could be undertaken at a number of different levels. These can be most easily understood by thinking about how we remember words; but they can be applied to other forms of information as well. As we saw in chapter 1, words have three encoding dimensions: orthographic, phonological, and semantic. Craik and Lockhart envisaged these encoding dimensions as a continuum stretching from 'shallow' to 'deep' levels. Orthography represented the shallowest level, followed by phonology, and, at the deepest level, semantics. They reasoned that retention of a stimulus would be a positive function of the depth to which a stimulus was processed during learning.

The authors were on safe ground in their assertion, because there was already an established literature supporting this claim. In the 1950s and 1960s there had been considerable interest in **incidental learning** – a learning paradigm which explored the extent to which people remember when they do not expect any memory test. Incidental learning makes use of a technique known as the **orienting task**. This is a task which requires a decision about one particular dimension of a stimulus, and it is assumed that the stimulus is encoded in away that is biased towards that dimension. Examples of these tasks are given below.

Many experiments showed that the type of orienting task undertaken during learning greatly affected the amount people remembered in an unexpected memory test. Figure 2.1 shows data from an experiment carried out by F. I. M. Craik (1977). Orthographic processing is seen to produce the poorest level of memory, then phonological processing. Semantic processing produces the greatest level of retention, and, interestingly, performance is as good as that found with intentional learning.

Craik and Lockhart explained these results by arguing that the processing of a stimulus was under the control of a **central processor** – a system with limited but flexible capacity that dealt with the processing of new information. Retention of a stimulus depended on the way in which the central processor was deployed during learning: the deeper the level, the better the retention. Embodied in this idea was the **co-ordinality assumption**, which stated that the nature of processing undertaken in response to an orienting task was directly related to the overt demands of the task. Thus, if you were asked whether the word 'table' was in upper- or lower-case letters, your processing was assumed to be restricted to the orthographic level.

The co-ordinality assumption, in its most extreme form, is patently wrong. There is abundant evidence that when we look at a word, we are automatically aware of its meaning. A clear demonstration of this is the **Stroop effect** (Stroop, 1935). This effect is most commonly shown

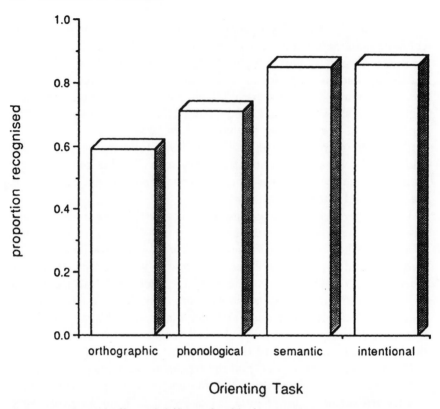

Fig. 2.1. Typical effect of different levels of processing on memory performance. Data from Craik, 1977.

by asking subjects to name the colour of the ink in which a word is written. If there is congruency between the ink and the carrier word – e.g. 'green' written in green ink – colour naming will be faster than in an incongruent condition in which 'green' is written in, say, red ink. A similar kind of effect can be observed by asking subjects to state the number of digits in an array. When both the number and type of digit are the same – e.g. 4444 – performance is quicker than when they are not – e.g. 444. The exact explanation of the Stroop effect has yet to be found; but what we can conclude is that human beings are not able to orient their attention precisely to task demands and that irrelevant information, particularly meaning, is processed regardless of instructions.

Phenomena such as the Stroop effect led Craik and Tulving (1975) to a revised version of the LOP model, illustrated in figure 2.2. They proposed that any stimulus first undergoes a **minimal core encoding**, which includes a degree of semantic analysis. This is followed by consciously directed processing appropriate to the task demands. These latter processes can be seen as effortful, in that they depend on some conscious

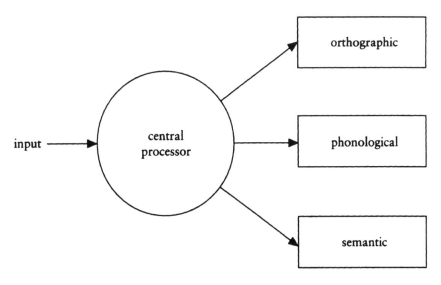

Fig. 2.2. The revised levels of processing approach to memory. Processing of new information is controlled by the central processor and can occur at one or more levels. From Parkin, 1987, p. 24. Reproduced with permission.

commitment by the subject. A second modification was to abandon the notion of a continuum between shallow and deeper levels of processing, and replace it with separable 'domains' of processing (Sutherland, 1972). This reflected the logical point that it was not possible to pass gradually from, say, orthographic to phonological levels of processing, because these contained qualitatively different dimensions of information processing, which could not merge with one another in any way.

Craik and Tulving (1975) carried out a large number of experiments which explored LOP in detail. They confirmed the **depth effect** by showing, under a variety of conditions, that semantic orienting tasks always produced better retention than non-semantic tasks. They also made comparisons within the semantic domain, and found that judging whether a word fitted the blank in a sentence (e.g. 'He met a —— in the street' – 'friend') produced better retention than judging whether a target item belonged to a particular category ('Is the word a type of fish?' – e.g. 'shark'). Craik and Tulving explained this by arguing that the sentence frame task achieved its results because it produced a more richly encoded or **elaborated** memory trace. Further experiments showed that this **elaboration effect** occurred only in the semantic domain, thus suggesting that the effect is dependent on the subject's ability to set up increasing numbers of associations with the stimulus.

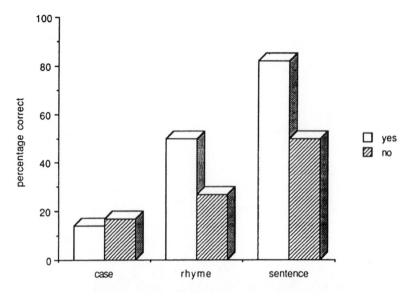

Fig. 2.3. The congruency effect. Subjects produce better performance when the initial orienting task evokes a 'yes' response, and the effect is most pronounced in the semantic domain. Case corresponds to an orthographic orienting task in which the subject decides whether or not each target word is printed in capital letters. Rhyme corresponds to a phonological orienting task in which the subject decides whether each word rhymes with a concurrently presented word. Sentence refers to a semantic orienting task in which a sentence is presented in which there is a blank space and the subject must decide whether the word fits the sentence. Data from Craik and Tulving, 1975, p. 280.

A second phenomenon of interest was the **congruency effect.** This is illustrated in figure 2.3, where it can be seen that retention is better for stimuli which evoke 'yes' responses during the orienting task than for those which evoke 'no'. The effect is most pronounced in the semantic condition, and was thought to arise because 'yes' responses are more likely to allow a coherent association between the stimulus and potential retrieval cues. Thus, if you answered 'yes' to the sentence 'Under the boulder there was a ——?' – 'snake', the sentence frame would, if you could remember it, be a good cue to what the word was. However, if a 'no' response was required – e.g. 'The man entered the room through the ——?' – 'snake' – then remembering this sentence would not be much of a cue for the target.

The levels of processing idea sparked off a large number of empirical studies all of which confirmed and extended the work of Craik and

Tulving. One interesting development was that levels of processing manipulations were found to be useful in investigating other forms of memory, most notably facial memory. Warrington and Ackroyd (1975), for example, presented subjects with faces to remember after giving them one of three types of learning instruction: judge each face as pleasant or unpleasant, decide whether each face is long or short; just try to remember the face. Subjects produced far fewer errors when instructed to rate the pleasantness of each face, as compared with the other two tasks. The contrast between pleasantness and length tasks was considered analogous to the semantic versus non-semantic distinction as applied to words: making a pleasantness judgement required a decision as to what the face meant to the subject, whereas the length task concentrated on the structure of the face. Better recognition following pleasantness judgements was therefore another expression of the superior learning produced by semantic orienting tasks.

Problems with Levels of Processing

As more and more studies demonstrated orienting task effects, a number of theorists became highly critical of the LOP approach (e.g. Baddeley, 1978; Eysenck, 1978; Nelson, 1977). The primary objection concerned the value of LOP as a *theory*. To be fair, Craik and Tulving (1975) never claimed specifically that levels of processing was a theory, preferring instead the term 'framework for memory research'. None the less, it was evident that many people were treating it as a theory, and as such it was a target for criticism.

A number of problems arose, but the most important concerned the circularity inherent in the LOP approach to the relation between learning and retention. The demonstration that semantic processing typically produces better retention than non-semantic processing was explained by asserting that semantic processing is deeper than non-semantic processing. However, the assumption of deeper processing under semantic orienting instructions was itself asserted on the basis of higher levels of retention.

Craik and Tulving were well aware of this circular reasoning, and attempted to break the circularity by devising an **independent measure of depth** – some index that could be measured during orienting task performance that would allow different depths of processing across orienting tasks to be established independently of the differences in retention that those tasks would be expected to produce.

The circularity problem was illustrated in a tongue-in-cheek study reported by Loftus et al. (1980) in which subjects viewed a series of landscapes and either counted the number of trees, decided how pleasant each landscape was, or thought about the meaning of life. Tree counting produced poorer subsequent recognition than deciding on pleasantness, but recognition in the latter case did not differ from that of the meaning of life group. Loftus therefore concluded that the meaning of life must be deep!

Craik and Tulving had noted that in all their experiments semantic orienting tasks always took longer to perform than non-semantic ones. From this they reasoned that **processing time** might be an effective independent measure of processing depth, with longer processing times indicating deeper processing and therefore greater retention. To test this idea, they devised a non-semantic task that took longer than a semantic task to perform. They reasoned that if processing time were a valid measure of depth, the non-semantic task should produce the best retention. Figure 2.4 shows that this was not the case. Despite taking less time to perform, the semantic task still produced the best results.

Failure to find a relationship between processing time and retention was in some ways fortunate for the LOP idea. For if processing time had predicted depth effects, it would have undermined the whole idea that memory can be affected by qualitative differences in the way information is encoded, since it could then have been argued that orienting task effects are merely one expression of the **total time hypothesis** (Cooper and Pantle, 1967), which states that learning is a positive function of study time *per se*. Failure to find any relation between processing time and memory means that the relationship between learning and memory is determined by more than just how long we spend attending to the stimulus.

I (Parkin, 1979) then took up the circularity problem in a series of experiments designed to test whether semantic and non-semantic processing tasks could be distinguished in terms of their ability to evoke associative processing. It is well established that if two related words are presented sequentially, identification of the second word will be made easier if it is associatively related to the first – e.g. 'table', – 'chair'. This is known as **associative priming**, and, logically, it must depend on processing of stimuli in the semantic domain. I reasoned that semantic orienting tasks should allow associative priming to occur, because they direct conscious processing into the semantic domain. Non-semantic tasks, by definition, should preclude the possibility of associative priming. In each trial in my experiment, subjects were first shown a single word, and were asked to make either a semantic or a non-semantic orienting decision about it. They were then shown a second word written

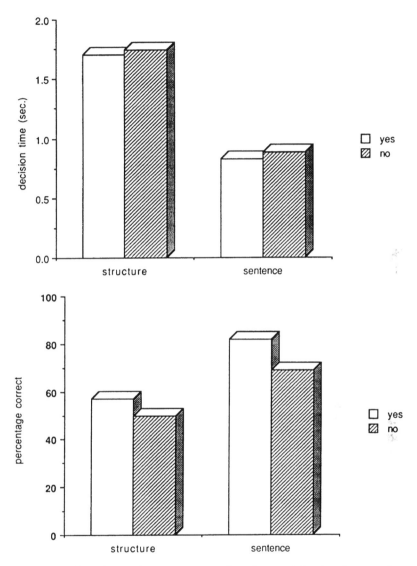

Fig. 2.4. a) The relation between processing time and levels of processing. b) The relation between retention and levels of processing. Note that the semantic task produces superior retention despite taking less time to carry out. Data from Craik and Tulving, 1975, p. 281.

in coloured ink; this was either an associated word or an unassociated word. On seeing this word, subjects had to name the colour of the ink as quickly as possible. The second part of the trial was thus a variant of the Stroop test, considered earlier, where the key factor influencing performance is the subject's ability to ignore the carrier word.

Subjects in the semantic orienting condition took significantly longer to name the colour of the ink when the second word was associated with the preceding decision word; whereas association between the two words had no influence in the non-semantic condition. The delay in naming the colour of the ink on the associated trials is evidence that associative priming has occurred, priming of the word in colour making it more easily identified and thus more difficult for the subject to ignore. The fact that this **associative interference effect** occurred only in the semantic condition indicates that only this task directed processing to the semantic domain and that recall from this condition should be superior – which it was!

My experiments indicated a solution to the circularity problem, at least in relation to depth; but these findings have not been followed up. In particular, no attempt has been made to specify the processing differences underlying demonstrations of elaboration and congruency, concepts which are equally circular. Perhaps one reason for this is that LOP ran into more serious trouble when further limitations of its explanatory value were exposed.

Transfer-Appropriate Processing

In a LOP experiment involving word stimuli, orienting tasks vary in the extent to which they force subjects to regard the stimuli as words. If you have to judge whether 'tiger' belongs to the category 'mammals', you have to know what the target word is. But what if you are asked whether or not it has two syllables? You will probably still be aware that 'tiger' is a word, but this is irrelevant to what you are required to do. Thus you will probably find it no more difficult to make the decision about syllables with the non-word 'riger'.

Morris et al. (1977) pointed out that the above observation has important implications for the explanation of LOP effects. For although orienting tasks vary in the extent to which they place emphasis on the **lexical** characteristics of the stimuli, retention tests always demand that the subjects remember *words*. Because semantic tasks always require attention to the stimuli as words, whereas non-semantic tasks do not,

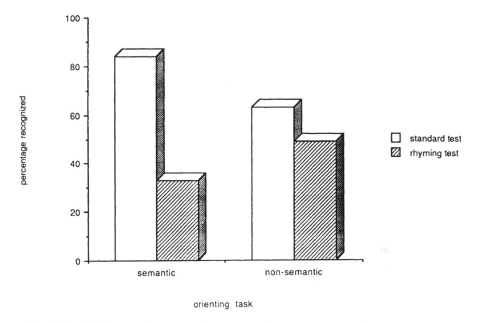

Fig. 2.5. With transfer-appropriate processing, memory performance depends on the relation between learning and test conditions. Data from Morris et al., 1977, p. 523.

Morris et al. argued that superior memory following semantic processing arises because the retention tests are biased towards the type of information that semantic orienting tasks force the subjects to encode.

To prove their point, they designed an experiment in which subjects first learnt target words under either semantic or non-semantic orienting conditions. The semantic task was a sentence-congruency task similar to that used by Craik and Tulving (1975), and the non-semantic task was a rhyming judgement – e.g. rhymes with 'legal'? – 'regal'. Two forms of retention test were used: a standard test of recognition – i.e. 'Indicate which of these words you saw in the orienting phase', – and one in which subjects searched a list of words and indicated words that sounded similar to words used in the orienting phase. Figure 2.5 shows that, with standard recognition, the expected depth effect was found, whereas on the rhyming recognition test, it was the non-semantic group that showed the best performance.

This experiment and several similar studies (e.g. Stein, 1978) demonstrate that enhanced retention following semantic processing depends critically on the type of retention test used. Thus semantic processing of words does not have any **absolute** advantage over non-semantic processing; it is merely more advantageous when the retention test involves recalling or recognizing words. If a retention test is biased in favour of the information addressed by the non-semantic task, it is this that will be remembered best.

Morris et al. referred to their discovery as the principle of **transfer-appropriate processing**. Stated simply, it asserts that the most appropriate learning strategy is the one that most closely addresses the information required at testing. This principle, which is difficult to dispute, deflated the LOP approach, which, until then, had asserted that semantic processing was always superior to non-semantic processing.

There was also disappointment when LOP effects in memory for faces were examined in more detail. In an elegant set of experiments, Winograd (1976) compared facial memory under three orienting conditions: a **trait** task, in which subjects judged each face along one of three personality dimensions; a **constrained feature** task, which required subjects to make a physical judgement about a specific feature of each face, and a **distinctive feature** condition, in which subjects decided for themselves which feature of a face was the most physically distinctive. Winograd found that the constrained condition produced poorer performance than the trait task, a finding one would predict from other LOP studies, but that, contrary to prediction, the distinctive feature task produced similar recognition to the trait task.

Winograd reasoned that the equal retention found with trait and distinctive feature conditions arose because memory for a face depended critically on subjects encoding the most distinctive feature of a face. By definition, the distinctive feature task ensured this; but so did the trait task, because, in making a personality judgement, the whole face must be scanned and the distinctive feature noticed. Constrained feature processing, in which no notice is taken of distinctive features, would thus be inferior, because the distinctive feature would not always be encoded. To prove this theory, Winograd devised a second version of the constrained feature task which ensured that subjects made a decision about the distinctive feature of each face; as predicted, this task now produced similar performance to the trait and distinctive feature conditions. Semantic processing of faces was not, therefore, qualitatively different from memory arising from orienting subjects to the physical dimension of faces.

The Legacy of Levels of Processing

It is quite easy to view the whole LOP idea as something of a blind alley in memory research. As a theory, it proved largely untestable; moreover, it failed to establish any absolute principles of learning. However, this rather dismissive view may not be justified. Until the advent of Craik and Lockhart's (1972) paper, memory theorists had paid little attention to the relation between perception and memory and to the idea that encoding processes could be flexible. Atkinson and Shiffrin (1968) had introduced the concept of 'control processes' in their version of STS, but in practice this had not advanced beyond the study of rehearsal. LOP showed the enormous variation in encoding that could occur, and all theorizing about memory now takes account of this basic observation. Furthermore, LOP provided the first substantial framework within which one could talk meaningfully of 'encoding deficits' as a reason for memory failure. Finally, as we shall see in the next chapter, the concept of processes, as opposed to systems, and the idea of transfer-appropriate processing have continued to be influential.

Overview

Proponents of levels of processing argued that the structural model of memory had outlived its usefulness and that further progress could be made only by examining how different processes applied during learning affected retention. Many experiments showed that semantic processing was superior to non-semantic processing, that elaboration in the semantic domain facilitated learning, and that response congruency also improved learning. However, objections were raised on the grounds that the levels approach was circular in its mode of explanation. These arguments were partially dealt with, but an equally important finding, the demonstration of transfer-appropriate processing, provided a major limitation on the explanatory power of levels of processing experiments

3

The Permanent Store

I have a memory like an elephant. In fact elephants often consult me.

Noel Coward

Consider these three questions:

> When did you last ride a bicycle?
> What is a bicycle?
> How do you ride a bicycle?

To answer the first question, you will need to reflect on some aspect of your personal past, and your answer will probably be accompanied by some image of you on a bicycle. Answering the second question is rather different. You will recall that a bicycle has two wheels, is propelled by pedals attached to a chain wheel, and so on. However, the answer does not require that you recall any personal events, even though, on logical grounds, we must presume that your recollections derive from personal experience; for you have not been innately endowed with information about bicycles, or anything else for that matter. To answer the third question is different again. Beyond stating that you sit on it, push off, start pedalling, and somehow stay upright, you will not be able to describe the acts of balancing and co-ordination that riding a bicycle entail, for these kinds of memories are not consciously accessible and cannot be described. Their existence is known only through the actions to which they give rise.

Observations such as these lead us to the view that our permanent, or long-term, store (LTS) of memories is not a single entity, but a composite of different kinds of memory, each with its own properties.

Knowing How versus Knowing That

Philosophers have given considerable thought to the possible organization of our permanent memories. One influential view, put forward by Ryle (1949), was that a fundamental distinction could be drawn between remembering based on 'knowing that' and remembering arising from 'knowing how'. Returning to our bicycle example, the answers to the first two questions are of the former type – 'I know that I rode a bicycle yesterday'; 'I know that a bicycle has two wheels' – whereas the answer to the final question is of the second kind – 'I know how to ride a bicycle'.

If we assume that Ryle's distinction has psychological reality – i.e. that the memory system subdivides memories into 'that' and 'how' types – this means proposing that LTS has two fundamental components and that the subjective difference we have highlighted in contrasting our answers to the first two types of questions is not functionally significant. Put another way, this dichotomy draws no distinction between recall associated with or not associated with some recollection of personal experience.

Episodic, Semantic, and Procedural Memory

Tulving (1972, 1983, 1987, 1989) put forward a different view of the organization of LTS, one that rejects the dichotomy suggested by Ryle's analysis and replaces it with a tripartite system in which a distinction is drawn between memories associated with personal recollection and others that are not. Tulving's account is properly considered a general one. However, being an experimental psychologist, he was particularly concerned with providing an account of LTS organization that would improve our understanding of memory as explored through verbal learning experiments.

Tulving argued that LTS has three distinct components: **episodic**, **semantic**, and **procedural memory**. In its original formulation (Tulving,

Fig. 3.1. Closure pictures, taken from the Gestalt Completion Test From Street, 1931.

1972) episodic memory was defined as an individual's autobiographical record of past experience and semantic memory as our knowledge of language, rules, and concepts. Episodic and semantic memory are similar, however, in that both can be consciously accessed. Within this system, remembering the last time you rode a bicycle accesses a different memory store from that containing information about what a bicycle is. Procedural memory is similar to Ryle's 'how' type of memory in that it is characterized as being consciously inaccessible. Thus it contains the information responsible for our bicycle-riding skill.

It is important to emphasize that procedural memory is not just motor skill memory, because other forms of memory unrelated to motor skills also fall within the category of procedural memory. Figure 3.1 shows a number of visual puzzles, each of which will take you some time to solve (providing you have not seen them before). Once you have solved them, close the book, wait a few moments, re-open it at this page, and examine each puzzle again. You will find that the solutions come to you fairly instantly, showing that you have obviously learned something. However, in achieving these solutions, you will not be aware of using any conscious knowledge. Indeed, if you try to describe the knowledge you have about each puzzle that enables you to solve it, you will be surprised at how superficial it is.

In a subsequent account, Tulving (1985) opts for a broader definition of semantic memory, defining it as the memory 'that allows the individual to construct mental models of the world . . . It makes possible the cognitive representation of objects, situations, facts and events.' Within this revised view, episodic memory is what enables us to be aware of having experienced something before. The important point about this revised view is that it allows us to have memory of an event without having any specific information about why we know that the event occurred in our past. Tulving labelled this form of memory experience **noetic** (knowing), by contrast with episodic experience, which he described as **autonoetic** (self-knowing). Memories retrieved without conscious recollection were held to be **anoetic** (not knowing).

Although episodic, semantic, and procedural memories are held to be functionally distinct, they are also interactive. All our acquired knowledge is derived initially from an experience or **learning event**, but retention of that episodic memory does not require that the event itself be retained. Remembering the meaning of a new word, for example, may not at first be possible without some episodic record confirming why the word means what it does. With time, however, the word's meaning is assimilated into semantic memory, and there is then no need for the episodic record to be maintained. The attraction of this system is that knowledge about the world can come to be represented independently of the events that gave rise to that knowledge in the first place. By not requiring that the representation of knowledge be linked to learning events, an enormous saving in storage is achieved, because memory for the events themselves can be discarded.

The episodic–semantic distinction makes a lot of intuitive sense. When remembering a fact or a rule, for example, we are rarely aware of the learning event in which we acquired that knowledge. The distinction also helps to clarify our thinking about what might be going on in a typical verbal learning experiment. In a test of free recall, a subject listens to a list of words and sometime later attempts to remember them; but only about half the words are remembered. Within the episodic–semantic framework, this can be seen as a failure of episodic memory. The subject has not forgotten the words completely – all subjects are able to read and understand them. What has happened is that the subject has failed to retrieve information regarding the fact that the word was one experienced in the original learning event. It is for this reason that accounts of verbal learning experiments often refer to the words that subjects are asked to learn as **word events**; for the word serves as the focus for a specific learning event.

It is also possible to see how procedural memory might interact with episodic and semantic memory. Learning a skill like touch typing, for example, might depend initially on retaining some record of the keyboard layout that can be recalled whenever you are uncertain about where to place your finger to type a certain letter. However, with repeated practice, this record is no longer needed and can be discarded. However, not all procedural memory is facilitated in this way, because sometimes the acquisition of skills occurs without any conscious mediation. A good example is the **pursuit rotor task**, in which the subject has to learn to keep a light beam on a moving target. Subjects learn this task well, but it is difficult to see how conscious memory could be helping, because what is being learnt, unlike touch typing, cannot be described in any way that could be entered into either episodic or semantic memory.

Experimental Evidence for Procedural Memory

Tulving's framework offers a plausible and intuitively appealing account of how LTS might be organized. But is there experimental evidence to support it? We will first consider the separate existence of procedural memory, because it is here that there is least controversy. Perhaps the best evidence for a separate procedural memory system comes from amnesic patients. We have already encountered amnesia in chapter 1, where we saw that amnesic patients could be regarded as having intact short-term storage but grossly impaired long-term storage. This latter point does requires clarification, however. Figure 3.2 shows the performance of HM and a group of control subjects on the pursuit rotor task. HM obviously learns the task, even though he has no recollection of having done it before. This phenomenon can also be demonstrated using the mirror drawing task (figure 3.3). This type of residual learning ability has been shown in many other amnesic patients and in a variety of other procedural memory tasks, such as mirror word reading and perceptual learning (Parkin, 1982; Parkin and Leng, 1993). These kinds of data are difficult to explain except by suggesting that procedural memory is a separate system which is selectively preserved in amnesic patients.

Experimental Evidence for Episodic and Semantic Memory

At the centre of Tulving's theory is the idea that the record of experience, episodic memory, resides separately from the knowledge gained

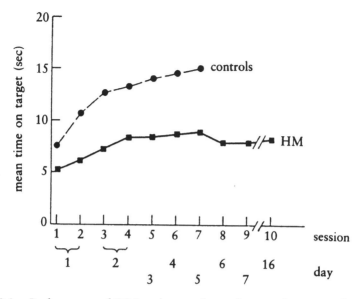

Fig. 3.2. Performance of HM and controls on the pursuit rotor task. Note retention of skill by HM after interval of 9 days. From Blakemore, 1977.

from experience, semantic memory. Finding experimental evidence from normal subjects to support this distinction is problematic, however, because of the interdependence that must exist between these two systems (e.g. McKoon and Ratcliff, 1979; McCloskey and Santee, 1981). In addition, the maintenance of the distinction in terms of the conscious awareness associated with retrieving information from the two systems – i.e. the contrast between noetic and autonoetic – might be considered rather vague even in the post-behaviourist era (however, see the section on recognition in chapter 4, in which a more operational definition of noetic and autonoetic remembering is considered). Once again, there-fore, it is evidence from amnesic patients that constitutes the primary support for separate episodic and semantic systems.

When you encounter an amnesic patient, there are good grounds for assuming that you have met someone with an intact semantic memory but highly impaired episodic memory. Many of the amnesic patients I have worked have completely normal conversational skills, for example, and it may be a little while before a stranger realizes that the person has a memory impairment (revealed when the patient starts to ask the same questions over and over again). These impressions are reinforced by the typical psychometric profile of an amnesic subject, which shows highly impaired memory performance on tests such as recalling an unfamiliar

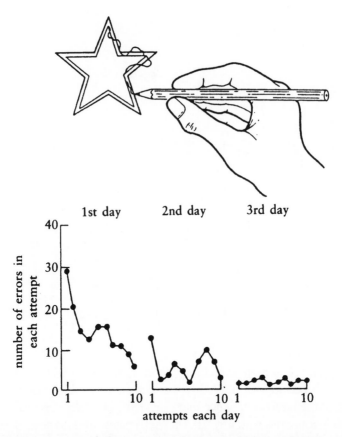

Fig. 3.3. Illustration of mirror drawing task and HM's performance. In the mirror drawing task the subject must trace a line in between the two lines depicting the star. The star is only visible to the subject via a mirror. From Blakemore, 1977. Reproduced with permission.

story even though he or she may be of normal intelligence, as measured by a standardized test such as the Wechsler Adult Intelligence Scale (WAIS; Wechsler, 1981) in which tests of verbal ability comprise over 50 per cent of the assessment. NA, another famous amnesic, was found to have an IQ of 103 three years after his brain injury. Yet, on a measure of story recall he recalled nothing after 10 minutes. However, is this kind of evidence sufficient to argue that semantic memory is preserved and functionally separate from episodic memory?

As well as having an inability to learn new information such as names and places, most amnesic patients suffer a parallel loss of the memories they acquired before the brain injury or illness that caused their loss of memory. This form of deficit, known as **retrograde amnesia**, takes a regular form, in that the deficit is more pronounced for memories acquired close to the onset of amnesia. Thus an amnesic patient may talk clearly and accurately about his or her childhood and early adult life, but be completely blank about the 20 years or so prior to the onset of amnesia.

For intelligence tests like WAIS to be general tests of intelligence, it follows that they must assess only those aspects of knowledge and ability that one could reasonably expect most people to have. Thus the WAIS concentrates on aspects of knowledge acquired during the relatively early stages of life. Normal performance on WAIS would therefore be expected in an amnesic patient, since early memories, whatever their type, are preserved in amnesia. But this finding does not allow the conclusion that semantic memory overall is preserved in amnesic patients; this would be the case only if it could be shown that semantic memory acquired later in life was normal, even though memory for episodes experienced at the same time was highly defective.

The Case of PZ

In trying to estimate the extent of retrograde amnesia in an amnesic patient, the experimenter is faced with a major methodological difficulty. Everyone's experience is different; so, if a patient fails to retrieve a fact from his or her past, it may be because he or she never learned it in the first place. This point applies particularly to patients who become amnesic due to excess alcohol intake, because it is distinctly possible that their alcoholism interrupted their learning processes long before their condition became severe enough to be called amnesia (see Parkin, 1991). A few years ago, however, psychologists were presented with a unique case known by the initials PZ (Butters and Brandt, 1985).

PZ was a science professor in a major American university. He had a severe drinking problem, which eventually lead to **Korsakoff's syndrome,** a neurological illness that has amnesia as its primary symptom. However, in the years immediately preceding the onset of amnesia, PZ wrote his autobiography. This, in combination with knowledge of his academic career, meant that researchers had reasonably accurate knowledge of what PZ once remembered about his life.

Figure 3.4 shows that, as expected, PZ showed very poor recall of events from most parts of his life except his early years, a finding consistent with impaired episodic memory. However, it also illustrates

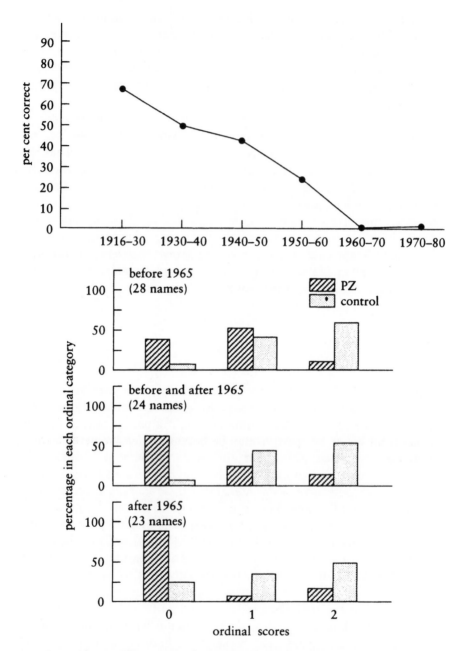

Fig. 3.4. Above, PZ's retrograde amnesia regarding information in his published autobiography. Below, performance of PZ and control on identification of famous scientists. Scores 0, 1 and 2 represent an ordinal scaling of the adequancy of the two subjects' responses (0 least adequate, 2 most adequate). From Butters, 1984, Alcoholic Korsakoff Syndrome: An Update. *Seminars in Neurology*, 4, 229–47. Reproduced with the permission of Theme-Stratton.

his very poor identification of scientists from his discipline at different times. Since we know that PZ was once familiar with these names and that this type of information would have been semantic rather than episodic in nature, we must conclude that his semantic memory is impaired as well.

If PZ has both an episodic and a semantic impairment, then parsimony in explanation leads us to conclude that these impairments might be two sides of the same coin – i.e. expressions of a single damaged LTS. Other data from retrograde amnesia studies also point in the same direction. We noted earlier that general tests of retrograde amnesia are difficult, because the knowledge being tested may never have been acquired by some subjects. One possible solution, however, is to examine the ability of patients to identify the faces of people who became famous in different decades. On the assumption that most people look at newspapers, films, and television, it can be assumed that people frequently in the news and entertainments would be familiar to most people, a fact we can confirm by testing faces on a wide range of normal subjects.

Figure 3.5 shows data from amnesic and control subjects on the Famous Faces Test devised by me and my colleagues (Parkin et al., 1990b). Performance of the amnesic group is poor, and shows the familiar **temporal gradient**, with poorer memory for the more recent past. On the assumption that the amnesic subjects once knew these faces, how might we explain this deficit? A deficit in episodic memory seems improbable. Consider what happens when you recognize somebody that you know. Is that recognition based on the last time you saw them? No. More likely it will seem to you like general knowledge and therefore best thought of as semantic memory.

Although the clinical impression given by amnesic patients is one of profound deficit in episodic memory, more fine-grained analyses of their memory deficits reveal that they also perform poorly on equivalent tests of semantic memory. Thus the data do not support a functional separation between episodic and semantic systems. Instead, it seems more correct to see these forms of memory as differing expressions of a single system.

Ryle Revisited: The Declarative–Procedural Distinction

The above discussion has indicated that, although intuitively plausible, the episodic–semantic distinction is not readily supported by experimental

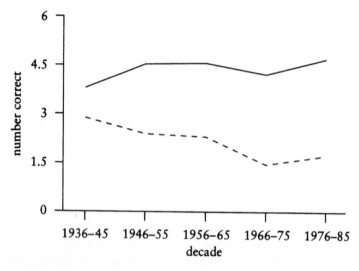

Fig. 3.5. Performance of amnesic patients and controls on the famous faces test. From Parkin et al., 1990b, p. 591. Reproduced with the permission of the Experimental Psychology Society.

evidence and that a more parsimonious account sees these two forms of memory as different aspects of the same system. This view was put forcefully by Squire and his colleagues (e.g. Cohen and Squire, 1980; Squire, 1987) using arguments of the type we have just considered. They suggested that the terms 'episodic' and 'semantic memory' should be replaced by a single term – **declarative memory**. This term refers to any memory that is consciously inspectable, and is conceptually the same as Ryle's 'knowing that' type of memory. Within this framework, declarative memory is contrasted with procedural memory, which is defined in the same way as in Tulving's system.

While the weight of evidence seems to be stacked against the episodic–semantic distinction, it may be premature to reject it completely. In subsequent chapters we will see that it may still have interesting implications for understanding certain memory phenomena. In addition, the terms 'episodic' and 'semantic memory' remain useful because, although they may not map on to different memory systems, they have important descriptive value in that they define different types of memory tasks.

Explicit and Implicit Memory

In the last few years an alternative approach to understanding the nature of LTS has been put forward. Unlike Tulving's approach, in which the emphasis is on defining the nature of different stores, this approach attempts to understand LTS by examining how it responds to different forms of memory test known as **explicit** and **implicit memory** tests (Schacter, 1987).

A test of explicit memory can be defined as one which requires the subject to recollect a previous learning event such as the presentation of a word list. Explicit memory can be tested using three different procedures:

Free recall: Subject attempts to remember the target information without any assistance from the experimenter.

Cued recall: Subject attempts to remember the target information in the presence of some specific cue (e.g. an associate of the word he or she is trying to remember).

Recognition: Subject is presented with a stimulus and must decide whether it is one that he or she was asked to remember. Recognition can be tested in either a **yes–no** procedure in which each item is judged individually or by **forced choice** in which one item from an array of items must be selected as the target.

Implicit memory refers to any memory task in which a subject's memory for a learning event is tested without specific reference to that event. Implicit memory tasks therefore test memory **indirectly**, as opposed to explicit memory tasks, which address memory for the learning event **directly**.

The idea that memory of an experience can be expressed indirectly is not new. Descartes (1649/1941) noted that frightening and aversive childhood experiences can remain imprinted on a child 'without any memory remaining afterwards'. Leibniz (1916) stressed the role of unconscious memories in everyday life, and argued that we can have 'remaining effects of former impressions without remembering them'. This point was nicely illustrated by Claparede (1911) in an anecdotal account of Korsakoff's syndrome:

> I tried the following experiment ... to see if she would better retain an intense impression that set affectivity into play. I pricked her hand forcibly with a pin hidden between my fingers. This little pain was as quickly forgotten as indifferent perceptions and, shortly after the pricking, she remembered no more of it. However, when I moved my hand near hers again, she pulled her hand back in a reflex way and without knowing why. If, in fact, I demanded the reason for the withdrawal of her hand, she answered in a flurried way, 'Isn't it allowed to withdraw one's hand?'

... If I insisted, she would say to me, 'Perhaps there is a pin hidden in your hand'. To my question, 'What can make you expect that I would like to prick you?', she would take up her refrain, 'It's an idea that came into my head' or sometimes she would try and justify herself with 'Sometimes pins are hidden in hands'. But she never recognized this idea of pricking as a memory' (from MacCurdy, 1928)

This kind of anecdotal information has subsequently been reinforced using more sophisticated methodology. Verfaellie et al. (1991) investigated an amnesic patient known as TR on a list learning experiment. After 30 minutes a recognition test was given in which both TR and the control subjects had to identify the targets in a multiple-choice test in which each target was embedded in a five-item sequence. As well as measuring accuracy, any change in the subjects' skin conductance, known as the **electrodermal response**, was measured as each test item appeared. An increase in skin conductance for a target relative to a previously unseen distractor item was taken to indicate that the individual had, in some sense, a record of encountering that stimulus before. Figure 3.6 shows that the extent of this 'electrodermal recognition' was similar in TR and the controls. This contrasts markedly with TR's poor explicit recognition of the same items.

The phenomenon of electrodermal recognition in the absence of explicit recollection seems consistent with the idea of separable implicit and explicit responses. However, an alternative possibility is that the electrodermal response occurring when a target fails to be recognized reflects the activation of an explicit trace which fails to reach conscious awareness because it is of insufficient quality. If correct, this argument would predict that electrodermal responses produced when targets are correctly identified should be greater. However, the researchers found that the magnitude of TR's electrodermal responses to targets was not correlated with overt recognition, thus suggesting that the electrodermal response is a consequence of a different form of memory to that used in explicit target recognition (see also Paller, 1990 for a further demonstration that implicit and explicit memory have different electrophysiological correlates).

In conversation you may have been struck by the following phenomenon: while speaking you may use an unusual word such as 'apoplectic'; a little later, someone else in the conversation uses 'apoplectic' as well, completely unaware of this 'conversational plagiarism'. This phenomenon is known as **cryptomnesia**, and was defined by Taylor (1965) as 'the presence of phenomena in normal consciousness which objectively are memories, but subjectively not recognized as such' (p. 1111). Cryptomnesia was investigated experimentally by Brown and Murphy

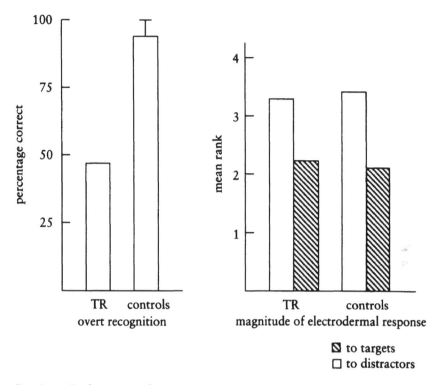

Fig. 3.6. Performance of patient TR and controls on overt verbal recognition (*left*) and electrodermal recognition (*right*) in a list learning task. Reproduced from Verafaellie et al., 1991, p. 15. Reproduced with the permission of Academic Press.

(1989). Groups of four subjects were asked to take turns in naming one item from a particular category, and after generating four exemplars each, they were instructed to recall the words they had generated and four new items. Plagiarism of each other's responses occurred at a level well above chance, even though subjects were specifically instructed not to recall information generated by another subject. In particular, there was a tendency for subjects to plagiarize the subject who responded immediately before them.

Tulving et al. (1982) devised an experimental procedure for investigating the implicit memory that might underlie phenomena such as cryptomnesia. It began by asking subjects to learn a list of multi-syllabic and relatively infrequent words such as 'toboggan'. Following an interval of either an hour or a week, subjects returned and underwent two types of memory test. The first was a yes–no recognition test which examined subjects' explicit memory for the target stimuli. The second was not ostensibly related to the original learning event, and involved a task known as **fragment completion**. Subjects were presented with incomplete words – e.g. _O_O_GA_ and asked to fill in the blanks to make a word. In this task the solutions to half the fragments were words from the target list, but subjects were not informed of this. Fragment completion therefore served as a test of implicit memory.

Tulving et al. found that subjects were more likely to complete fragments correctly when the solution corresponded to a target word – a phenomenon known as **repetition priming.** You may not find this result surprising. One might, for example, argue that subjects notice that some of the solutions are target words and use their explicit recollection to help them do the test. If correct, this argument would mean that repetition priming was just another form of explicit memory. However, an ingenious aspect of Tulving et al.'s study ruled out this simple interpretation. In the experiment each target word was tested for recognition and fragment completion, and it was shown that the probability of correct fragment completion was no greater for target words that were recognized than for target words that subjects failed to identify. This **stochastic independence** indicated that the repetition priming effect was unrelated to explicit memory performance. Fragment completion therefore served as a valid implicit memory test; furthermore, the demonstration of stochastic independence suggested that explicit and implicit memory tasks measured different forms of memory.

The claim that stochastic independence between recognition and fragment completion is a sufficient basis for concluding that different forms of memory underlie explicit and implicit memory performance has been seriously questioned. Briefly, it has been argued that many factors influence subjects' ability on these two tasks and that failure to control for these may have masked a real relationship between recognition and fragment completion (Hintzman, 1991, Hintzman and Hartry 1990 but see Flexser, 1991 and Gardiner, 1991).

Fortunately we do not have to rely on stochastic independence data to conclude that explicit and implicit memory tasks test different forms of memory. In chapter 1 we saw that one approach to establishing the existence of different forms of memory was the method of functional double dissociation. To recap, this method assumes that if two different memory systems exist, they must have different properties and that it must be possible to find experimental variables which affect the two systems differently.

We saw that Tulving et al. examined both recognition and repetition priming at retention intervals of a hour and a week. Figure 3.7 shows

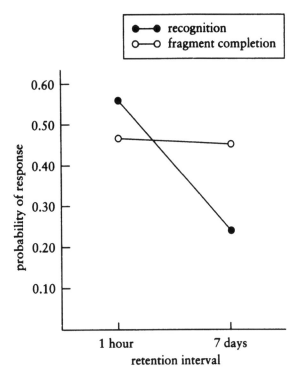

Fig. 3.7. The influence of retention interval on fragment completion priming and recognition. From Tulving et al., 1982, p. 339. Reproduced with the permission of the American Psychological Association.

that recognition declined significantly after a week, but that the extent of priming did not change significantly. This demonstration that tests of implicit memory are far less affected by time than measures of explicit memory has been repeated a number of times. It is now known, for example, that repetition priming effects can be detected after intervals of up to 16 months (Sloman et al., 1988) in normal subjects, and a single case study of amnesia found reliable priming effects after 12 months (Tulving et al., 1991).

Demonstration that implicit and explicit memory change differently over time suggests that they are separate forms of memory, but tells us little about the nature of the difference, between them. Recent research, however, has begun to tell us more about the processes underlying these two forms of memory. It is a well-known characteristic of explicit memory tasks that they depend on the degree of conscious effort expended during learning. This was demonstrated in a study by Anderson and Craik (1974) in which subjects studied a series of target words while carrying out an additional **secondary task** which involved monitoring the pitch of a random tone sequence. When recall was tested, the subjects performing the secondary task performed much more poorly than control subjects allowed to devote all their attention to learning the words.

My colleagues and I (Parkin et al., 1990c) examined how the imposition of the same secondary task would influence fragment completion priming. It was found that the secondary task significantly reduced recognition performance, but had no effect on repetition priming. This finding has been replicated using a different form of implicit memory test known as **picture completion priming** (Parkin and Russo, 1990; see chapter 7), and collectively the data indicate that the memory tested under implicit memory conditions is formed *automatically*, by contrast with explicit memory, which is dependent on the degree of conscious effort. This conclusion is consistent with Nissen et al.'s (1987) finding that scopolamine, a substance known to inhibit effortful memory functions such as free recall (see chapter 1), has no effect on fragment completion priming.

Graf et al. (1984) examined repetition priming using a variant of the fragment completion paradigm known as **stem completion**. Subjects again study a list of words, such as 'watch', and then, sometime later, are confronted with a series of word stems, e.g. wat——? The stem can serve as an explicit memory test by acting as a cue for recall or as an implicit test by requiring the subject to report the first word that 'pops' into mind beginning with those three letters. Graf et al. found that cued recall instructions resulted in better recall for words learned under semantic than under non-semantic orienting instructions, – a finding consistent with the levels of processing research considered in chapter 2. However, when the word stems were used as an implicit memory test, subjects completed the stems more often with target than non-target words, a repetition priming effect; but this was uninfluenced by the level at which these target words were processed during learning.

In an early study Warrington and Weiskrantz (1970) showed that amnesic patients showed priming in a task similar to fragment completion. Target words were pre-exposed, and patients were then asked to identify degraded versions of these words. Performance was much better for pre-exposed than novel words, even though the patients had no testable explicit recollection. Studies using conventional fragment completion and stem completion priming have also shown the preservation of implicit memory performance in amnesic subjects (Graf et al., 1984; Graf and Schacter, 1985).

So far, we have identified a number of factors that appear to influence explicit memory but not implicit memory. To these we can add a number of further factors, including more exotic manipulations such as hypnosis and surgical anaesthesia (Kihlstrom, 1980; Jelic et al., 1992). For a functional double dissociation, however, we need to find a variable that influences implicit memory but not explicit memory.

Jacoby and Dallas (1981) used an implicit memory test called **perceptual identification**, in which subjects are exposed to a stimulus briefly and then required to identify it. Priming is shown in terms of increased accuracy in identifying repeated items as compared with new items, – a phenomenon that has been termed **perceptual fluency**. In one experiment the modality of presentation was varied across repetitions of the same item. Thus on first presentation an item would be visually presented, whereas on second presentation it would be spoken. This **modality shift** greatly reduced the extent of priming compared to when the modality was unchanged. However, the same modality shift had little or no effect on subjects' explicit memory for the target stimuli. Modality shifts also reduce performance on other types of implicit memory test, such as stem and fragment completion (e.g. Bassili et al., 1989), and it has even been demonstrated that shifts within a modality can influence performance. Repetition priming in fragment completion, for example, is substantially reduced if there is a change in the typescript used at learning and test (e.g. Roediger et al., 1989).

In sum, it appears that explicit memory is sensitive to a range of variables, including secondary tasks, levels of processing, and retention interval. Implicit memory, by contrast, appears much more sensitive to the perceptual or **surface features** of stimuli. These differences thus give us some idea about how the forms of memory underlying implicit and explicit performance might be organized, and we return to this in a later section.

Implicit Memory and the Learning of New Information

The implicit memory studies we have looked at so far have all involved the modification of existing responses – e.g. the priming of a known word so that it can subsequently make fragment completion easier or be identified more readily when presented in a degraded form. An important question, however, is whether the learning exhibited under implicit memory testing conditions also applies to the learning of new information. To test this possibility, Graf and Schacter (1985) first presented subjects with word pairs, and then asked them either to produce a sentence that brought the two words together (e.g. 'She had a good *reason* for opening the *window*') or to judge whether the two words had the same number of vowels. In the second phase of the experiment, subjects were given trials on which a stimulus word from the first phase was paired with a word stem and the subject was asked to produce the first word he or she could think of to fit the stem. For half the words the paired stem corresponded to the word that the first word had been paired with at learning (e.g. *window era——?*), whereas on the other half there was a different pairing (e.g. *mother rea——?*).

The results showed that the extent of priming was greater when the stem was paired with the same word than with a different word (a phenomenon that has been termed the **word enhancement effect**), but only when there was elaborative encoding (see chapter 2) during learning. These results were interpreted as showing that some novel contextual association between the two unrelated words can be formed under implicit learning conditions, but only if elaborative encoding takes place. Other studies have supported this original finding, although there is now doubt as to whether elaborative encoding during learning is a necessary condition for demonstrating implicit memory for new associations (see Micco and Masson, 1991).

The learning of new associations via implicit memory may have important implications for helping people with impaired memory due to brain damage. As we have seen, amnesic patients still have intact implicit memory, and it may therefore be possible to teach them new information using this available function. Indeed, Glisky et al. (1987) have presented data using the 'vanishing cues' technique, in which an implicit learning procedure appeared able to impart new information to amnesic subjects very effectively.

Implicit Learning versus Implicit Memory

So far we have been considering experiments that examine implicit memory, but, parallel to these, there has been growing interest in various phenomena referred to as **implicit learning**. This can be defined as learning that occurs without the subject being able to explain how. Two types of experimental tasks have been used to investigate implicit learning: artificial grammar learning and the control of complex systems. In the former, subjects are asked to learn strings of letters generated by a synthetic grammar which defines what letters are permissible and the sequences between them. Next they are told that the strings of letters are rule-governed, and are required to categorize new strings of letters as grammatical or ungrammatical. There are now many demonstrations that subjects can learn to do tasks such as this even though they cannot explain the rules they are using (Reber, 1989; Berry and Dienes in press).

A typical complex control task is one in which subjects take on the role of managing a sugar production factory. They are required to maintain a specified level of sugar output by manipulating the number of workers. Several studies have shown that subjects can learn to perform optimally on this type of task even though they cannot explain the principle that is governing their performance (e.g. Berry and Broadbent, 1984).

An important issue is whether implicit learning and the memory demonstrated on implicit memory tests are similar, because, if so, the two sets of phenomena could be incorporated in a single explanatory framework. This question is most straightforwardly addressed by examining whether implicit learning exhibits similar properties to those we identified earlier for implicit memory.

Research on complex control tasks has revealed that there may be a degree of independence between the explicit and implicit learning components of these tasks similar to that found in the repetition priming paradigm. Berry and Broadbent found that practice on a control task improved performance on the task, but not the subjects' ability to explain what they were doing. Verbal instruction improved knowledge about task performance, but not performance itself. Furthermore, subjects with better knowledge of the principles underlying task performance tended to perform slightly worse or no better than subjects with poor task knowledge (Berry and Broadbent, 1984).

Allen and Reber (1980) measured the durability of information acquired under implicit learning conditions. They recalled subjects who had learned an artificial grammar two years previously, and found that subjects could still classify grammatical and ungrammatical strings of letters accurately. Levels of processing effects have not been formally investigated in implicit learning, but what little evidence there is suggests that, like implicit memory, the imposition of different learning strategies has no effect on the rate of learning. Instructing subjects to use a deliberate hypothesis-testing approach, for example, does not improve artificial grammar learning (Reber, 1976).

The effect of modality shifts on implicit learning have not been specifically investigated, but there is some indication that surface features are important in task performance. Berry and Broadbent (1988) examined performance on two successive control tasks which involved learning the same underlying principle, and found that learning of the second task was quicker if the tasks were perceptually similar.

Finally, we saw that amnesic patients often show preserved perform-ance on implicit memory tasks, so it is of interest to see whether a similar preservation exists in implicit learning. Squire and Frambach (1990) examined the ability of amnesic patients and controls to learn the sugar production task. It was found that patients and controls learned at a similar rate in the first session but that, at a follow-up, the patients performed more poorly, a finding that was attributed to some explicit influence on performance.

From the above, it seems reasonable to propose that implicit memory and implicit learning tests are sensitive to the same kinds of factors and that they are reflections of the same type of memory ability; that is, that implicit learning gives rise to implicit memory.

What is Implicit Memory?

So far, tests have revealed a number of features of implicit memory. It appears to be uninfluenced by secondary tasks and manipulations of processing strategy; what is learned seems highly durable; performance is sensitive to surface features; and amnesic patients tend to show preserved implicit function. Earlier we considered the concept of pro-cedural memory, and noted that the strongest evidence for it came from studies showing preserved performance by amnesic patients on tasks like motor skill and perceptual learning. These are also tasks that do not benefit from conscious intervention and that can be described with-out reference to any prior learning event. As such, they are functionally indistinguishable from the implicit memory tasks that we have considered in this section.

We now have a whole range of tasks that can be viewed as tests of implicit memory; but does this imply that there is only one implicit memory system? The answer to this is no, because there is no reason to suppose that the actual mechanisms responsible for the learning are the same. Common sense, for example, tells us that the processes re-sponsible for learning a motor skill are unlikely to be the same as those responsible for repetition priming in fragment completion. Similarly, it is hard to believe that the kind of representation responsible for repetition priming is the same as that underlying accurate performance on the sugar production task.

The proposal that all implicit memory might be mediated by a single form of memory was formally evaluated in a study by Witherspoon and Moscovitch (1989) in which they examined the statistical relation between priming effects in fragment completion and perceptual identification. Subjects were presented with a list of words and were then examined on both fragment completion and perceptual identification priming tests. If the priming observed in these two tasks were mediated by a single form of memory, one would expect performance on the two tasks to be correlated; that is, if a stimulus results in fragment completion priming, it should also show priming by enhancing perceptual identification. In fact, the results showed largely the opposite, in that priming in the two tasks was found to be uncorrelated. Hence, it was concluded that different forms of memory were responsible for priming in the two tasks.

A single account of implicit memory thus seems ruled out, and separate accounts of the various forms of implicit memory are required. Hayman and Tulving (1989b) conducted a repetition priming experiment in which a target word (e.g. 'caterpillar') was presented and priming was measured by examining subjects' fragment completion responses. An important feature of this study was that priming was measured twice for each target, using different, but equally hard, fragments (e.g. '_at_r_ _ll_ _'?; c_ _e_pi_ _ar'?). The idea behind this was to see whether priming of 'caterpillar' was mediated by some activation of the word's internal representation. If so, this would predict that the two different fragments, all other things being equal, would be just as effective in showing priming, because the critical factor determining priming is the likelihood of the fragment making contact with the activated word representation.

Priming effects were observed, but no correlation was found between the effectiveness of two fragments addressing the same target. Tulving and Hayman therefore concluded that priming in fragment completion was not mediated by some activation of a word's internal representation. Instead, they suggested that repetition priming was mediated by a 'traceless quasimemory' (QM) system in which learning occurs not by the establishment of traces representing the original stimulus, but by changes in processes that operate on the stimulus when it is perceptually present. Changes in the QM system do not record that a particular stimulus has been presented; rather, they increase the probability or speed in responding to a stimulus when it reoccurs, and it is this that facilitates priming. Since there is no reason to suppose that two different fragments of the same word map equally on to presumed changes in the QM system that took place when the target was presented, there is no basis for expecting them to be equally effective in contacting the target word during fragment completion.

The QM system thus suggests that implicit memory, as measured by fragment completion priming, has its origins in changes that occur in

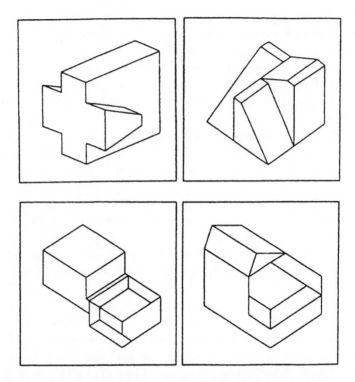

Fig. 3.8. Possible and impossible stimuli used in Schacter et al.'s experiment. The upper stimuli are possible objects, the lower ones impossible objects. From Schacter et al., 1990, p. 7. Reproduced with the permission of the American Psychological Association.

the perceptual system itself. This type of memory is typically known as **data-driven**, because it is critically dependent on the stimulus or some part of it being perceptually present. This contrasts with explicit memory, which is held to be **conceptually driven** – i.e. related to internal mental processes such as the meaning extracted from a stimulus. Schacter and his colleagues (e.g. Schacter, 1992; Schacter et al., 1990) have put forward a related view of implicit memory effects in which learning again depends on modification of perceptual processes. In a representative study, subjects studied line drawings of novel visual objects half of which were 'possible' objects, the other half impossible objects (see figure 3.8). Explicit memory for the objects was tested by yes–no recognition, and implicit memory by means of an **object decision task**. In the latter, subjects were exposed to studied and non-studied objects for 50 milliseconds, and were then asked whether or not each object was possible. Implicit memory is indicated when decisions about studied objects are significantly more accurate than those regarding non-studied objects.

Four key findings emerged from these experiments. First, reliable priming effects were obtained only for possible objects. Second, priming of possible objects occurred only when using study tasks that required subjects to appreciate the global, three-dimensional nature of the object. When subjects concentrated on two-dimensional features (e.g. judging the relative number of horizontal and vertical lines in an object), no priming took place. Third, the priming effects observed were not enhanced, and were sometimes reduced, by the subjects' attempts to form semantic descriptions of the objects. Finally, priming on the object decision task was preserved in amnesic patients (see Schacter, 1992).

Schacter et al. (1991) proposed that object decision priming is mediated by a **perceptual representation system** (PRS) whose primary role is to compute the structural description of objects. On this account, priming of impossible objects is not observed because it is difficult to represent internally the global structure of an object for which no coherent description is possible. Learning strategies addressing only two-dimensional aspects of the stimulus fail to produce priming, presumably, because, they fail to activate a structural description. Global strategies applied to a possible object result in the formation of a structural description, and subsequent perception of such objects is facilitated by the record of this processing. Mediation of the effects at the level of structural description is assumed, because semantic orienting strategies do not enhance object decision priming. This latter assumption is backed up by substantial neuropsychological data indicating that knowledge about the structural description of objects can be dissociated from knowledge about an object's semantic properties (e.g. Humphreys and Riddoch, 1987).

It should also be noted that, in terms of the explicit/implicit dichotomy, tasks featuring semantic information are also implicit, because no overt reference to a learning event is made. Furthermore, reliable priming effects involving semantic knowledge can be observed. Gardner et al. (1974) exposed Korsakoff patients to unusual exemplars of categories (e.g. 'fruit' – 'mango'). Subsequent recall of these words was extremely poor, but when asked to name exemplars from the various categories, they produced these unusual items much more often than the controls. McAndrews et al. (1987) presented two amnesic patients with sentences in which the meaning was not immediately apparent but which could become meaningful with context words present (e.g. 'The person was unhappy because the hole closed' – 'pierced ears'). Subsequent testing showed poor recognition of these sentences, but they patients were able to give the contextually derived meaning of these sentences more quickly than that of comparable sentences they had not seen before. More impressively, amnesic patients have even shown the ability to learn mathematical formulae (Milberg et al., 1988).

In modern Japanese, words taken from foreign languages are usually written in *Katakana* script, although it is possible to write them in *Hiragana* if required. Komatsu and Naito (1992) exploited this fact in an interesting implicit memory study in which subjects were asked to generate a borrowed foreign word from its definition and were then tested for fragment completion priming. Priming was observed for Hiragana as well as Katakana fragments. Since the subjects would have been highly unlikely to have ever seen the target words written in Hiragana, the priming of these fragments could only have come about via some kind of semantic process.

Data-driven perceptual learning processes cannot, therefore, account for all demonstrations of implicit memory, so some other form of memory must be responsible for what is learned. Progress in describing other possible forms of implicit memory has been slow, although there have been attempts to explain the implicit memory underlying learning of control tasks such as sugar production. One class of theory is the **instance theory** in which subjects construct a 'look up' table which would determine the appropriate action by matching the current situation with the most similar entry in the table. Evaluation of this and contrasting theories designed to account for this type of learning are beyond our present scope (see Berry and Dienes, in press, for a discussion). What should be clear, however, is that these theories are of a different kind from those used to account for implicit memory tasks such as repetition priming.

Systems versus Processes

Although we initially defined the terms 'explicit' and 'implicit memory' in terms of task demands, the foregoing discussion illustrates very clearly that these terms have come to be considered as coextensive with different memory systems. The explicit system appears to be singular, but it is clear that the systems account must propose a number of implicit memory systems to handle the various learning phenomena.

Roediger (1990; see also Roediger and Blaxton, 1987; Roediger et al., 1989; Srinivas and Roediger, 1990) has raised doubts about the systems approach to implicit memory, on the grounds that the various systems postulated do not meet the criteria for separable memory systems (Sherry and Schacter, 1987). Instead, he and his colleagues have proposed a **transfer-appropriate processing** (see chapter 2) account of implicit and explicit memory. Their argument is that memory for a prior occurrence results from the overlap between the retrieval processes induced by a memory test and the encoding operations undertaken during learning. Within this framework, memory tests are either conceptually driven, in that performance depends on some recapitulation of the elaborative process that took place during encoding, or data-driven, in that performance depends on the overlap between perceptual processing at encoding and retrieval.

Most tests of explicit memory tend to be conceptually driven, whereas those of implicit memory are data-driven. Roediger's point, however, is that these relationships are not exclusive, and do not, therefore, meet the strong criterion for a multiple memory system which requires that the operating characteristics of the two systems be mutually exclusive of one another (Sherry and Schacter, 1987).

Roediger et al. operationally define conceptually driven and data-driven tasks using the study manipulations devised by Jacoby (1983). Jacoby's subjects studied words in three different conditions:

No context condition: 'xxx' – 'cold'
Subject reads word aloud.
Generate condition: 'hot' – ?
Subject generates an association.
Context condition: 'hot' – 'cold'
Subject reads word out in presence of semantic associate.

Jacoby found that the no context condition facilitated later perceptual identification, whereas the generate condition produced the best recognition performance. Extrapolating from these data, a memory test is considered data-driven when performance in the no context condition exceeds that in the generate condition. Conversely, when performance in the generate condition is better than performance in the no context condition, a memory test is considered conceptually driven.

Blaxton (1985) compared five memory tests, three of them explicit, two implicit. Two of the explicit tasks were considered to be conceptually driven (free recall and cued recall), but the third (graphemic cued recall) was assumed to be data-driven. One of the implicit tasks (fragment completion) was considered data-driven, the other, answering general knowledge questions, conceptually driven. Blaxton found better performance in the generate condition compared to no context on all conceptually driven tasks, regardless of whether they were classified as explicit or implicit, and better performance in the no context relative to the generate condition in the implicit and explicit tasks assumed to be data-driven.

Examples of the tasks used by Blaxton, all referring to the target 'copper' are as follows:

1   Graphemic cued recall: 'chopper' (explicit; data-driven).
2   Free recall: no cues given (explicit; conceptually driven).
3   Fragment completion (implicit; data driven).
4   General knowledge test: what makes up 10 per cent of yellow gold? (implicit; conceptually driven).

Findings such as these suggest that functional dissociations between memory tests depend on whether the tests require different modes of processing rather than on whether they meet the criterion of implicit or explicit. There are difficulties, however, with this approach. First, can we be sure that the data-driven explicit task (graphemic cued recall) is really what it says it is? Looking at the letters 'chopper', it is quite easy to imagine that correct recall of 'copper' arises via priming. Another problem is that it is difficult to see how the process approach can explain the pattern of preserved implicit memory in amnesic patients. Although it has not been tested formally, it is highly unlikely that amnesic subjects would perform at all well on graphemic cued recall, if it were a genuine explicit test, we know because they have highly defective memory for previous events even though they perform well on repetition priming. To account for amnesia, therefore, we would have to argue for a dissociation between different types of data-driven processes. A model of implicit memory based on different types of systems therefore seems preferable (see also Schacter, 1992, for further arguments against the process approach and Poediger and McDermott (in press) for a review of implicit memory research including a discussion of different theoretical approaches).

Overview

In this chapter we have considered different approaches to the organization of long-term store. There seems to be general agreement that procedural memory is independent of consciously accessible memory. However, the view that consciously accessible memory can be further divided into episodic and semantic forms is debatable. Memory can also be classified in relation to implicit and explicit memory tests, and there is a growing belief that these types of task map on to different memory systems. An alternative process approach has been put forward, but this has trouble accounting for the nature of preserved implicit memory in amnesia. At present, explicit memory is treated as a single system, whereas implicit memory is divisible into a number of independent subsystems.

4

Remembering and Forgetting

Ah, Jeanne, anyone who says to me, 'Do you remember?', has my heart. . . . I remember everything.

Katherine Mansfield

The existence of forgetting has never been proved: we only know that some things don't come to mind when we want them to.

Friedrich Nietzsche

On 22 September 1969 Susan Nason disappeared while running an errand for her mother, and two months later her body was found in a ravine outside her home town in California. Despite the presence of many clues, Susan's murderer was not found, and the crime remained unsolved until a curious sequence of events 20 years later.

Eileen Franklin-Lipsker, a childhood friend of Susan, was feeding her young son one day when her older daughter, Jessica, looked up at her and asked her a question. For some reason the look on her daughter's face suddenly brought back images of Susan's final moments of life, and for the next few months Eileen began to reassemble detailed recollections of the events leading up to Susan's death. She recalled her father taking both of them for a car ride, stopping in the countryside, her father attempting to rape Susan, and, finally, Susan's brutal murder. Almost a year after recalling these events, Eileen contacted the police and told them everything. Her father was arrested, tried, and is now serving a term of life imprisonment.

This story emphasizes that forgetting can often be a case of failing to remember. Eileen's story is extremely unusual but by no means unique, and represents the phenomenon of **repression**, a form of forgetting we will tackle later in the chapter. It is also the kind of story that gives rise to the idea that all forgetting can be explained as a failure to remember.

Is All Forgetting Failing to Remember?

In chapter 1 we encountered a surgical procedure known as temporal lobectomy as a means of treating severe epilepsy. In the early years of this operation the procedure was somewhat risky, because neurosurgeons did not have sufficient information about the functions carried out by different parts of the temporal lobes. One method whereby surgeons attempted to evaluate the consequences of removing a certain part of the brain entailed **brain stimulation**. Briefly, the patient was first fully anaesthetized, and the part of the skull covering the target brain region was exposed. The patient was then allowed to regain consciousness, and his or her brain was stimulated in different areas. The resulting effects were noted, and some idea of the functional proprieties of that area of the brain were established.

In right-handed patients a frequent consequence of stimulating the left temporal lobe was spontaneous speech. One surgeon, Wilder Penfield, became fascinated by what patients said (Penfield, 1958). He noted that the patients' utterances were often recollections and, what's more, that they were largely very trivial: 'I just heard one of my children speaking. . . . It was Frank, and I could hear the neighbourhood noises'; 'Something brings back a memory. I can see the Seven-Up bottling company. . . . Harrison Bakers'. Penfield used these observations to argue that the brain contained a permanent record of all experiences (the 'stream of consciousness') and that any forgetting was simply due to retrieval failure.

Penfield's views were peculiarly influential considering the rather weak basis on which they were formed. In 1980, for example, Loftus and Loftus found that Penfield's ideas about memory were accepted by the majority of professional psychologists and that only experimental psychologists were, rightly, sceptical. Loftus and Loftus set about re-examining Penfield's data, and found them to be far less convincing than had originally been thought. Of the 520 patients at whose brains were stimulated only 40 appeared to show any recollection, and of these, only 12 seemed to be genuine cases of recall. Furthermore, when the content of these 12 patients' recall was explored in detail, the 'memories' were found to resemble dreams rather than the recollection of events.

Storage versus Retrieval Failure

If we dismiss failing to remember as the sole basis of forgetting, we must entertain two distinct possibilities. The first is **storage failure**, which can be defined as some inability of the memory system to produce a permanent memory trace of a given event. Storage failure might occur either because no transfer from STS to LTS was initiated or because the permanent memory trace formed was lost for some reason. By contrast, forgetting due to **retrieval failure** has its origins in some inability of the memory system to locate an existing memory trace.

Forgetting due to storage failure is most easily demonstrated in experiments in which the normal biological processes of learning are nterfered with in some way. In a unique study, Yarnell and Lynch (1973) investigated memory processes in American football players. In this game, players form a huddle, in which they receive a coded sequence which specifies the forthcoming play. With this in mind the players then face the opposition, and when play commences, each player acts according to the specified play. Unfortunately, a player may collide with one of the opposition players and suffer concussion (or are 'dinged' in the parlance of the game). Dinged players are easy to spot as they wander aimlessly around the field, and the investigators were curious to know what these unfortunate men could remember about the 'play'. Intriguingly, they found that the players had very good recall immediately after being dinged, but by the time they reached the touchline for treatment, all memory for the 'play' had gone.

Yarnell and Lynch's study is most easily interpreted as forgetting due to storage failure brought on by concussion disrupting the mechanisms of consolidation. The study also has the advantage of ecological validity (see chapter 1), although many would argue that the conditions under which the study was carried out were rather uncontrolled. More convincing evidence of storage failure comes from studies such as that carried out by Calev et al. (1989) into the effects of the anti-depressive drug **imipramine**. In chapter 1 I emphasized the importance of acetylcholine in the memory process and how drugs which antagonize the action of this substance impair memory. Imipramine is also known to have anticholinergic effects, and the study examined the drug's effects on both new learning and subjects' ability to remember events prior to administration of the drug. Patients given imipramine were compared with patients rendered temporarily amnesic following **electroconvulsive therapy** (ECT) – a treatment for depression involving the administration of an electric current to the temporal lobes. Imipramine subjects were found to be as impaired as ECT patients at learning new verbal and visual information. However, when asked to remember events from before their treatment, the performance of the imipramine group was close to normal. The ECT group, by contrast, showed a pronounced inability to remember prior events, particularly in the period immediately before ECT treatment commenced.

The results obtained with imipramine are found with other drugs as well (e.g. benzodiazepines and marijuana), and provide a clear indication that forgetting can be caused by storage failure. However, although they provide a *prima facie* case for this kind of forgetting, these studies do not tell us much about the psychological factors that determine this storage failure under normal conditions. Indeed, one might even argue that forgetting due to storage failure occurs only under conditions of abnormal brain function. Confronted with this kind of view, we are forced to argue that the 'video record' account of memory is intuitively implausible, because it is difficult to understand why any organism should store away every single event it experiences, and that, from an adaptability point of view, a memory system that stores away only what is relevant is decidedly more efficient in terms of both the storage space required and organization.

But if we are to accept the concept of a memory system which results in only a fraction of our experiences being selected for permanent storage, we must offer some pyschological theory as to how the selection occurs. One possibility is to invoke the notion of **intention**. It is a truism to say that if we try to learn something, we are more likely to remember it subsequently but intention cannot be the only factor determining learning. In chapter 2, for example, we saw that incidental learning can be as effective as intentional learning provided our processing of information occurs at a particular level. An alternative proposal is that STS exerts some form of executive control over what information is stored in memory. Intention is one aspect of this control, but other factors such as the individual's past experience and current and future goals also determine what aspects of experience are remembered. Such an arrangement clearly makes a lot of sense, and shows that selective storage failure is an asset rather than a disadvantage.

How, then, might we explore the psychological basis for storage failure? We could, for example, conduct an experiment in which subjects were shown a list of 30 words and, after an interval, give them a recall test. The subjects would not be expected to recall all the words, so for those that they fail to recall, we provide additional cues. After extensive cueing, we find we cannot facilitate recall of some of the words; can we now conclude that memory for these words has been subject to storage failure and investigate why it has occurred? The answer is no, because we cannot be sure that our attempts to facilitate recall have been exhaustive.

It is therefore difficult to provide a psychological explanation of why storage failure occurs, because any forgetting attributed to this cause could also be attributable to retrieval failure – how often have you tried desperately to remember something, only for it to come to mind much later? Indeed, there is a well-established phenomenon called **hypermnesia**, in which the amount remembered about a given event increases across time (see Payne, 1987). Only studies involving some physical intervention in the biological mechanisms underlying memory enable us to be confident that forgetting due to storage failure can occur; but these kinds of experiments do not help us to understand the psychological factors that might determine storage failure under normal conditions. For this reason, most psychological investigations of forgetting have concentrated on different aspects of retrieval failure. But to understand these accounts, we must first consider the nature of retrieval in greater detail.

Generation–Recognition Models

One of William James's many great insights was his awareness that retrieval of past experiences must be guided in some way: 'Suppose I am silent for a moment and then say . . . Remember! Recollect! Does your . . . memory obey the order, and reproduce any definite image from the past? Certainly not. It stands staring into vacancy, and asking, What kind of a thing do you want me to remember?' (James, 1899, pp. 117–18). James's point is that retrieval is essentially a **reconstructive** process, involving an interaction between information currently available and that stored in memory. Modern approaches to explaining retrieval are still based on this fundamental axiom that retrieval is a guided search process.

The first systematic attempts to explain retrieval as a reconstructive process were the **generation–recognition** (GR) models (see Watkins and Gardiner, 1979 for a detailed account). Although they vary in their exact specifications, they all operate in essentially the same way. At the outset of the retrieval process, the system **generates** possible candidates for the memory that is being sought. These candidates are then subjected to a **recognition** process, which, if successful, results in that candidate being retrieved as a memory.

The best-known examples of GR models are those of Anderson and Bower (1972) and Kintsch (1970). These models specifically address how subjects retrieve words in a verbal learning experiment; but it must be borne in mind that the intention was to produce a general account of retrieval. The models assume a structure rather like semantic memory, in which each known word is represented by a **node**. When a subject studies a word, it is assumed that some form of 'occurrence marker' or 'tag' is set up, to indicate that the word was part of the target list. When recall is attempted, various candiates are generated, and the corresponding nodes are examined for markers, which, if detected, result in recognition and hence retrieval. In recognition, access to the node was considered to be automatic, and recognition was dependent simply on detection of a marker.

In chapter 3 I drew a distinction between implicit and explicit memory tests, and pointed out that explicit memory can be tested in three ways: by free recall, cued recall, and recognition. Under normal conditions these three types of task are related in an orderly way. Free recall will always produce poorer retrieval than cued recall, which, in turn, is inferior to recognition. Any model of retrieval must therefore account for this consistently observed relationship. GR models explain it on the grounds that, in free recall, the generation phase has less information to guide it than is available when a cue is present. Recognition produces even better performance, because the fallible generation stage is bypassed altogether and the subject simply has to detect evidence that the presented item is a target.

GR models are able to account for a number of other findings as well. A well-established finding is that words used with high-frequency in the language (e.g. 'table', 'dog') are easier to recall than low-frequency words (e.g. 'barge', 'pine'), whereas the reverse is true of recognition memory. The better recall of high-frequency words can be attributed to the greater probability of them being generated as candidates for recognition. The poorer recognition, in turn, arises because higher-frequency words may be expected to be associated with a greater number of occurrence markers, making it more difficult to decide whether that word was presented in a specific list.

Another important finding explained by GR models is the influence of **extra-experimental association** on cued recall. If subjects are given a stimulus word (e.g. 'table') and are asked to free associate, they will produce some words (e.g. 'chair') far more often than others (e.g. 'glue').

A number of studies have shown that this measure of extra-experimental association is an accurate predictor of cued recall performance, in that cues with a strong extra-experimental association with their target word are far more effective than cues where this relationship is weak (e.g. Bahrick, 1970). In terms of GR theory, this effect of extra-experimental association arises because the generative process is governed by the same principles that operate in free association.

The Encoding Specificity Principle

The GR theory was a good theory in that it gave rise to a testable prediction. According to the theory, recall of an item involves both successful generation and successful recognition, whereas recognition involves just the latter stage of the retrieval process. From this it follows that any item we are able to recall must be capable of being recognized, because the recognition process must have been involved in recall.

This prediction was the subject of a series of experiments carried out by Tulving and his colleagues (e.g. Tulving and Osler, 1968; Tulving and Thomson, 1973). The basic experiment consisted of four phases. In phase 1 subjects were presented with a target word along with a cue word which they were asked to attend to but not try to remember. The target and cue words were not closely associated with one another, e.g. 'engine' – 'black'. In phase 2 subjects were given another list of words, each of which was a strong associate of one of the target words in the learning list (e.g. 'steam'). For each of these phase 2 words subjects had to generate several associations, and because of the list's construction there was a high probability that subjects would produce target items from the list as associations (e.g. 'steam' – 'engine'). In phase 3 subjects were asked to indicate whether any of the words they had generated were target words from the list presented in phase 1. Finally, they were given the low-value cue words and asked to recall which items were paired with them during phase 1.

According to GR theory, any target word recalled successfully in phase 4 should also have been recognized in phase 3; this follows on the assumption that the recognition process undertaken as part of cued recall in phase 4 is the same recognition process as is carried out when only recognition is required in phase 3. The results contradicted this prediction however, in that words recalled in phase 4 were often not recognized in phase 3 – a phenomenon that has been termed 'recognition failure of recallable words' or, for short, **recognition failure**.

On the basis of these recognition failure results, Tulving and Thomson (1973) put forward the **encoding specificity principle** (ESP), which proposed that recall and recognition are different manifestations of a single retrieval system and that the retrieval of information depends critically on the degree of overlap between these features encoded in the memory trace and those present in the retrieval environment (e.g. the information provided by a recognition probe or a cue). To explain their own data, Tulving and Thomson proposed that the learning manipulation in phase 1 resulted in an encoding of the target word which emphasized its featural overlap with the low associative cue. When recognition was tested in phase 3, the target was presented in a retrieval environment specifying a different pattern of featural overlap to that encoded during learning (i.e. one emphasizing the target's relations with a strong associative cue), with the result that insufficient overlap existed for a successful recognition response to occur. By contrast, the potentially more difficult cued recall task was in fact easier, because the cues had a high degree of featural overlap with the target memory trace. Recall and recognition were thus independent of one another, because they had differing featural overlap with the target as encoded.

Other findings also seemed consistent with ESP. The superiority of strong associates over weak associates as retrieval cues could be explained by assuming that, without any constraints imposed, subjects will tend to encode the dominant meaning of a stimulus during learning. Now, because pre-experimental associative strength and semantic overlap are highly confounded (e.g. 'table' is not only the commonest associate of 'chair', it also shares a large number of semantic features), it follows that any strong associative cue will also have a high degree of featural overlap.

The encoding specificity principle also accounted for the general relationship between recall, cued recall, and recognition, by arguing that, on average, recall tests provide a more impoverished retrieval environment than cued recall tasks, which, in turn, provide less information about target memory than a recognition test (see figure 4.1). The essential proposal, however, is that the contrast between recognition and recall is not a matter of qualitative differences in the underlying memory system. Rather, it reflects the operation of a single retrieval system whose prime determinant is featural overlap between memory trace and retrieval environment. Recognition superiority is therefore the norm, because, as a form of testing, it usually provides the most featural overlap with a target trace. However, as Tulving and Thomson's demonstration shows, memory can be manipulated so that cued recall for an item can be better than recognition.

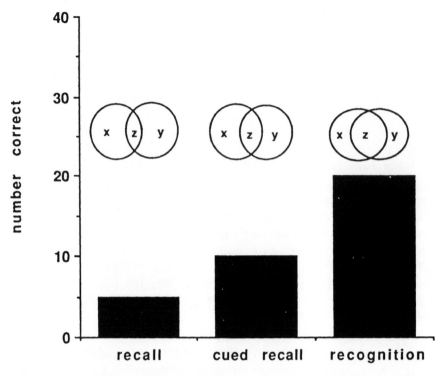

Fig. 4.1. The typical relationship between recall and recognition according to the encoding specificity principle, where x = trace, y = retrieval environment, z = overlap.

The Tulving–Wiseman 'law'

The major empirical fact supporting encoding specificity and undermining generation–recognition models came from the findings of recognition failure experiments. During the 1970s there was quite an industry in demonstrating recognition failure under a variety of circumstances, and Flexser and Tulving (1978) were able to examine 89 sets of data in which recognition failure had been measured. Figure 4.2 shows the relationship between recognition and recall in these studies; it appears that the two measures are independent of one another. Figure 4.3 shows a different plot from these data, with the probability of recognition plotted against the probability of recognizing word that has been recalled. The broken line indicates the values that would obtained if recall and recognition were independent of one another. Values falling above

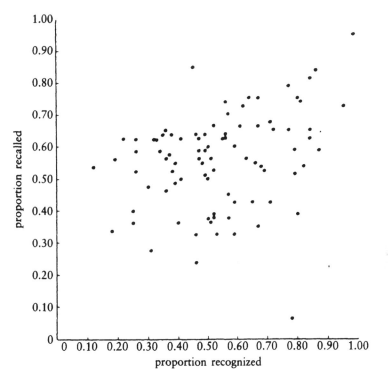

Fig. 4.2. Probability of recall of target words as a function of the probability of recognition of the same words. Each data point represents a separate experiment or condition in an experiment. From Tulving, 1983, p. 294. Reproduced with the permission of the American Psychological Association.

the line thus indicate that recall is dependent on recognition. It is evident from figure 4.4 that the values tend to fall above the line; but the distribution is not what one would expect if GR theory were correct. For if recalling a word depends on successful recognition, it follows that the proportion of items recalled and recognized should be close to 1, regardless of the absolute level of recognition performance. Instead, it appears that there is only a limited, if significant, relationship between recall and recognition (indicated by the solid line), a finding that has variously been termed the Tulving–Wiseman function, or 'law', after the original study in which it was described (Wiseman and Tulving, 1975).

Figures 4.2 and 4.3 appear to present an impressive set of data arguing against any strong relationship between recall and recognition, but various objections to these findings have been raised. Santa and Lamwers

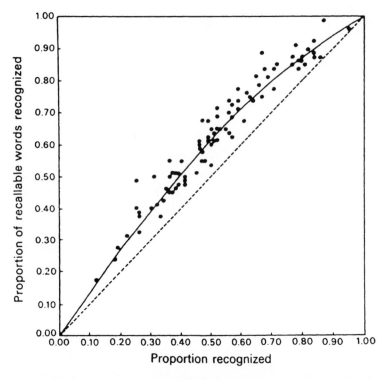

Fig. 4.3. Probability of recognition of recallable target words as a function of the probability of recognition of all target words. Each data point represents a separate experiment or condition in an experiment. From Tulving, 1983, p. 294. Reproduced with the permission of the American Psychological Association.

(1974) took the view that in recognition failure experiments subjects were simply confused about what was required of them in the recognition phase of the experiment, and that when different instructions were issued the critical effect was not demonstrated. More recently, Hintzman (1992) argued that the Tulving–Wiseman function 'is an artifact, essentially a visual illusion caused by mathematical constraints' (p. 536). He maintained that these constraints arise in data sets in which recall exceeds recognition because, under these conditions, it is logically impossible for the proportion of words recalled and recognized to be 1. This in turn creates a 'ceiling', which prevents the generation of data points that would be more indicative of a dependence between recall and recognition.

Tulving and Flexser (1992) have responded to Hintzman's criticisms by dividing the original 89 studies into those in which recall exceeded recognition and those in which recognition equalled or exceeded recall. Analysis showed that the two subsets of data did not differ significantly from one another, and on this basis the authors argued that the Tulving–Wiseman function, and hence its implications for the relationship between recall and recognition, were still valid.

Context

Encoding specificity experiments were important, because they alerted theorists to the importance of **context** in determining remembering. Context is a much used and, according to some, much abused term which can be defined in a number of ways. One useful approach, first put forward by Hewitt (1973), draws a distinction between **intrinsic** and **extrinsic context**. Intrinsic context refers to various features that are an integral part of a target stimulus. For a word, the intrinsic context constitutes the particular subset of features encoded about that word at the time of learning (e.g. those features that associate 'train' with 'black'). Extrinsic context represents those features that are present when the target is encountered but are not, themselves, an integral part of the stimulus. Examples of this include the place and time where the stimulus was encountered, plus other associations such as the experimenter's mannerisms.

Returning to the encoding specificity results, it is clear that they were obtained by manipulations of intrinsic context. It also becomes apparent that a modification of generation–recognition theories could accommodate Tulving and Thomson's result. Prior to the encoding specificity experiments, generation–recognition theorists had operated under what we will term the **trans-situational identity assumption**. This is the assumption that words are represented by 'atomistic' nodes and that, whenever a given word is learned in an experiment, this node, representing all aspects of the word's meaning, is activated. The encoding specificity work suggested that this assumption was wrong and that remembering a target word involved encoding only a subset of the features potentially available about that word. It was but a small step to provide a modification of GR theory to accommodate the effects of intrinsic context. All that was needed was to modify the model so that it operated at the level of individual features rather than atomistic word units (Reder et al., 1974).

A feature-based GR model could thus handle the data from encoding specificity experiments by arguing that under certain cued recall conditions the cue can generate more features in common with a target than a recognition probe presented under conditions designed to de-emphasize its relationship with the target. A problem, however, is that this modification brings to the GR model a major theoretical weakness of the ESP namely, – **circularity of explanation**. Consider a hypothetical experiment in which a subject learns some new information. Two cues, X and Y, are then presented successively, but only Y results in correct recall. ESP asserts on the basis of this that Y must have an overlap with the target trace, whereas X does not. However, if X were singularly successful, the opposite conclusion about the nature of the memory trace would be reached. A modified GR theory falls into the same trap, in that successful recall would be attributed to the featural similarity between target and retrieval environment, which, in turn, is inferred from whether or not recall is successful.

Although ESP and GR accounts of retrieval now seem much more similar than when we started out, they still differ in important ways. The ESP account proposes that retrieval is a direct result of the interaction between the retrieval environment and the stored trace and that recall and recognition are different manifestations of a single retrieval process:

trace ← – – → retrieval environment

Retrieval is achieved when the overlap between the stored trace and the retrieval environment reaches some critical value. The important point to note is that only information in the retrieval environment can facilitate trace retrieval.

GR theory specifies a different relationship between trace and re-trieval environment. Information in the retrieval environment constitutes the stimulus for a generative process whose output is tested against the contents of memory. Recall occurs when a recognition match between the generated information and the trace reaches a critical level; recall and recognition are thus separate stages in retrieval:

trace ← – – → generative mediation ← – – → retrieval environment

Under these conditions the information provided by the retrieval envir-onment may influence retrieval directly, because part of what it repre-sents is generated in an attempt to contact the target trace. However, the retrieval environment can also facilitate retrieval indirectly, by caus-ing the generative mediation stage to produce information that, al-though not specified by the retrieval environment, overlaps with the trace.

To understand the above difference, consider an imaginary situation in which the subject learns the word 'chair' as a target, and, because a non-semantic orienting task was imposed during learning, the target trace comprises only phonological information. At test the cue 'table' is presented, and is successful in facilitating recall. On the basis of ESP one would have to argue that 'table' succeeded as a cue because, despite the imposition of non-semantic orienting conditions, semantic processing sufficient to realize the meaningful overlap with 'chair' was still carried out. The GR account is perhaps less strained, because it can be argued that no relationship exists between 'table' and 'chair' as encoded but that, on presentation, 'table' led to the generation of 'chair' and that this internal representation included phonological information, which, in turn, caused trace overlap and successful retrieval.

It can be seen that GR imparts a degree of flexibility to the retrieval process that is not possible in the ESP account. This flexibility would certainly be an advantage to an organism, because the latter's ability to retrieve information would then not be strictly bound by its immediate external environment. However, what evidence is there to indicate a generative stage in recall? The evidence showing that cued recall is positively correlated with pre-experimental associative strength does not bear on the issue (see above). The existence of a generative stage can be effectively demonstrated only under conditions where informational overlap between target and trace is held constant but the probability of a cue generating a target is manipulated.

I carried out an experiment of this type in 1981. In the first part, subjects were presented with a series of words (e.g. 'leak') and asked for the first word they could think of that rhymed with each one. A sufficient number of words generated two rhyming responses which differed greatly in the probability with which subjects generated them but differed from the cue word by just the initial letter (e.g. 'beak'; 'teak'). All else being equal, it was assumed that the two response words had equal informational overlap with the cue word. On the basis of ESP, therefore, it was predicted that recall of both items would be equiprobable in the presence of the rhyming cue word.

An experiment was then constructed in which a different group of subjects attempted to learn target words known to have either a high or a low probability of being generated by rhyming cue words but matched in terms of informational overlap. Figure 4.4 shows that associative strength had no effect on recognition, but was a powerful determinant of recall performance, even when informational overlap was held constant. This finding points toward a generative component in recall, although there may well be limitations in the extent to which

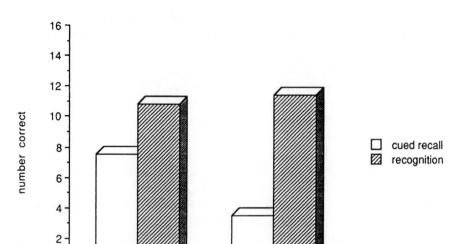

Fig. 4.4. Data from Parkin, 1981, p. 295, showing the influence of cue-target strength on recall and recognition. Reproduced with permission.

generation strategies can be used. In the bulk of our remembering we are not aware of any generation, so it is possible that generative effects, such as those I reported in 1982, may represent just an auxiliary, voluntary retrieval strategy (e.g. Rabinowitz et al., 1979) rather than providing an indication that generation is an integral part of retrieval per se.

Before leaving this issue, there is one more point of similarity between GR and ESP approaches that must be emphasized. Both accounts involve a reconstructive approach to retrieval in which a hypothesis is formed about the nature of the target memory trace. At some point, both approaches assume that a decision is made about the current reconstruction, which results either in a conscious recollection or in a continuation of the retrieval process. Explaining how this decision is reached presents a major theoretical problem, which has, as yet, failed to receive any solution. GR models side-step the issue by referring to 'list' or 'node' markers subject to a 'recognition check' as the basis on which an item is accepted as a memory. Tulving (1983) is perhaps a little more direct, in that he attributes the determination of conscious recollection to a 'general abstract processing system', – an entity whose acronym, GAPS, he considers an appropriate summary of our knowledge about this aspect of the memory process.

The Complexity of Recognition

Up to now, we have considered recognition as a single process, but there is mounting evidence that it involves two components. This approach to understanding recognition owes much to the work of Mandler (1980), who introduced his account by asking us to:

> Consider seeing a man on a bus whom you are sure you have seen before; you 'know' him in that sense. Such a recognition is usually followed by a search process asking, in effect, Where could I know him from? Who is he? The search process generates likely contexts . . . [and] . . . eventually may end with an insight, That's the butcher from the supermarket! (pp. 252–3)

Mandler argued that this indicated two stages to recognition: an initial **familiarity** response and identification following **context retrieval**. On this theory, then, recognition can be either **context-free**, when only familiarity information is available, or **context-dependent**, when the prior occurrence of a stimulus has to be specified in place or time.

The example of recognizing someone as familiar but not being able to place them in context is rather atypical, in that, normally, we are not aware of any dissociation between familiarity and context-dependent aspects of recognition. Experiments show, however, that these two processes underlie recognition memory. Mandler and Boeck (1974) asked subjects to sort 100 randomly selected words into categories, and found significant variation in the number of categories that individual subjects invoked. In line with earlier studies, they found that subjects who used more sorting categories achieved better recall and recognition performance; this was attributed to better initial organization and differentiation of the words. A recognition test was given a week later in which the speed of subjects' recognition responses was recorded. Each subject's reaction times were divided into slow and fast before examining how initial organization affected recognition speed. For slow responses the effect of organization was again evident, in that subjects who sorted the words into fewer categories had longer reaction times. However, for the fast responses, the organizational factor had no effect.

Discussing their results, Mandler and Boeck concluded that the slow recognition responses were indicative of the context-retrieval process operating in recognition and that this was slower for memories that were less well organized. Faster responses, by contrast, were assumed to reflect familiarity responses, and for this reason were not sensitive to the organization factor.

Although the Mandler and Boeck study and other similar studies (e.g. Atkinson and Juola, 1974) could be interpreted in terms of a dual process theory, they did not provide direct evidence that recognition based on familiarity could be dissociated from that based on context retrieval. A recent study by Rugg and Doyle (1992) provides electrophysiological evidence for two forms of recognition memory. It has been proposed that words with low frequencies of occurrence (e.g. 'barge') are more likely to be recognized on the basis of familiarity than high-frequency words (e.g. 'table'), the argument being that the fewer past encounters with a low-frequency word mean that, on exposure, its absolute familiarity will be increased by a proportionately greater amount than a high-frequency word. In Rugg and Doyle's experiment, subjects were asked to recognize high- and low-frequency targets while at the same time measuring **event-related potentials** (ERPs). This is a form of electroencephalography in which the brain's electrical activity is measured in a number of different places at the precise point moment that a stimulus is encountered. Recognition of low-frequency targets produced larger ERPs than low-frequency distractors, but no difference was found between high-frequency targets and distractors. These data, combined with other findings indicating that increased ERP is associated with familiarity-based responding, led Rugg and Doyle to conclude that the recognition advantage for low-frequency words was due to greater reliance on familiarity.

Evidence for separable familiarity and context-dependent aspects of recognition was provided in a study by Huppert and Piercy (1978) in which the recognition memory of amnesic Korsakoff patients and controls was investigated. On day 1 of the study, subjects were given picture postcards to try and remember. Half of these were shown only once, and half three times. On day 2 another set of postcards was presented, and, as before, half were presented once and half three times. All subjects were then given a recognition test for the postcards, and whenever they identified one, they were asked to indicate whether they had seen it on day 1 or day 2.

Figure 4.5 shows the results. Control subjects performed very well, in that they easily discriminated day 1 targets from day 2 targets. Korsakoff patients performed very differently. They were comparable to controls in classifying targets presented three times on day 2, but could not distinguish between items presented once on day 2 from those presented three times on day 1. On the assumption that familiarity fades with time, the performance of the Korsakoff patients indicates that their judgement as to which day a picture was presented was based solely on

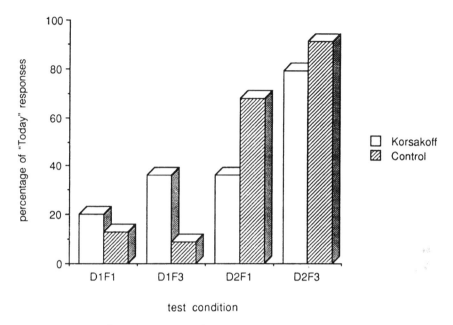

Fig. 4.5. Data from Huppert and Piercy, 1978, p. 349. Key: D1 = day 1, D2 = day 2. F1 = pictures presented once, F3 = pictures presented three times.

familiarity. Thus pictures presented three times on day 1 seemed as familiar as those presented once on day 2, and were thus indistinguishable. Controls, by contrast, have contextual recollection available as well, and can therefore distinguish the two situations.

Other findings from amnesic subjects also suggest that responding based on familiarity is preserved independently of context-based recognition. I and my colleagues (Parkin et al., 1990b), for example, found that Korsakoff patients were able to identify target items from an array of distractors after a short interval without difficulty as long as the distractor items had not been seen previously. However, when the distractors had been exposed on previous trials and thereby made familiar, Korsakoff patients found the task largely impossible because of their inability to retain any contextual memory (see also Hunkin and Parkin, in press).

We thus have converging evidence that recognition can be based on two types of processes: familiarity and context retrieval. The next task is to explain how these different components of recognition operate.

One idea developed by Johnston and his colleagues (Johnston et al., 1985, 1991) is that context retrieval is essentially a search process, hence its sensitivity to factors such as organization during learning. Familiarity is held to be dependent on perceptual fluency. This, it will be recalled, refers to the increased speed with which a previously exposed stimulus will be identified if re-presented. It is assumed that the locus of perceptual fluency effects lies within the perceptual system itself and that any cue arising from perceptual fluency will be reduced if the stimulus is re-presented in a different format from that used initially.

In the first phase of their experiment Johnston et al. (1985) asked subjects to read some words. During the test phase, these 'old' words were re-presented along with 'new' words. Both old and new words were severely degraded at first, but gradually they became clear enough for subjects to identify what they were. The subjects' task was to identify each word as soon as possible and then to say whether or not it was an old word. It was assumed that the time taken to identify each word was a direct measure of perceptual fluency – the faster the identification, the greater the amount of perceptual fluency available. Four types of response were therefore possible: hits (old words correctly identified as old), misses (old words incorrectly identified as new), false alarms (new words incorrectly identified as old), and correct rejections (new words correctly identified as new).

The logic of the experiment was that if perceptual fluency does provide a cue to recognition, then items identified as old should be associated with greater perceptual fluency irrespective of whether that decision is correct or not. The results of the study confirmed this prediction, and although objections to this early finding have been raised (Watkins and Gibson, 1988), more recent findings have confirmed and extended it (e.g. Johnston et al., 1991).

The perceptual fluency theory therefore proposes that familiarity judgements are data-driven, in that they appear to be dependent on the perceptual qualities of the stimulus. As we saw in chapter 3, implicit memory also exhibits data-driven qualities, so it is not a difficult step to considering familiarity-based responding as a form of recognition memory arising from the output of implicit memory. This conclusion also explains the relatively good performance of amnesic patients when they are able to respond on the basis of familiarity information, because, as we saw in chapter 3, amnesic patients tend to have preserved implicit memory abilities. However, we are not in a position to state that all familiarity-based responding is data-driven. Indeed, the fact that certain aspects of implicit memory are free from data-driven influences suggests that a similar state of affairs might apply with familiarity.

Subjective Differences in Recognition Memory

So far we have been considering objective evidence for the existence of two forms of recognition memory. Tulving (1983) introduced a new methodology for understanding the nature of recognition. This methodology originated from his view that memory for an event could be derived either from its representation in semantic memory or from episodic memory (see chapter 3). Tulving presented pilot data suggesting that subjects could reliably classify their recognition responses as either based or not based on conscious, episodic recollection. To achieve this, subjects were required, on recognizing a stimulus, to classify their response as either 'remember' (R) or 'know' (K). An R response represented recognition, the response being associated with some episodic recollection of the word's prior occurrence (e.g. an image or emotion it evoked), whereas a K response represented recognition without any specific recollection.

A number of recent studies have collectively demonstrated a functional double dissociation of processes underlying R and K responses (see Gardiner and Java, in press, for a review). Gardiner and I (1990) asked subjects to learn a list of words under either focused attention conditions or while performing a secondary task. At test the level of R responding was directly related to the demands of the secondary task, whereas K responding was unaffected. This suggests that R responses are dependent on consciously mediated processing operations, whereas K responses are not – a conclusion supported by additional findings that R responses are also affected by levels of processing, intentional learning instructions, and by tranquillizers that affect conscious processing resources (Gardiner, 1988; Gardiner and Java, 1992; Curran et al., 1992).

Several studies have now identified variables which have opposite effects on R and K responding. Russo and I (Parkin and Russo, in press) examined how spacing influenced the distribution of R and K responses. A well-established finding is that if items are repeated during a learning sequence, they will be remembered better, and that the beneficial effects of repetition will be greater if other items are presented in between – a phenomenon known as the **spacing effect**. Russo and I examined the effects of spacing on the pattern of R and K responses produced as a function of item spacing. For items classified as R, a conventional spacing effect was found, but for items classified as K, there was a 'reverse' spacing effect, with more items being classified as K when repeated immediately. Our data thus suggest that different types of process give rise to R and K recognition responses.

If we accept that R and K responses are qualitatively different, our next task is to explain in more detail what is reponsible for these two kinds of recognition memory. An important clue lies in the nature of the variables affecting the two types of response. The factors affecting R responses are all factors that we know influence performance on measures of explicit memory (see chapter 3), so it is reasonably straightforward to equate R responding with the memory processes responsible for explicit memory performance.

Can we, as suggested above, argue that K responding is a form of implicit memory? Many of the variables known to influence explicit memory (e.g. retention interval, levels of processing, divided attention, spaced repetitions) have no effect or the opposite effect on the level of K responding. Evidence that K responding is data-driven – i.e. influenced by perceptual fluency – is less compelling, however. Gardiner and I (Parkin and Gardiner, in prep.) failed to find any effects of modality shifts on the relative distribution of R and K responses. However, one study has provided some evidence that K responses are data-driven (Rajaram, in press). But, given our acceptance of the fact that objective measures of familiarity need not be data-driven, it follows that K responding may be similarly unconstrained.

One problem in describing K responding as a form of implicit memory testing is that the conditions at test are not implicit in nature. Subjects are told to give a K response to any item they remember seeing, where this recollection does not involve any specific memory of having seen the word. It is therefore tempting to see K responding as noetic – i.e. based on the semantic representation of an event (see chapter 3). However, in doing this, we once again encounter problems concerning arguments against the episodic–semantic distinction.

Overview of Retrieval

Generation–recognition theory proposes that retrieval involves two stages. Recall also involves these two stages, but recognition proceeds without generation. Experiments on encoding specificity suggest, by contrast, that recall and recognition reflect a common retrieval process. The debate as to which of these theories is correct continues. Experiments on recognition memory indicate that two independent processes can contribute to recognition: context retrieval and familiarity. Context retrieval is dependent on explicit recollection, whereas the processes underlying familiarity-based responding bear a considerable similarity to those responsible for implicit memory phenomena. Context-retrieval and familiarity-based recognition are associated with different experiential awareness.

Context Effects

Regardless of which particular model of retrieval eventually proves correct, it is clear that context plays an important role in our everyday memories. I remember watching a travel programme on TV in which the director focused on what he thought was a typical inhabitant of the Loire Valley, who was, in fact, one of my departmental colleagues. Given this unlikely context, it took me about 30 seconds to carry out a recognition response that would normally occur almost instantly.

There are many formal demonstrations that context exerts powerful effects on our ability to identify things. In a classic experiment, Light and Carter-Sobell (1970) demonstrated how changes in the intrinsic context associated with a target could reduce recognition memory. Subjects studied simple sentences which biased subjects towards encoding one particular meaning of an ambiguous word (e.g. 'They were stuck in a traffic *jam*'). Retention testing involved subjects identifying the target words, which were again embedded in biasing sentences but, in half these, the sentence was biased toward a different meaning from that used at encoding (e.g. 'They enjoyed eating the *jam*'). It was found that recognition of the targets was significantly reduced when the biasing context at test was different from that at learning.

Disruptive effects of changing intrinsic context between learning and test are perhaps not surprising, because, in effect, what is being shown is that subjects are worse at remembering a different stimulus from the one they studied. More interesting, and potentially more relevant, is the possibility that extrinsic context could exert effects on remembering.

State-Dependent Memory

Godden and Baddeley (1975) examined memory performance in two distinct environments: on land and under water. It was found that free recall was better when the learning and the test environments were the same than when they were different. However, they found no evidence of this **state-dependent memory** when a recognition test was used (Godden and Baddeley, 1980).

S. M. Smith (1986) reports a similar study in which subjects were put through a number of memory span trials, either in a room or while immersed in a flotation tank. They were then given an unexpected final memory test for the items, and a significant state-dependent effect was found for both recall and recognition. A subsequent study examined whether changing rooms could exert state-dependent effects on recall and recognition. Memory span again served as the basic task, but half the subjects were told that memory for the words would be tested again later. Here it was found that a state-dependent effect occurred only when subjects did not know that recognition would be tested later.

Environmental context also appears to influence eyewitness accuracy. Smith and Vela (1992) staged an incident in which a confederate entered an introductory psychology class and announced that it was a fictitious person's birthday. He asked the class if 'she' was present, and when no one came forward, he left. After varying intervals the subjects were given a recognition test for the confederate in either the same room or a different one. Some of those in the different room were asked to try to reinstate mentally the original encounter with the confederate, while others were left to their own devices. Correct identification of the confederate was significantly better for the group in the same room. Moreover, subjects in the different room asked to reinstate the original context did particularly poorly – an interesting finding given that mental reinstatement under other conditions is held to improve eyewitness memory (e.g. Malpass and Devine, 1981).

There is a widespread belief that various psychoactive states, particularly states involving alcohol, can result in state-dependent learning. Goodwin et al. (1969) studied recall and recognition data for subjects who had recently consumed either a soft drink or a substantial amount of high-strength vodka. The next day the subjects were required to perform the same tasks again, either in the same state or a different state. A change in state (e.g. learn sober, test intoxicated) produced reliably lower recall performance, but there was no state-dependent effect on recognition.

During the next decade there was considerable interest in the ability of various drugs to induce state-dependent effects, but the results were very inconsistent. Analysing these studies, Eich (1980) noticed that 88 per cent of studies showing evidence for state-dependent effects had measured free recall, whereas 90 per cent of the studies failing to show state-dependency had used either cued recall or recognition.

There has also been substantial interest in the idea that mood can exert state-dependent effects on memory (e.g. Ucros, 1989). Bower (1981) asked subjects to keep a diary of the emotional aspects of their lives.

After one week, they were subjected to a **mood-induction** procedure in which hypnotic suggestion was used to make subjects either 'happy' or 'sad'. Subjects were then required to recall events, and it was found that there was a **mood-congruency** effect, with subjects in a happy mood recalling more pleasant memories and those in an unhappy mood recalling more unpleasant memories. A second study, by Bower et al. (1981), again used mood induction to create 'happy' or 'sad' subjects, and the subjects then listened to a story about Paul Smith. Half the events be falling Paul were positive and half negative, and a mood-congruency effect at recall was again found.

Findings like these were incorporated in a network model, in which mood selectively biased which aspects of an experience were remembered (Bower et al., 1981). However, since then, there has been controversy as to whether mood-congruency effects occur regularly. Hasher et al. (1985), for example, reported three failures to replicate findings of the type reported by Bower et al. (1981), and Bower himself also reported a failure to replicate his findings (Bower and Mayer, 1985). Discussing this, it was concluded that mood-congruency effects were 'evanescent will-o'-the-wisp' phenomena and that this 'spotty record of success' was 'Nature's way of telling us that our questions about mood-dependent memory are formulated too simplistically' (p. 42).

Many investigators regard the mood-induction procedure used in mood-congruency investigations as the major cause of inconsistent findings (e.g. Hasher et al., 1985). Bower and Mayer, for example, consider that their studies showing positive evidence for mood congruency used subjects who were highly familiar with hypnotic procedures and had greater rapport with the hypnotist. Hypnosis may have a strong compliance aspect (see below), so it is possible that positive evidence for mood congruency reflects the operation of **demand characteristics**. Experiments can be regarded as a social contract in which human subjects agree to be investigated. It has been argued that this co-operation may sometimes be extended so that the subject attempts to identify the hypothesis being tested and to respond accordingly. Consistent with a demand characteristics explanation of mood-congruency effects, Perrig and Perrig (1988) demonstrated that mood-congruent learning can also occur if subjects are simply instructed to behave *as if* they were happy or sad.

Doubts about possible compliance and demand-characteristic factors present in hypnotic induction procedures did not deter Rinck et al. (1992) from trying to demonstrate mood-congruency effects. After becoming either 'happy' or 'sad', subjects rated words on a seven-point scale ranging from −3 (very unpleasant) to +3 (very pleasant). Four

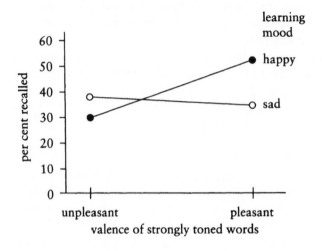

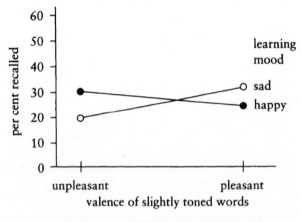

Fig. 4.6. Data from Rinck et al., 1992, p. 37, showing that mood-congruency effects occur with strongly toned words (*top*) but not with slightly toned words (*bottom*). Reproduced with the permission of the Psychonomic Society.

types of words were used: strongly unpleasant (e.g. ulcer), slightly un-pleasant (e.g. dirty), slightly pleasant (e.g. avenue), and strongly pleas-ant (e.g. beauty). Next day, free of induced mood, subjects were given an unexpected recall test. The results are shown in figure 4.6. For strongly toned words there is a mood-congruency effect, but for slightly toned words there is a **mood-incongruency** effect: subjects recalled more words incongruent with the mood they were in during learning.

Rinck et al.'s data are difficult to explain in terms of demand characteristics, because it is quite implausible that subjects could have noticed the difference between strongly and slightly toned words and responded accordingly. Instead, the authors suggest that while mood does have an effect, it is dependent on the emotional valence of the stimulus. Strongly toned words exert a mood-congruence effect, whereas slightly toned words result in either no effect or a mood-incongruency effect. However, the manner whereby the latter comes about is not very well specified by the authors.

Eich and Metcalfe (1989) reasoned that 'internal events', events that originate from mental operations such as reasoning or imagination, might be more influenced by current mood state than externally mediated events. If true, memory for these internal events should be more susceptible to mood-congruency effects than memory for external events. To test this idea, subjects were first put in either a happy or a sad mood by first listening to appropriate classical music (e.g. Mozart's *Eine kleine Nachtmusik* or Albinoni's *Adagio in G minor*). During the learning phase, subjects either read a target item paired with a category name and a related example (e.g. milkshake flavours: chocolate – *vanilla*) or generated the target item with a high probability when given the initial letter (e.g. milkshake flavours: chocolate – *v*-?). The researchers assumed that production of the response under the latter condition would correspond to an internal event, whereas that under the former conditions would correspond to something external. A subsequent retention test free of mood bias revealed two principal findings: that mood-congruency effects were much more substantial for generated than for read items, but only when free recall was measured. No effect of mood emerged with recognition testing.

While we may have some doubts about whether mood can affect memory in normal people, there seems little doubt that abnormal moods have a profound effect on memory. Lloyd and Lishman (1975) found that the time taken by depressed patients to recall negative experiences decreased as they became more depressed. Clark and Teasdale (1981) exploited the natural mood swings of depressed patients. They found that when the patients were relatively happy, they recalled more pleasant than unpleasant memories; but that when they sank into deep depression, unpleasant memories dominated their recall (see also Williams et al., 1988, for a recent review of this area). Williams and Broadbent (1986) found that depressed, suicidal patients found it more difficult to retrieve memories when prompted with positive cue words and that, even when successful, these memories were less specific (see chapter 6 for a further discussion of this last result). In a similar kind of study, Burke and Mathews (1992) presented clinically anxious and non-anxious subjects with neutral cues, and found that the anxious subjects produced more anxiety-related memories. Collectively these studies indicate that clinical mood states exert important influences on the pattern of memories retrieved – findings that may be significant for understanding the nature and maintenance of these disorders.

Overview of State-Dependent Effects

State-dependent effects thus seem to occur under a variety of different circumstances, but are found regularly only when memory is measured using free recall. When either cued recall or recognition is tested, the influence of context is extremely variable. Several factors may explain the state-dependent sensitivity of free recall. Psychoactive states may lead subjects to adopt unusual encoding or retrieval strategies which are incompatible with those adopted when sober. It is known, for example, that marijuana intoxication causes people to make unusual associations to stimuli (Block and Wittenborn, 1985). This would be critical in free recall, because here the subject must generate appropriate contextual information to aid remembering. In cued recall and recognition, however, information is provided about the targets, and the potential for mismatches between encoding and retrieval operations is substantially reduced, because a certain amount of information at learning and test is invariant. In addition, recognition memory has a strong familiarity component, which is context-free (see above) and so not vulnerable to context effects. Thus, with recognition, a state-dependent effect is likely to occur only when memory is too weak to support reliable context-free identification or when the context-associated target memory is so dominant that recollection enhances memorability.

Hypnosis

There have long been claims that hypnosis can enhance memory, and these claims have become particularly important with the suggestion that hypnosis can be used to enhance eyewitness memory. Odd things can certainly happen when people are hypnotized, but what exactly is going on? Contemporary research into hypnosis is organized around two competing accounts: the **state**, or **special-process** view and the **non-state, social-psychological** view (Spanos, 1986). According to the special-process theory, hypnosis produces involuntary behaviour that differs qualitatively from that in the non-hypnotic state. The social-psychological view argues that hypnotic behaviour is purposeful, in that subjects deliberately comply with the aims of the hypnotic situation: the hypnotized subject may know that the raw onion he or she is eating is not an apple, but the power of **compliance** (Wagstaff, 1981) ensures that he or she continues to act as if it was. The idea of extreme compliance may seem difficult to believe, but if we look at the power of psychology experiments as compliance situations, we are left in little doubt of the possibility. Orne (1962), for example, designed an amusing experiment which measured the ability of American college students to eat fried locusts. When subjects were just asked to eat locusts, no one did; but, told it was an experiment, subjects ate a substantial number of locusts (see Milgram, 1963, for more frightening examples of compliance).

In a **hypnotic amnesia** experiment, subjects are given material to learn and then some hypnotic instruction to forget part or all of the information. They are then challenged to recall the material, and are subsequently given a 'cancellation cue' and again asked to recall the material. Hypnotic amnesia is demonstrated when the subject fails to recall the information until the cancellation cue is given. Special-process theorists argue that this amnesia represents a genuine dissociation of memory involving the creation of 'amnesic barriers'. Social-psychological theorists argue simply that the hypnotized subjects are complying with the experimenter's wish for them not to recall while apparently hypnotized. Which of these theories is correct?

One widely used method of evaluating hypnotic amnesia is the 'owning up' control in which subjects failing to remember information following a hypnotic suggestion are given an opportunity to admit that they are faking and to recall the information in the absence of the cancellation cue. These studies typically show a lessening of hypnotic amnesia but, significantly, the amnesia persists in subjects who are known to be highly susceptible to it (e.g. Kihlstrom et al., 1980). Special-process theorists interpret subjects behaving in this manner as showing a genuine interference 'with the usual processes of information retrieval' (ibid., p. 291). Social-psychological theorists, by contrast, argue that attempts to 'breach' hypnotic amnesia merely provide highly suggestible subjects with a further opportunity to comply with what they perceive to be the aim of the experiment.

A different approach is to consider whether hypnosis can facilitate the recall of normal memories. Zelig and Beidelman (1981) showed subjects a distressing film of an industrial accident, and then tested subjects' memory in either a hypnotic or a normal state. Hypnotized subjects were found to make more errors on leading questions, and their confidence was correlated with their degree of hypnotic susceptibility, but not the accuracy of their memory. Sheehan and Tilder (1983) found that hypnosis did not enhance memory, but did enhance confidence. These findings suggest that hypnosis does nothing more than give a false boost to subjects' confidence in their own memories; but a more recent review suggests that some real effects of hypnosis may occur. Geiselman and Machlovitz (1987) examined 38 studies to determine whether hypnosis could act as a memory aid. Five studies showed positive results, and they concluded that these were the studies in which the methods employed most closely resembled conditions under which hypnosis is used in real-life witness interviews. However, the question of whether hypnosis is acting as a special process or merely providing a more relaxed environment for recall is not clear.

Repression

The concept of **repression** as a means of forgetting stems from the work of Sigmund Freud (1915, 1943). Freud's basic idea was that memories injurious to the ego might be suppressed in order to reduce anxiety. The ideas underlying Freudian theory are extremely complex, and we cannot go into them in any detail here. However, in order to understand some of the experimental investigations of repression, we must familiarize ourselves with one tenet of Freudian theory, the **Oedipus complex.** According to Freud, personal development passes through three stages before reaching its final, sexual phase. The first phase is the **oral phase,** in which psychological activity is focused on the nipple. Next comes the **anal phase,** in which the child becomes aware of basic bodily functions. The third state is the **oedipal stage** which is associated with the first awakenings of sexual desire. In boys (the position is much more complicated for girls, and Freud never really sorted it out) the oedipal stage results in sexual desire towards the mother and jealousy towards the father. The anxiety produced by this conflict is normally resolved, however, by the boy's fear of his father's possible retribution; because of the sexual focus, these fears are expressed as a fear of castration. Resolution of the oedipal conflict allows progression to the **sexual phase,** but failure to resolve it leads to regression, either to the oral or to the anal phase, states that are thought to be reflected in behavioural traits such as excessive smoking or extreme tidiness.

On the assumption that, within any group of young men, a certain proportion will not have resolved the oedipal conflict, Wilkinson and Cargill (1955) reasoned that memory for stories containing oedipal material would be worse in men than women – the argument being that the oedipal material might be repressed because of its anxiety-provoking qualities. In the study, men and women listened to two stories about a dream. One story contained fairly obvious sexual imagery relating to the oedipal conflict – e.g. 'I got into the nice warm bed with my mother. She smiled, put her arms around me, and drew me close to her warm body. Her soft skin felt good against my warm body. . . . The next thing clear to me was the sensation of climbing a long stairway up a hill to the beautiful temple situated on top. The stairs led to the temple door. All around the temple were shrubs, trees, and heavy foliage.' The control story was similar in structure, but had no oedipal content.

Wilkinson and Cargill found that men recalled less of the oedipal story than women, and interpreted this as evidence of repression operating in memory. However, McCullough et al. (1976) put a different interpretation on this result. They pointed out that the subjects had been told that the experiment was about 'personality'. As a result, the men may have spotted the obvious sexual innuendos and failed to report them on the grounds that reporting them might bear unfavourably on their personality. McCullough et al. supported their response-bias interpretation by showing that the oedipal and control stories were remembered equally well when subjects were not told that the experiment was concerned with personality.

McCullough et al.'s finding is just one of many studies casting doubt on the value of Freudian theory in the explanation of normal mental processes. For some years, however, a study by Levinger and Clark (1961) stood as perhaps the best example that some kind of repressive process might operate in human memory. In the study, young nurses were presented with either neutral (e.g. 'frog') or emotionally laden (e.g. 'love') stimulus words, and were asked to produce an association. During this task the subjects' electrodermal responses were measured, providing a measure of **arousal**. Perhaps unsurprisingly, the nurses appeared to be more aroused when making associations to emotional stimuli. The subjects were then shown the stimulus words again and asked to reproduce the response they had previously made. It was found that associations made to emotional words were remembered less well than those to unemotional words.

Levinger and Clark avoided a Freudian interpretation of their findings, suggesting instead that the lower recall of emotional associations stemmed from some form of 'emotional inhibition'. However, an alternative explanation was that the results were due to the differing levels of arousal caused by emotional and neutral associations. A variety of studies have shown that increases in arousal, no matter how they arise, have differing effects on immediate, as opposed to delayed, recall, with higher levels of arousal inhibiting immediate recall but facilitating longer-term, recall (Eysenck, 1982). The lower recall of words with emotional associations might therefore be just one instance of the inhibitory effect of higher arousal on immediate memory.

I and my colleagues (Parkin et al., 1982) repeated the study by Levinger and Clark, and found that when retention was tested immediately, associations to neutral words were recalled better than those to emotional words. However, when tested 7 days later, a different group of subjects showed the opposite result. This study thus supports an arousal-based interpretation of the Levinger and Clark finding. Similar results have been published more recently by Bradley and Baddeley (1990) and Contini and Whissell (1992). However, it should be noted that other authors have found a general suppression of emotional responses at all retention intervals (Jones et al., 1987; Rossmann, 1984; but see Parkin, 1984). The question of emotional inhibition remains open.

Psychogenic Amnesia

Keller and Shaywitz (1986) described the following case of RF, a 16-year-old male found lying entangled in shrubbery. He had maps and food, but no identification. On admission to hospital, he knew his age, but denied any knowledge of his identity or personal past. Physical examination revealed him to be normal, and there was no sign of any brain damage. His photograph was then shown on the evening news, and his parents recognized him. They revealed that a close relative of the boy had just died and that the boy's mother had just learned that she had cancer.

RF was suffering from a form of **psychogenic amnesia** known as **fugue** (from the Latin *fugere*, 'to flee'). Psychogenic amnesia is loss of memory due to a negative life event. In RF's case it was a combination of a relative's death and his mother's illness; but it can also be caused by things like rape and murder. In fugue the patient somehow dissociates from his personality, and may under some circumstances adopt a new personality. The fugue state is not usually permanent, and the patient's memory returns. In RF's case his memory started to return two days after his admission to hospital.

The view that we can repress our memories of adverse events is further illustrated by the phenomenon of **multiple personality**, in which a person manifests a number of different personalities. The outcome is somewhat bizarre, and in one recent case a multiple personality asked to give evidence in court had to be sworn in six times! Coons et al. (1982) describe the case of Lucy. Hospitalized as the result of a drug overdose, Lucy was found to have suffered memory lapses and hallucinations for two years, as a consequence of being raped. Psychiatric examination revealed that she had four personalities. Aside from her normal, friendly personality, there was 'Linda', an aggressive woman who emerged when she recounted the physical and sexual abuse she had endured as a young child; 'Sally', a distrustful, isolated woman who gave the accounts of the rape incident; and 'Sam', an imaginary man who rescued her when she was feeling suicidal.

An important feature of multiple personality is that the various personalities have only varying degrees of knowledge of each other's activities. Nissen et al. (1988) investigated a woman who had manifested 22 different personalities. These included 'Alice', who was studying to be a ministerial counsellor; 'Charles', a profane and aggressive heavy drinker; 'Ellen', who enjoyed birdwatching; and 'Gloria', an artist and one of three left-handed personalities. Gloria was the only one to have adopted a different surname so that she could get her own social security number. The patient was able to change personalities at the request of her psychiatrist, and Nissen et al. used this to examine what one personality might be able to remember about information presented to another. On tests of explicit learning, there appeared to be little transfer across personalities, in that successive presentations of, for example, a short story to several of the personalities did not result in an upward trend in the amount retained. Implicit memory testing yielded a different picture, however. Both perceptual identification (see figure 4.7) and fragment completion were facilitated when the priming stimulus was presented to a different personality. But on implicit tests involving more conceptual information (e.g. interpreting an ambiguous paragraph) there was little evidence of transfer. Nissen et al. concluded that interpersonality transfer occurred only for information that could not be differentially interpreted by the different personalities.

Fugue and multiple personality are very unusual memory disorders, and their study is complicated by many problems – not least the possibility that the amnesia may in fact be fake. A more common and genuine psychogenic disorder is **event-specific** amnesia. Here memory loss is restricted to a particular period of time. Event-specific amnesia is often reported by violent criminals who claim that they cannot remember the crime they have been charged with (Kopelman, 1987). Violent crime is often carried out by drunk or drugged individuals, which may explain why some of them cannot remember. Wolf (1980)

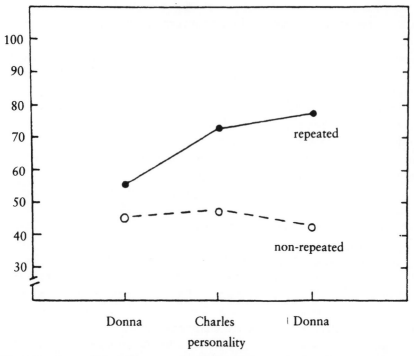

Fig. 4.7. Data from Nissen et al. (1988) showing results of a perceptual identification experiment involving two personalities contained within the same person. Words shown initially to 'Donna' were subsequently identified more easily by 'Charles', and this effect remained when the words were shown a third time to 'Donna'. Reproduced with the permission of Academic Press.

investigated six convicted Eskimo murderers, all of whom had been extremely drunk when they committed their crimes. He got them all drunk again, but found no evidence that the subjects could now recall their crimes. These findings suggest that extreme drunkenness prevented memory formation, rather than exerting a state-dependent effect (see above). Criminals may also fake memory loss as a way of gaining sympathy and reduction of sentences. However, when both intoxication and malingering have been ruled out, there are still a substantial number of criminals who seem to have repressed memory for crime.

Event-specific amnesia is observed in soldiers and others who have experienced extremely violent episodes. Grinker and Spiegel (1945) studied a large number of men who had developed amnesia following traumatic wartime episodes. They made use of the **sodium pentothal interview**, in which the subject is sedated by slow intravenous injection of the drug. Its first effect is to relieve any anxiety that the subject may have. This is followed by the onset of drowsiness. At this point the injection is halted, and the interview begins. Because the interviewer knows the circumstances, he can start to cue the patient about the traumatic incident. As recall becomes more detailed, the subject is likely to become more and more agitated, as this passage shows:

> The terror exhibited in moments of extreme danger, such as the imminent explosion of shells, the death of a friend before the patient's eyes ... is electrifying to watch. The body becomes increasingly tense and rigid; the eyes widen and the pupils dilate, while the skin becomes covered in fine perspiration. The hands move about convulsively, seeking a weapon, or a friend to share the danger. The breathing becomes incredibly rapid and shallow. The intensity of the emotion sometimes becomes unbearable; and frequently, at the height of the reaction, there is collapse and the patient falls back in bed and remains quiet ... usually to resume the story at a more neutral point. (Grinker and Spiegel, 1945, p. 80)

Sodium pentothal is one of a number of barbiturates that have been found to facilitate the recall of emotionally disturbing memories. The most commonly used alternative is sodium amytal (amylbarbitone). These drugs are assumed to have their effect by reducing anxiety to the point where the patient can tolerate the recollection of experiences which are too painful to recall in the normal conscious state.

Finally, there is recent evidence that repressive mechanisms may play a beneficial role in enabling victims of massive traumatic events to adjust. These people often present what is known as **post-traumatic stress disorder** (PTSD), which is characterized, by, among other things, poor sleep patterns and disturbed dreams relating to their trauma. Kaminer and Lavie (1991) examined sleep patterns and dream recall in well-adjusted and less-adjusted survivors of the Holocaust. The less-adjusted group took longer to get to sleep, and their sleep pattern was more disturbed. However, when both groups were woken up at a point where their eye movements indicated that they were dreaming, the well-adjusted survivors were significantly less able to recall their dreams. The authors argue that the decreased dream recall may be one factor in enabling better adjustment and that this may be attributable to some form of repressive mechanism operating.

Faced with this range of findings, it is hard to deny that we can, in extreme circumstances, repress memories that are disturbing. Fugue, multiple personality, and event-specific amnesia reflect varying degrees of dissociation between self and memory. The term 'repression' has been used to describe these phenomena but it is important to stress that we are not thereby subscribing to a Freudian interpretation. Rather, we are simply acknowledging that memory has the ability to render part of its contents inaccessible as a means of coping with distressing experiences. The mechanism by which memory achieves this, however, is, an elusive one.

5

Imagery

Were you to say you were near blind, you should be sent for spectacles; that you have no visual imagery, to the laboratory to invent metaspectacles.

Herbert Crovitz

The first issue of Psychological Review, published in 1894, included an article by A. C. Armstrong entitled 'The imagery of American students'. This was a study based on 'intelligent self-observation' in which young college students were given the following instructions: 'Think of some definite object – suppose it is your breakfast table as you sat down to it this morning – and consider carefully the picture that rises before your mind's eye.' They were then required to answer a series of questions, such as 'Is the image dull or fairly clear? Is it's brightness comparable to that of the actual scene? Are all the objects pretty well defined at the same time or is the place of sharpest definition at any moment more contracted than it is in a real scene? Are the colours of the China, of the toast . . . quite distinct and natural?' Armstrong then analysed the answers to these and other questions, in order to quantify the 'imaging power' of the students. Using this method, he came to a number of conclusions about the nature of the images, including, for example, the fact that the clarity of objects depicted in an image was related to the degree of illumination present.

Armstrong's study represented a form of psychology known as

introspectionism, which can be defined as the study of the mind and its contents, 'the science of mental life'. In introspectionism the primary mode of investigation is observation of one's own mind, and images are an essential aspect of this – internal representations of the world that can be perceived and manipulated in the mind's eye. Observing the properties of images, therefore, was a legitimate form of scientific investigation.

Introspection failed, however, for a number of reasons. Although it is reasonably easy to 'observe' images, it is less easy to produce accurate observations of emotions and more complex thought processes. It is also clear that many psychological processes are not open to conscious inspection. Consider the mess that introspectionists would have got into trying to understand implicit learning (see chapter 3). Introspectionism is also a biased form of investigation, in that observers are often guided by some presupposed theory about what is going on in their minds.

Introspectionism came under particularly fierce attack in North America during the early part of the century, and this discontent gave rise to **behaviourism**. The position of the behaviourist is that unobservable events such as images and emotions can never be the basis of scientific psychology. Real progress can be made only by studying **behaviour**. In the words of John Watson, the founder of behaviourism:

> Psychology, as the behaviorist views it, is a purely objective, experimental branch of natural science, which needs introspection as little as do the sciences of chemistry and physics . . . the behavior of animals can be studied without appeal to consciousness. The position is taken here that the behavior of man and the behavior of animals must be considered on the same plane . . . It is possible to define [psychology] as the 'science of behavior' and never to . . . use the terms consciousness, mental states, mind, content, will, imagery. (Watson, 1914, pp. 9, 27)

The Rebirth of Mental Imagery as a Scientific Subject

Until about the mid-1960s, behaviourism was the dominant force in experimental psychology, particularly in the United States. However, disillusionment began to set in when it came to be realized that the theoretical framework offered by behaviourism, in which explanation is couched purely in terms of observable relationships between stimulus and response, is inadequate as a means of explaining most aspects of human mental processes.

This point was made very forcibly by the linguist Noam Chomsky in his review of B. F. Skinner's book Verbal Behavior. Chomsky pointed out, for example, that language acquisition by children could not be explained in purely behaviourist terms. When learning language, children do, at a certain stage, produce **over-generalizations**, using a regular plural construction 'mouses' instead of the correct 'mice', for example. Chomsky's point was that children would not have heard 'mouses', so their response could not have been acquired through experience. Rather, it reflected some internal construct they had developed about forming plurals.

Objections like those of Chomsky led to the view that a proper psychological explanation could be achieved only by developing theories about the internal representations, processes, and structures underlying mental activities such as memory, language, and thinking. The stage was thus set for mental imagery to once again become a central topic in experimental psychology.

Imagery as an Experimental Variable

The revival of imagery as an experimental issue is largely attributable to the work of Allan Paivio (Paivio, 1971, 1986). Paivio's approach was to show that mental imagery could be studied within an experimental framework that behaviourists would find acceptable (see Richardson, 1980). In early studies Paivio (1969) used the **paired associate** (PA) learning task to explore the value of imagery as a factor in verbal learning. The PA task is a stimulus–response method for investigating memory for associations, and was used extensively by behaviourists in their attempts to understand forgetting (for a full description of PA learning, see chapter 6). Paivio examined the ease with which subjects could learn associations when the stimulus and response terms were either **concrete** or **abstract** words. A concrete word is one that can be assumed to evoke a visual image (e.g. 'piano'), whereas an abstract word is one that does not bring an obvious image to mind (e.g. 'justice'). The results showed that subjects found it much easier to learn associative pairs based on concrete words, as compared with abstract words.

Paivio's initial results were confirmed by other investigators, who examined the effect of instructing subjects to use mental imagery while they were learning. Bower (1970) required subjects to learn a list of thirty word pairs of concrete words (e.g. 'piano' 'cigar') under one of three kinds of instruction:

Rote learning: Repeat word pairs aloud as they appear.
Interactive imagery: Imagine the objects defined by the words acting
together in some way.
Separate imagery: Make separate images of the two objects defined by
the words.

The three types of instruction had no differential effect on recognition,
but interactive imagery produced far better recall. The benefits of interactive imagery were particularly evident in a study by Schnorr and
Atkinson (1970), who found that the technique allowed subjects to
recall around 75 per cent of the 96 stimulus–response pairs they had
been instructed to remember.

Interactive imagery is thus a powerful means of improving memory,
but how does it work? One possibility is that interactive images are, by
their very nature, *bizarre*. This view is certainly held in the classical
anonymous work Ad Herennium, which includes rules for the use of
imagery. It says that we remember what is 'exceptionally base, dis-
honourable, unusual, great, unbelievable or ridiculous'. Returning to
Bower's experiment, bizarreness may well have been a factor, because
subjects may have formed unusual images when attempting to link together functionally unrelated objects such as a piano and a cigar. However, experimental evidence appears to argue against bizarreness having
any real value in promoting learning. Wollen et al. (1972) tried to
enhance paired-associate learning by instructing subjects to use bizzare
imagery, but this had no effect over and above that of interactive imagery
itself.

The Dual Coding Hypothesis

To account for the effects of imagery on verbal learning, Paivio put
forward the **dual coding hypothesis**. According to this, mental activity
involves the interaction of two interconnected but functionally independent subsystems: a **non-verbal imagery system**, which processes information about objects and events, and a **verbal system** specialized for
handling speech and writing (Paivio, 1986). Within the verbal system
each known word is assumed to be represented by a **logogen** – a
concept borrowed from Morton's (1970; 1979) recognition model.
Images are represented in a similar discrete unit system in which each
image is related to a specific **imagen**. Logogens and imagens are assumed to be connected by **referential links** which allow a word to be
associated with its relevant image and vice versa.

The dual coding hypothesis provides a convenient account of various experimental findings. The better learning of concrete words can be attributed to their ability to induce both verbal and non-verbal codes, whereas abstract words are more poorly recalled because only a verbal code is available. It is also known that pictures are easier to memorize than words representing those pictures (Paivio, 1971). This finding can be explained by arguing that presentation of a picture is more likely to elicit a verbal code in addition to an imaginal one, as compared with word presentation, where imagery is less likely to occur.

Exploring the Properties of the Mental Image

Paivio's dual coding hypothesis is based on the idea that mental images are separate and functionally distinct from the representations underlying our verbally based knowledge. This is an appealing idea; all of us experience mental imagery, and images often seem involved in the decisions we make. It is a little surprising, therefore, to find that the concept of a mental image is somewhat controversial.

One way of defining a mental image is to think of it as an 'internal percept' – some embodiment of what it is like to see the object we are thinking about (one can, of course, have images related to the other senses, but these have been far less investigated, and we will not consider them here). Images are therefore assumed to be dependent, to some extent, on the same system that underlies perception itself. In particular, images and percepts are thought to share one important quality in that both are **analog** representations.

An analog representation is one in which each part of the depicted object is represented only once and the spatial relationships between different elements of the representation correspond, in proportional terms, to the relationships in the object itself. The idea of an analog representation can be understood by imagining a map of England. As well as the general shape, various towns are identified, the distances between them on the map being proportional to the actual distances. Within the image, the perceived distance between the towns also reflects their actual distance apart. Thus, the distance between London and Brighton in the image will appear less than the distance between London and Edinburgh.

A second property of a mental image is that it can be rotated in a way similar to rotation of the object itself in space. If you hold a pencil horizontally in front of you and rotate it around its central point, you observe a continuous transformation of the object. You can also imagine the same thing, and observe the same continuous transformation in your mind's eye.

Images are therefore assumed to be analog representations of objects which can undergo transformation. The ability of mental images to undergo **mental rotation** was explored in a series of classic experiments by Roger Shepard and his colleagues (e.g. Shepard and Chipman, 1970; Shepard and Cooper, 1983; Shepard and Metzler, 1971). In the first of these experiments, subjects saw pairs of two-dimensional drawings (see figure 5.1), and had to decide whether the drawings showed the same object from different orientations (if you have ever played the computer game Tetris, you will have some idea of what it is like to perform mental rotations). The graph shows the time it took subjects to decide that two drawings were of the same object as a function of the angular disparity between them (angular disparity represents the amount one object would have to be rotated so as to be at the same orientation as the other). Correct reaction time was found to have a linear relationship with angular disparity: the more rotation needed, the longer the reaction time.

A second study, the nature and results of which are shown in figure 5.2, required subjects to decide whether an angularly displaced letter was the correct way round or not. The results were similar to those for object rotation: correct reaction time was predicted by the degree of angular disparity between the letter as presented and its normal upright position.

One problem for the image-based account of mental rotation experiments is that, in order to explain the linear relationship between angular disparity and reaction time (e.g. that shown in figure 5.2), the subject must always choose the correct direction in which to rotate the image. Thus, if an image has a disparity of 240 degrees, it should be rotated clockwise; but with a disparity of 60 degrees, the rotation should be anticlockwise. How does the subject know which way to rotate the image? If imagery alone is involved, there is no way of knowing in advance whether the quickest rotational direction has been chosen. Some other source of information must decide the direction of rotation. Thus, although it can still be argued that an analog representation is used in performance, the mental imagery account must accept that other knowledge not based on imagery also contributes to task performance.

Mental rotation experiments were interpreted as showing that subjects imagine the located objects in an internal three-dimensional space and that one object is rotated until it matches the other. The demonstration of a linear relationship between reaction time and angular disparity also suggests that the image rotation process itself operates at a

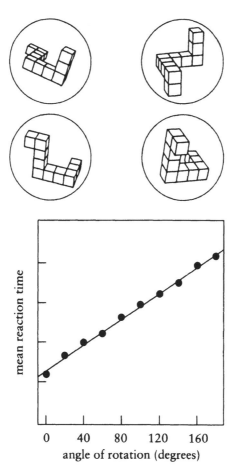

Fig. 5.1. Above, stimuli used by Shepard and Metzler, 1971, p. 157. The top pair differ by an 80-degree rotation in depth, whereas the bottom pair cannot be rotated into congruence. Below, the mean reaction time taken to determine whether two objects are the same shape as a function of angular disparity. From Metzler and Shepard, 1974, p. 161. Reproduced with the permission of Lawrence Enlbaum Associates.

constant speed. Shepard's mental rotation experiments were enthusiastically received, and one commentator was led to conclude that mental rotation experiments 'show beyond any reasonable doubt that when one rotates a mental image from one aspect to another, the representation of the object is in fact going through all of the intermediate aspects in a continuous manner. I have no idea how anybody could possibly account for these results without postulating an analogue representational medium' (Attneave, 1974, p. 498). In a subsequent section

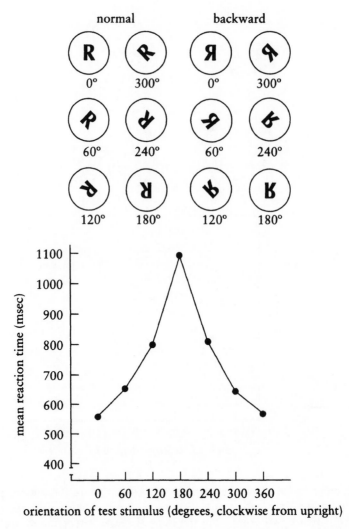

Fig. 5.2.   Above, normal and backward versions of one of the stimuli in the mental rotation study of Cooper and Shepard (1973). Below, mean reaction time for judging the normality of a letter as a function of orientation. From Cooper and Shepard, 1973, p. 95. Reproduced with the permission of Academic Press.

we will see that there is another explanation for mental rotation effects, but, before considering this, we must first look at further developments of the imagery concept.

A Computational Model of Imagery

The concept of mental imagery has been developed in Kosslyn's (1980) computational model. This model assumes that mental images exist in a spatial medium which has a number of essential properties. Like physical space, the spatial medium has a limited extent, which, in turn, limits its capacity to hold information. It resembles the visual field in having its highest resolution at the centre; the medium also has 'grain', which limits the extent to which small details can be represented. Finally, once generated, images fade from the medium much in the same way as after-images fade from the visual system.

In Kosslyn's model there are two permanent stores of information about objects: **image files** and **propositional files**. Image files contain information about how the image of part or the whole of a particular object is represented in the spatial medium. Certain **image files**, known as **skeletal files**, describe the basic shape of the object, but not any specific details. Information about specific visual details is obtained from other image files. The basic shape of a bee, for example, can be enhanced by the addition of certain features, such as a black and yellow stripes on the body.

Propositional files are not linked to a specific sensory modality (i.e. they are **amodal**) and contain information only about meaning. The files are collections of **propositions**, a proposition being defined as the smallest unit of knowledge that can stand as an individual assertion and about which we can make the decision 'true' or 'false'. Propositional files list the various properties of an object in relation to a foundation part, e.g. black and yellow stripes – location – sides – body. Information in propositional files is linked directly to the relevant image file. Thus a foundation propositional file describing a bee would be linked to the appropriate skeletal image of that object. Additional information about the bee would be stored in associated propositional files, which, in turn, would be linked to the image files containing information about how to depict those details.

When asked to produce an image of an object, the system first establishes whether there is a propositional file corresponding to a skeletal image. If located, the skeletal image is placed in the area of the spatial medium with the highest resolution. Other processes then access further propositional information about the object, and additional parts of the image are constructed in the spatial medium from associated image files. Once fully established, the image can be operated on in various ways, using processes such as scan, zoom, and rotate.

Kosslyn and his colleagues (see Kosslyn, 1980) conducted a series of experiments on mental imagery, carrying them out very much in the introspectionist tradition exemplified by Armstrong's study nearly 100 years earlier. In an **image scanning** study, subjects were asked to memorize a fictitious map of an island on which there were several prominent landmarks (see figure 5.3). In the next phase, subjects were asked to form an image of the map and focus on one of the landmarks. Having done this, a second landmark was named being and subjects had to focus on that, the time taken to do this being recorded. The time taken to focus on a second landmark was found to be a linear function of its distance from the first landmark. The performance of subjects thus suggested that the image formed of the map was an analog of the actual map, because processing operations performed on it appeared governed by the actual distances depicted on the map.

A second set of experiments examined how the assumed limited size of the spatial medium affected subjects ability to 'see' detail in mental images. Subjects were asked to imagine pairs of animals standing next to each other. One animal, the critical animal, was always imagined alongside another animal that was either much bigger or much smaller. A rabbit, for example, might be imagined alongside a bee or an elephant. The assumption was that when imagining a rabbit next to an elephant, the amount of spatial medium available for representing the rabbit would be small because of the large space taken up by the elephant. By contrast, a rabbit imagined next to a bee would have much more spatial medium allocated to it. On the assumption that the spatial medium was also granular – i.e. that there was a finite limit to its powers of resolution – it followed that more details about a rabbit should be available when imagined alongside a bee as compared with an elephant. To examine this hypothesis, Kosslyn asked subjects to indicate when they could 'see' a specific feature of an imagined rabbit and he found that subjects took longer when the rabbit was imagined alongside an elephant, a finding Kosslyn attributed to the poorer resolution of the rabbit image in the spatial medium.

In a third set of experiments, subjects were asked to close their eyes and imagine walking towards animals of different sizes. They were asked to stop 'walking' when they could 'see' all the animal simultaneously and to estimate how far away they were at that point. If you

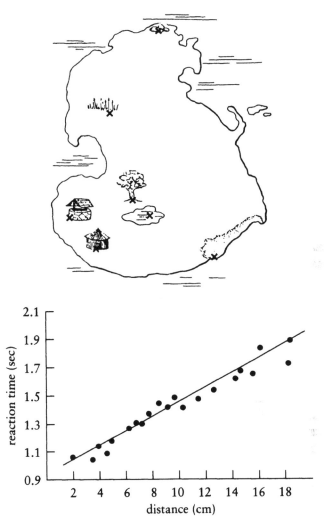

Fig. 5.3. Above, fictitious map used by Kosslyn et al. (1978) to determine differences in processing time relative to the distance between images to be recalled. Below, time to scan between two points of mental map as a function of the distance between the points. From Kosslyn et al., 1978, p. 51. Reprinted with the permission of the American Psychological Association.

were to carry out this task looking at real animals, you would obviously need to stand further away from an elephant than from a rabbit because, if you got too close, the elephant's size could not be incorporated within your visual field. The results showed that subjects doing the task on an imaginal basis performed exactly as if they were actually looking at the animals, the distance from the animal that subjects estimated stopping at being a linear function of the animal's size.

The findings we have considered so far appear to make a fairly convincing case for the existence of mental images as functional representations. Under varying conditions it appears that subjects are responding on the basis of internal analog representations which share many of the qualities of percepts. This positive view of mental imagery is not universal, however.

Arguments against Mental Imagery

Pylyshyn (1973, 1979, 1981) has put forward a number of criticisms of mental imagery. A primary argument is that images are **epiphenomena** – experiences that are the end result of, rather than the basis of, mental activity. They are like the exhaust fumes of an engine perhaps; they tell you that the engine is working, but not how it works.

We saw in our discussion of mental imagery experiments that it is necessary to propose the existence of knowledge other than an image to explain mental rotation findings. Pylyshyn's view is an extreme form of this view, in that he ascribes all phenomena attributed to mental imagery to the operation of a representational system based exclusively on propositional knowledge. The basis of his argument is as follows. If it is accepted that we can have a propositional representation of an object, it is also possible to have propositional knowledge about how we might respond if we had an analog representation of that object. To understand this, let us return to Kosslyn's image scanning experiment described earlier. It is not difficult to argue that the information contained in the map about the distances between landmarks could be represented in propositional terms. Pylyshyn argued that subjects could use this distance information as a basis for responding as if they actually had a functional image; again, the greater the computed distance between objects, the longer the response time should be. Similar arguments could also, of course, be made about other imaginal judgements apparently influenced by perceived distance or size.

Pylyshyn's argument seems plausible; but then, why do subjects decide to behave in this way? One strong possibility is that results obtained in image scanning and other similar studies are due to the demand characteristics of the experimental procedures (see chapter 4). Indeed, Kosslyn et al. (1978) conceded that their scanning results may have reflected 'nothing more than the enthusiastic co-operation of our subjects'.

Richman and Mitchell (1979) employed the 'non-experiment' technique (Orne, 1962) to establish the extent to which demand characteristics might explain the image scanning results of Kosslyn et al. Subjects were presented with the written instructions used in the experiment and information about the relative distances on the fictitious map, but not the map itself. They were then asked to estimate what their scanning times would be, and it was found that subjects produced significantly longer estimates for scanning between landmarks that were furthest apart. Pylyshyn (1981) also gave evidence supporting a demand-characteristics interpretation of image scanning studies. Using experimental instructions similar to those of Kosslyn et al., requiring subjects to imagine a spot moving from one specified landmark to another, Pylyshyn found the same kind of linear relationship between scanning time and map distance. However, when subjects were asked to focus on one landmark and then decide as quickly as possible what the compass bearing of a second landmark was, there was no relationship between map distance and response time.

How exactly do demand characteristics exert their influence on the pattern of results obtained in imagery experiments? Intuitively, it seems unlikely that subjects could have consistently devised conscious processing strategies for generating the systematic relationships evident in mental rotation and image scanning experiments. To solve this difficulty, Pylyshyn proposed that subjects also possess **tacit** (i.e. unconscious) propositional knowledge of how their visual systems behave, and, in response to the demand characteristics of the experimental situation, allow this knowledge to simulate image-based responding. Thus, in a mental rotation experiment, subjects tacitly know that when they actually see an object rotating, it will do so continuously and take an amount of time directly proportional to the angle through which it has to rotate. This tacit knowledge then provides the basis for determining subjects' reaction times.

The tacit knowledge theory can account for all instances where subjects' response patterns appear to suggest that an image is the basis of performance. Furthermore, much of this knowledge is held to be unconscious, making it impossible to establish independently whether or not any particular subject possesses this knowledge. The propositional knowledge account of mental imagery cannot, therefore, be refuted by any experiment involving normal subjects and mental imagery.

Neuropsychological Evidence for Mental Imagery

Farah (1988) has produced various arguments in favour of mental imagery based on neuropsychological evidence. The first source of evidence she considers comes from studies that examined the brain regions that become active when subjects are perceiving, compared with imaging, stimuli. Goldenberg et al. (1992) compared the patterns of **regional cerebral blood** (rCBF) flow while subjects tried to answer questions which either did or did not require the use of imagery. Regional cerebral blood flow is a reasonably precise technique for measuring the extent to which different regions of the brain are active at any time. The imagery questions were of comparable difficulty to the non-imagery questions, but they evoked significantly different patterns of regional blood flow. Imagery questions resulted in increased brain activity in the visual areas of the brain, such as the occipital lobes, but this was not the case with non-imagery questions.

Whereas Armstrong's early study attempted to measure people's imaging power in an introspective manner, psychometric tests have now been devised to estimate the degree to which a person can use imagery to carry out a mental task (e.g. Vandenberg and Kuse, 1978). Charlot et al. (1992) used two tests to classify subjects into low and high imagers, and then measured rCBF while subjects performed an image scanning task or a verb conjugation task. The results showed a number of differences between high and low imagers; in particular, low imagers showed a general increase in rCBF during both tasks, whereas high imagers showed a specific increase in rCBF to the right visual association cortex in the verb conjugation task. While it is not clear why the right visual association cortex should be particularly active during verb conjugation, the data none the less point to markedly different patterns of brain activity in high and low imagers, the former appearing to be more reliant on visual areas of the brain.

The visual areas of the brain have also been implicated in imagery using a technique known as **electroencephalography** (EEG), in which the electrical activity of the brain is monitored. In EEG techniques, suppression of the alpha rhythm emanating from a specific brain region is an indication that the region has become more active. Several studies have examined how imagery affects EEG. Davidson and Schwartz (1977) simultaneously measured the alpha rhythm arising from brain regions associated with visual imagery (occipital lobes) and tactile imagery (parietal lobes). When subjects were carrying out a visual task, there was maximal suppression of the alpha rhythm in the visual areas, whereas when they were carrying out a tactile imagery task, there was maximum suppression in the tactile areas.

Farah et al. (1988) measured event-related potentials (ERPs; see chapter 4) while asking subjects either to read words or to read them and form images of the words' referents. During the first half second or so of performing these tasks, the ERPs generated were the same; but sampling at a later point indicated that the imagery task produced a highly localized increase in the size of ERPs in the occipital lobes which was not produced in the reading only task. Other ERP studies (e.g. Farah et al., in press) have also indicated that visual areas of the brain show a selective increase in activity during imagery-based tasks, and in combination with rCBF and EEG studies strongly suggest that the visual areas are active when subjects are using imagery. However, can we conclude from this that images therefore have the same properties as the percepts that are also processed by these brain regions? This is certainly one interpretation, but an alternative is that this activation corresponds to the epiphenomenal aspect of imagery; that is, it is an index of what we experience as a consequence of carrying out image-based tasks, rather than an indication that the visual areas of the brain are the neural substrate of the processes leading to responses in an imagery-based task.

Farah maintains that this epiphenomenal argument can be countered only by demonstrating that damage to the visual areas of the brain produces deficits in mental imagery that parallel the nature of the perceptual deficits observed in the unfortunate patient – the argument being that if activation of visual areas during image-based responding is epiphenomenal, damage preventing that activation should not preclude performance of the task, because this presumably depends on structures elsewhere in the brain.

Farah (1988) reviews a whole range of studies which show a relationship between colour vision and colour imagery. Several studies demonstrate that patients with colour blindness also lose the ability to make comparable colour-based imaginal judgements, such as judging the colour of cement (see Humphreys and Riddoch, 1987; see also De Vreese, 1991). A recent study by Dittuno and Mann (1990) also suggests a link between vision and imagery. Mental rotation performance was examined in six patients with right-hemisphere lesions that compromised the parietal lobes, six left-hemisphere parietal patients, and controls. Figure 5.4 shows that the patients with right-hemisphere parietal damage performed more poorly than the left-lesion group and controls. Studies of vision also suggest that the right-hemisphere parietal cortex is involved in spatial processing. Warrington and Rabin (1970) compared

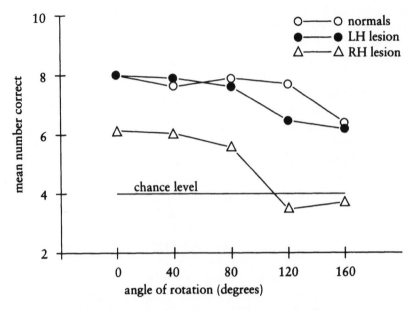

Fig. 5.4. Data from Dittuno and Mann, 1990, p. 181, showing performance of patients with right (RH) and left-hemisphere, (LH) damage on mental rotation. Reproduced with the permission of Masson Italia.

the ability of left- and right-hemisphere parietal patients to judge whether two dots, presented one on each of two cards, occupied the same position or not. Right-hemisphere parietal patients performed this very poorly, as compared with the left-hemisphere parietal group.

Taken together, these studies suggest that the neural substrates underlying visual processes are also involved in imagery. Thus, when colour vision is affected, colour imagery is also impaired; and when our spatial vision is damaged, we also have difficulty in manipulating images in mental space. Neuropsychological data thus allow us to conclude that people certainly seem to be doing something different when performing mental imagery tasks, as compared with tasks that do not demand imagery. However, can we further conclude that images are therefore analogical? This conclusion would be valid only if our additional assumption that percepts are analogical is also valid. We can conclude that the retinal image is an analog, but the processes that derive the percept may or may not be. There are, for example, a number of propositional theories of perception; that is, the ones in which the percept itself is represented as a list of propositions (see Humphreys and Bruce, 1989). The experience of mental imagery might therefore reflect the operation of a specific propositional system underlying perception.

Eidetic Imagery

Allport (1924) discovered three American children who, despite no knowledge of German, could spell the word Gartenwirtschaft both forwards and backwards after seeing it only very briefly. A few years later the Russian psychologist Luria started working with an extraordinary man known as S (see Luria, 1975). In one study S was shown a large, meaningless table of numbers, and spent 3 minutes looking over it. Three months later he was able to reproduce this table without any difficulty. When recalling the table, he reported that he could once again 'see' it and that remembering was merely a process of 'reading off' the information.

Both these examples are most probably instances of **eidetic imagery** (from the Greek eidos, 'that which is seen'), which can be defined formally as a 'visual image representing a previously scanned stimulus, persisting for up to several minutes, and phenomenologically in front of the eyes'. This contrasts with conventional images which are perceived as 'inside our heads'. Eidetic imagery has been extensively investigated by Haber (1979), and it is estimated that around 8 per cent of children are eidetic, but only 0.1 per cent of adults. Reasons for the gradual disappearance of eidetic imagery are not clear, but one possibility is that, despite the apparent advantages of a photographic form of memory, the retention of large numbers of eidetic images might actually be a hindrance because, without a system to interpret them, they have no value. In terms of mental development, therefore, it is more cost-effective to represent knowledge in a propositional way which enables assertions about the external world to be made. It is therefore not surprising that Luria's S never developed a successful career and ended up becoming a 'memory man'; even so, he ran into problems, because he could not forget images of information learned in previous shows. Interestingly, eidetic imagery has also been proposed as one basis of the *idiot savant* phenomenon – people of exceptionally low intelligence who none the less have one extraordinary mental power such as calendar calculating (see Treffert, 1988).

There has been little experimental investigation of eidetic imagery. Experiments on children have proved difficult because of problems in getting them to provide reliable subjective reports. Stromeyer and Psotka (1970; see also Stromeyer, 1982) reported the case of Elizabeth, a university teacher who appeared to have remarkable eidetic abilities. She claimed to be able to mentally project beards on to men's faces and leaves on to barren trees. Her eidetic imagery was tested more formally using random dot stereograms; these consist of a pair of apparently random patterns of dots. When presented using a stereoscope, so that one pattern projects only on to the left eye and the other only onto the right eye, a figure can be seen in depth. One half of a 10,000 dot stereogram pair was projected onto Elizabeth's right eye, and 10 seconds later, a second pattern was presented to her left eye. She was asked to superimpose the eidetic image from her right eye on to the pattern she could see in her left eye, and, without hesitation, she correctly identified the pattern produced by combining the stereograms.

Overview

Imagery has re-emerged as a major area of experimental psychology. The imageability of material greatly influences how well something will be remembered, and instructions to use imagery greatly enhance retention. Mental rotation and image scanning experiments have led many to argue that subjects can form internal analog representations; but others have argued that all internal representations are propositional in nature and that demonstrations of imagery are experimental artefacts. There is considerable evidence, however, that when subjects use imagery, they make use of the visual areas of the brain, whereas non-imagery tasks maximally activate other regions. This suggests, at the very least, that image-based mental processing is in some way different from mental processing not based on imagery.

6

Working Memory

Courtney Young...was the undisputed Security Service cross-word king. He always claimed it was too easy to do the [Times] crossword with a pencil. He claimed to do it in his head instead. For a year I watched him do this, until finally I could resist the temptation no longer. I challenged him, whereupon he immediately wrote in each answer without hesitation.

Peter Wright

In 1969 Warrington and Shallice reported the case of KF, a young man who suffered a closed-head injury after falling off his motor bike. KF developed a number of deficits as a result of his brain damage, but we shall concentrate on how this injury affected his memory span. Figure 6.1 shows that KF had a reliable digit span of only one. Normal people, you may recall, typically have a memory span of seven plus or minus two (see chapter 1), so clearly something has gone terribly wrong.

So far, our account of memory has taken the line that a single structure underlies the memory capacity essential for normal conscious mental activity. We have variously called this primary memory, short-term store, or central processor; but all these concepts share the view that this memory system is a single, indivisible entity. Memory span has been taken as a definitive measure of short-term storage, so the fact that KF's is performance on the digit span task is so poor suggests that he experiences problems with mental activities, including those resulting in normal long-term storage.

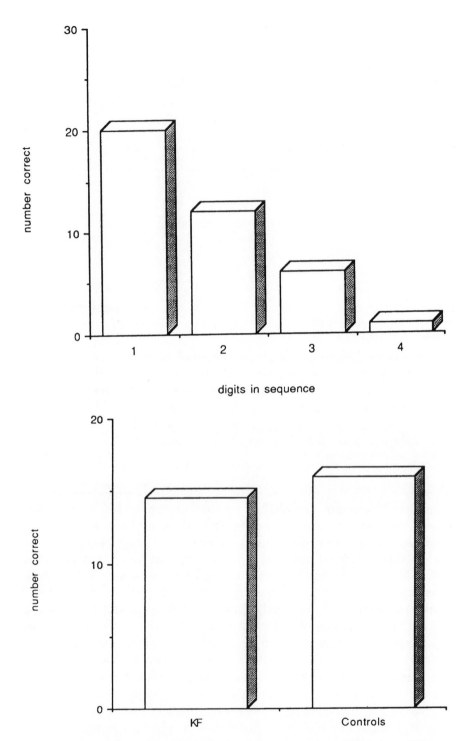

Fig. 6.1. Results of digit span and paired-associate learning tests on KF and controls. Data from Warrington and Shallice, 1969, p. 887.

Figure 6.1 also shows KF's ability to learn **paired associates**. In this task the subject first listens to pairs of unrelated words (e.g. 'nail' – 'map'). After three trials involving 20 pairs, KF's performance was only slightly poorer than that of the controls, and was certainly much better than one would expect if he had a highly defective capacity for conscious mental activity. KF required fewer trials than controls to learn a 10-word sequence, and when tested two months later, he still remembered seven of the words.

What are we to make of KF? One interpretation might be that his short-term storage processes are impaired but that long-term storage is normal. However, this would require us to revise our organizational concept of memory, which, as we have seen, assumes an orderly transition from short-term to long-term storage. An alternative view, and one which we shall develop in this chapter, is that short-term storage does not rely on a single structure or process. We will examine the possibility that, instead, short-term storage involves a complex system in which different components carry out different tasks. Seen in this light, KF's deficit becomes easier to interpret, his memory span difficulties now being seen to arise because some specific subcomponent of STS has been affected.

The Working Memory Model

The idea that short-term storage involves a number of subsystems has been most actively developed by Alan Baddeley and his colleagues (Baddeley and Hitch, 1977; Baddeley, 1986, 1990, 1992). His model is termed **working memory**, because the emphasis is on how the memory system is adapted to meet the needs of real-life conscious mental activities such as reading, thinking, and doing *The Times* crossword in your head!

Our starting point for understanding the origin of the working memory model is Baddeley and Hitch's assumption that if digit span reflects the capacity of STS and, in turn, if STS is a single structure, any task requiring the subject to retain a sequence of digits comparable to his or her memory span should make it extremely difficult for the subject to carry out any other task requiring STS capacity at the same time. To test this hypothesis, it was necessary to devise a **dual task paradigm** in which the subject performs a primary task while carrying out, simultaneously, a secondary task. In one study subjects were given the primary task of learning lists of visually presented words while at the same time

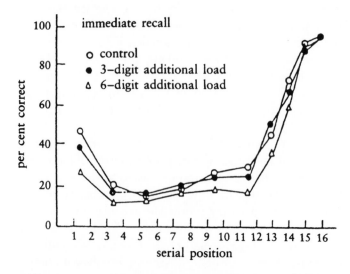

Fig. 6.2. The influence of a secondary digit span task on free recall. From Baddeley, 1986, p. 43. Reproduced with the permission of Oxford University Press.

either retaining a sequence of three or six auditorially presented digits or copying down pairs of digits as they were spoken.

If performance of the digit span task reflects maximum STS capacity, we should expect subjects learning the lists and retaining six digits at the same time to be quite impaired on the word task because we are using up most of the available STS capacity. Figure 6.2 shows that the additional load of six digits generally reduced performance, but to nowhere near the extent one would expect if STS capacity was largely absorbed with retaining the digits. Furthermore, the recency effect, which we attributed to short-term storage processes, remained robust under the six-digit load.

Baddeley and his colleagues went on to explore the influence of secondary task performance on primary tasks involving other kinds of conscious processing. In one study subjects were asked to verify sentences of the kind 'Canaries have wings', 'Dogs have feathers'. Before each of these sentences was presented, subjects were given a sequence of digits to remember which ranged from none to eight numbers. The subjects had to repeat the sequence continually until they had verified the sentence in front of them. Even when subjects were keeping in mind seven or eight random digits, it was found that they could still perform a reasoning task in 2 seconds with 95 per cent accuracy. It is extremely difficult to reconcile this and other similar results (e.g. Baddeley and

Hitch, 1977) with a unitary concept of STS in which digit span is assumed to be a measure of capacity, because, if so, one would expect verification performance to be severely disrupted when subjects were repeating seven or eight digits.

The Articulatory Loop

The results of these early experiments led to the view that the system responsible for memory span, as measured by the digit span task, was not the same as the system supporting all our conscious mental activity. Instead, it seemed possible that the task of retaining short sequences of digits might, to a large extent, be carried out by a different system from that involved in tasks such as learning word lists and reasoning.

Using a variety of lines of evidence, Baddeley and Hitch (1977) suggested that the system underlying the retention of digits was speech-based, and they named it the **articulatory loop**. In chapter 1 we discussed the phonological confusability effect – the finding that memory span is adversely affected if the items to be recalled have similar sounds (e.g. 'mad', 'man', 'mat'). These data strongly suggest that the mechanism underlying memory span makes use of a sound-based code, but it does not allow us to conclude that it is articulatory.

Evidence for the existence of an articulatory system underlying memory span came from an elegant series of experiments by Baddeley et al. (1975). The experiments were based on the observation that memory span for sequences of short words (e.g. 'sum', 'wit'), is better than for long words (e.g. 'aluminium', 'university', 'mechanism'). Baddeley et al. then asked whether this **word length effect** depended on the number of syllables in short and long words or on differences in the spoken duration of the words. To examine these two possibilities, they compared memory span for items that have equal numbers of syllables but relatively shorter or longer spoken durations (e.g. 'wicket' versus 'harpoon'). They found that memory span was shorter for words with longer spoken durations, and therefore concluded that the system underlying memory span was speech-based.

More evidence for an articulatory loop came from a second study, in which the word length effect was examined under conditions of **articulatory suppression**. In this study the subject had to repeat a meaningless spoken sequence (e.g. 'the, the, the . . .) while carrying out a primary task. Figure 6.3 shows that articulatory suppression causes the word length effect to disappear. Note in particular that performance on short words is reduced to the same level as that on long words. This is

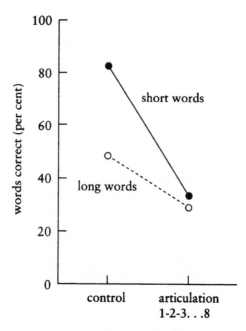

Fig. 6.3. The influence of articulatory suppression on the word length effect. Data from Baddeley et al., 1975, p. 584. Reproduced with the permission of Academic Press.

rather nice evidence that the advantage in recalling short words in a memory span task depends critically on the availability of an articulatory coding system. When this is not the case, as with articulatory suppression, memory for short and long words is dependent on the same processes, and they are therefore recalled to the same degree.

Hulme et al. (1984) provided developmental evidence for an articulatory component in memory span. They examined the relationship between speech rate and memory span as a function of age. Figure 6.4 shows that as we get older, our memory span increases in parallel with increases in our speech rate. This finding alone does not allow us to conclude that the relationship is causal, however. It could be, for example, that speech rate is a measure of some other more abstract verbal function which itself influences memory span performance. To examine this possibility, Raine et al. (1992) examined memory span in both normal children and those with pathologically slow speech on a memory span task that did not require verbal responding. The speech-disordered subjects were found to have reduced spans, reduced word length effects, and tended to rehearse less during learning. These differences were not

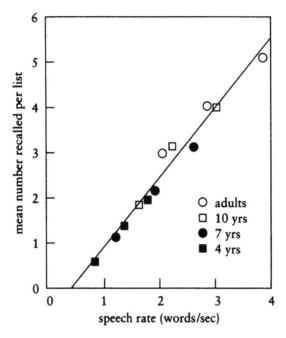

Fig. 6.4. The relationship between speech rate and memory span as a function of age. From Hulme et al., 1984, p. 244. Reproduced with the permission of Academic Press.

attributable to differences in intelligence or motor speed, but appeared to be directly determined by speech rate.

The first specific model of working memory, which is illustrated in figure 6.5, identifies three components: an articulatory loop, a **visuo-spatial scratch pad**, and a **central executive**. On the basis of experimental evidence, the articulatory loop was characterized as a structure capable of holding and recycling a small amount of speech-based information, and was assumed to underlie subjects' ability to perform mental tasks relatively easily while simultaneously holding digits – the argument being that part or all the digit load could be placed in the articulatory loop, thus making little or no demand on other components of working memory. Similarly, the phonological confusability effect was thought to arise because subjects unavoidably make use of the loop when carrying out memory span tasks – a conclusion supported by Murray's (1968) finding that this effect disappears under conditions of articulatory suppression.

Before moving on, we should note a couple of refinements to the articulatory loop concept. First, the loop is now thought to comprise

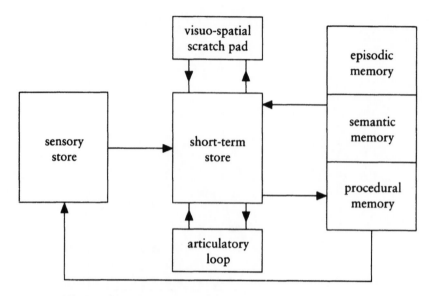

Fig. 6.5. The working memory model.

two components: a **phonological store**, which holds speech-based information, and an **articulatory control process**, which recycles a limited amount of speech-based information. This distinction is necessary to account for the fact that under conditions of articulatory suppression, subjects are still able to make certain judgements about phonology. For example, Besner et al. (1981) showed that subjects undergoing articulatory suppression at the same rate as Baddeley et al. (1975) reported had no difficulty judging whether non-words (e.g. 'pallis') sounded like real words. This indicates that the effect of articulatory suppression is to prevent transfer of information from the phonological store to the articulatory control process.

Baddeley (1986) has coined the term 'inner voice' for the articulatory control process, which suggests a direct relationship between the articulatory control process and the mechanisms governing overt speech. This possibility was investigated in a study by Baddeley and Wilson (1988) which examined working memory in a patient with **anarthria**, a complete inability to speak, despite intact language comprehension and production by other means. This patient had a normal digit span, and showed both phonological confusability and word length effects. These findings indicate that the articulatory control process is not linked to the mechanisms of overt speech, but instead reflects some more central form of motor programming that precedes speech production.

What is an Articulatory Loop For?

With the working memory model in mind, we can reinterpret KF's poor memory span performance in terms of an impairment to the articulatory loop. This would explain why, despite poor memory span, he showed normal learning on other memory tasks, because learning on these is not helped by the presence of an articulatory code. KF's case also raises another issue. If normal learning can occur with a defective articulatory loop, what is the loop for? So far, we have implicated the loop only as a system involved in performing memory span tasks. However, memory span tasks do not bear much resemblance to the kinds of task for which we use our memory in everyday life. As we noted earlier, the motivation for the working memory idea was to establish how memory was adapted to mental tasks we routinely carry out.

The Articulatory Loop and Reading Development

An important characteristic of children with developmental dyslexia is that they have greatly reduced memory spans. This suggests a possible link between a failure to develop an effective articulatory loop and the presence of dyslexia. This was supported by Shankweiler and Liberman (1976), who found that superior readers showed a much greater phonological confusability effect (see p. 13) than poorer readers. This result complemented an earlier study by Conrad (1971) which demonstrated that phonological confusability effects start to appear only around the time that children start to learn to read, suggesting that a speech code may be essential for normal reading development.

The above evidence implicates the articulatory loop in language development; but what is its exact role? One possibility is that the articulatory loop is essential for encoding sequences of spoken sounds (**phonemes**) in the correct order. Consider a relatively simple word like 'cat'. In order to read it aloud, the visual input must be converted into a sequence of phonemes which are then blended in the correct order to produce the word. A poorly developed articulatory loop may make this task much more difficult, and so lead to reading retardation.

The Articulatory Loop and Fluent Reading

A plausible case can be made for the role of the articulatory loop in reading and other aspects of reading development. But what role does the articulatory loop play in fluent reading? When we read silently, we still experience an inner voice, and it has often been speculated that this inner speech has some functional significance. Huey (1908), for example, noted that

> The carrying range of inner speech is considerably larger than vision. . . . The initial subvocalization seems to help hold the word in consciousness until enough others are given to combine with it in touching off the unitary utterance of a sentence which they form. . . . It is of the greatest service to the reader or listener that at each moment a considerable amount of what is being read should hang suspended in the primary memory of inner speech.

Hardyk and Petrinovich (1970) carried out an interesting study in which students read essays judged as either easy or hard in content. All subjects were wired up to apparatus which measured both throat muscle and forearm muscle activity. One group of subjects (the normal group) simply read, with the inconvenience of being attached to the apparatus. A second, feedback group was told not to subvocalize, and if they did, a buzzer sounded. A third, control group read while maintaining their forearms at a particular level of flexion. Subsequently, subjects answered questions on the essays. The results are shown in figure 6.6. They indicate no difference between the three experimental conditions when reading easy passages; but subjects forced to suppress vocalization were found to remember considerably less about the hard passages.

Although one might argue that measurement of throat muscle activity is not the most direct means of assessing whether articulatory activity is relevant to comprehension, the Hardyk and Petrinovich result does at least suggest that the articulatory loop may be more important when reading material that is complex. This view is supported by some experiments carried out by Slowiaczek and Clifton (1980). They presented subjects with a passage which they either listened to or read. Within each group, half suppressed vocalization and half were silent. They were then given a series of statements about the passage and asked to verify them. Some statements were simply a paraphrase, whereas some required the integration of concepts across the passage. The results showed no differences between reading and listening groups with paraphrase questions. However, with more complex questions, subjects who read while carrying out articulatory suppression were found to be impaired.

Both these studies suggest that the articulatory loop is particularly useful when dealing with more complex material, perhaps because it

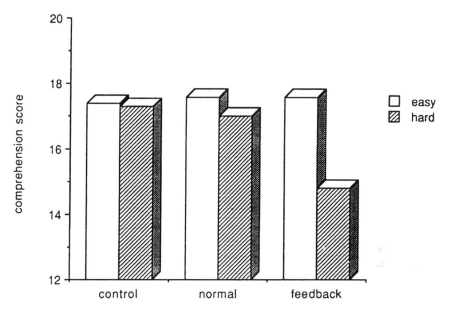

Fig. 6.6. Data from Hardyk and Petrinovich, 1970, p. 650, showing that only comprehension of hard material is impaired when vocalization during learning is prevented by the use of feedback.

provides a useful memory system for retaining word order. In addition, it may also be a means of holding the **intonation contour** – those aspects of phonology that enable different meanings of the same basic sentence to be understood. However, both tasks assess reading comprehension by means of a memory measure; hence the observed effects may be due to the effects of articulatory suppression on reading or on memory storage subsequent to reading.

This difficulty can be circumvented by taking on line measures of reading ability under both suppression and control conditions. Kleiman (1975) found that subjects repeating aloud digits as a secondary task did not differ from controls in their ability to detect a category instance in a sentence. However, when the same secondary task was imposed on subjects asked to judge whether sentences such as 'Pizzas have been eating Jerry' were anomalous, control subjects performed significantly better.

Baddeley and Lewis (1981) examined how articulatory suppression interfered with subjects' ability to detect anomalous words in a piece of text. Test sentences were quite complex (e.g. 'She doesn't mind going to the dentist to have fillings, but doesn't like the pain [rent] when he gives her the injection at the beginning'). Anomaly detection was less accurate if subjects engaged in articulatory suppression, but this did not affect their ability to classify meaningful sentences correctly. In a second study Baddeley examined how articulatory suppression affected subjects' detection of word order errors in real text. Here performance was compared with both a silent control condition and a condition in which subjects had to tap their fingers in time with a metronome. Only the articulatory suppression condition produced an increase in error rate.

Articulatory Suppression – A Cautionary Note

One of the problems with the dual task paradigm is teasing out the general distracting effect of a secondary task from any specific effect assumed to arise from the particular mental operations demanded by that task. In relation to articulatory suppression, this poses the question of whether the effects of articulatory suppression are due to some specific interference with the ability to use articulatory coding or merely to the general distraction caused by asking subjects to do two things at once.'

Margolin et al. (1982) re-examined a study by Levy (1977) which had shown that subjects' memory for visually presented sentences declined when they undertook articulatory suppression at the same time and had concluded that articulatory coding was specifically involved in carrying out the task. Margolin et al. replicated this effect, but also included a 'pseudo-suppression' task in which subjects pressed a button every time they sensed a mild electric shock. Surprisingly, this manipulation produced identical results to the real articulatory suppression task.

This shows that we must exercise caution in interpreting the results of articulatory suppression experiments. We did note, however, that Baddeley et al. used a secondary tapping task as a potential control for effects due to general distraction. However, use of this control is effective only if it can be shown that the alternative secondary task has the same general distracting qualities as articulatory suppression. At present, an independent measure of the distracting qualities of secondary tasks is not possible; yet it is necessary if the effects of these tasks on mental processes are to be interpreted accurately.

Reading without an Articulatory Loop

The above comment indicates certain difficulties in inferring the role of the articulatory loop in fluent reading from experiments involving articulatory suppression. These objections do not apply to people who can be assumed to have a defective articulatory loop on the basis of their severely reduced memory span, however. One such patient was PV (Vallar and Baddeley, 1984, 1987). PV was asked to classify as true or false simple sentences such as 'Plants grow in gardens', verbose simple sentences such as 'There is no doubt that champagne is something that can certainly be bought in shops', and complex sentences such as 'It is fortunate that most rivers are able to be crossed by bridges that are strong enough for cars'. Whether tested for auditory or written comprehension, PV had no difficulty with the simpler sentences, but performed at close to chance levels when trying to classify the complex sentences. The data from PV are therefore consistent with the data from articulatory suppression experiments on normal subjects, and suggest that articulatory encoding may be important only when dealing with more complex sentences in which the memory load is high. It is also important to note that PV's comprehension difficulties were not worsened by articulatory suppression, a finding one would expect in someone without an articulatory loop.

Vallar and Baddeley's interpretation of PV's performance has been questioned by Howard and Butterworth (1989), however. Their point is that the co-occurrence of a comprehension deficit and an impaired memory span does not, of necessity, mean that the latter deficit underlies the former. Brain lesions rarely have an isolated effect on mental processes, and it could be that PV's two problems have independent causes. Howard and Butterworth also claim that defective memory span cannot be the basis of comprehension deficits, on the basis of work with a patient known as RE (Butterworth et al., 1986). This patient had a memory span deficit similar to that of PV, but no comprehension difficulties.

Howard and Butterworth also suggest that the arguments for the involvement of the articulatory loop in comprehension are not motivated by any independently derived theory as to the role of phonological storage in comprehension. As a result, the claim that phonological storage is essential to comprehension arises only because evidence of defective memory span is associated with comprehension difficulties. Vallar and Baddeley produce various counter-arguments, including, for example, the fact that RE's memory span deficit dates from birth. Neuropsychological impairments can either be **acquired** – i.e. arise when a normal brain is suddenly damaged – or be **developmental** – i.e. due to defective development. Vallar and Baddeley argue that only acquired deficits shed light on the organization of mental processes because, in developmental disorders, the whole basis of mental processes may have developed atypically.

Vallar and Baddeley do not, however, provide any additional discussion as to how phonological storage might be relevant to comprehension. This issue is addressed in a study by Waters et al. (1991) in which the comprehension abilities of another patient with severely reduced memory span, BO, were investigated. BO was given a wide range of sentences to comprehend, and in general her performance was excellent. However, she did have some difficulties. For example, she had more difficulty understanding a sentence such as 'Patrick said that Joe kicked Eddie' than a syntactically comparable one using animal names rather than proper nouns – 'The monkey that kissed the elephant scratched the frog'. On the basis of these findings, Waters et al. suggested that deficit affects 'post-interpretive processes', elements of comprehension that occur once the basic meaning of an utterance has been encoded. Without the help of phonological coding, holding proper nouns in memory may be more difficult than holding real nouns, because the former have a less elaborate representation in memory.

Visuo-spatial scratch pad

Baddeley (1986) extended the concept of working memory with the addition of a second structure, the visuo-spatial scratch pad (VSSP). Imagery is a prominent feature of our mental life, and, as we saw in the previous chapter, there is some reason to believe that it has a separate status from other, non-image-based mental processes. The idea behind the VSSP is that working memory has a specific component that provides a work space within which a visual image scan be stored and manipulated in order to carry out a particular task. The VSSP thus has much in common with the spatial medium in Kosslyn's computational theory of imagery.

Evidence for a VSSP comes from dual task studies such as that by Brooks (1968). Subjects were asked to keep in mind a letter F and then imagine an asterisk travelling around the F (see figure 6.7). At each change of direction, subjects had to indicate whether the asterisk was at an extreme or intermediate point of the F. Three modes of responding were used: vocal yes–no, tapping – one tap for yes, two taps for no – and a pointing response. In the latter, subjects had a visual array of spatially distributed Y and N symbols in front of them. As they imagined the asterisk moving, subjects indicated their response by pointing to the next Y or N location available as they worked their way down the array.

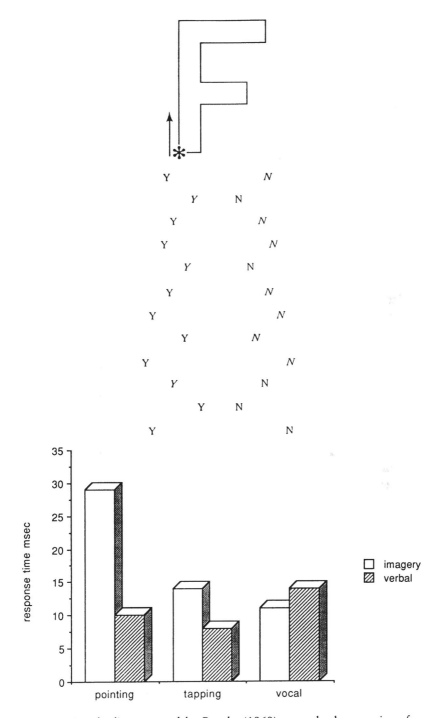

Fig. 6.7. Simple diagram used by Brooks (1968) to study the scanning of mental images (*left*). Pointing response arrangement (*middle*). Response times in the different experimental conditions (*right*). From Brooks, 1968, pp. 350–3. Reprinted with the permission of the University of Toronto Press.

These three modes of responding were also used in a verbal task in which subjects had to work through a proverb and indicate whether or not each successive word was a noun. For the verbal condition, the three response modes produced comparable reaction times. For the visual condition, however, the pointing response produced far slower reaction times than the other two response modes. The fact that the pointing task caused a significant delay only when responding in the visual condition suggests strongly that subjects were retaining a spatial image and that this interfered with responding that was also determined by spatial constraints.

The Central Executive

The components of working memory that we have identified so far, the articulatory loop and the visuo-spatial scratch pad, contribute to only a small percentage of our conscious mental activity. In terms of the model, the bulk of what we do is carried out by the central executive. Because it is the most complex component, it is perhaps not surprising that it is also the least understood.

One approach to understanding the central executive can be described as the 'psychometric' approach. The basis of this idea is that the executive must, under a given set of conditions (e.g. reading comprehension), have a fixed capacity. Daneman and Carpenter (1980) have termed this the **working memory span**. They measured it by presenting subjects with a sequence of sentences and asking them to retain the last word of each. Thus subjects might see or hear the sentences 'The sailor sold the parrot', 'The vicar opened the book'. Afterwards, they are asked to recall the final words ('parrot', 'book'). This constitutes a measure of working memory span, and it was subsequently correlated with each subject's score on a reading comprehension test. The correlation was found to be high, indicating that reading comprehension is a positive function of working memory span.

The idea that the capacity of the central executive is related to reading ability gains support from other studies involving both adults (Baddeley, et al., 1985) and children (Oakhill, 1984; Oakhill et al., 1986). However, these studies measured working memory in purely quantitative, capacity-related terms, and some account of how the executive actually works must be provided if the working memory model is to be a proper account of memory.

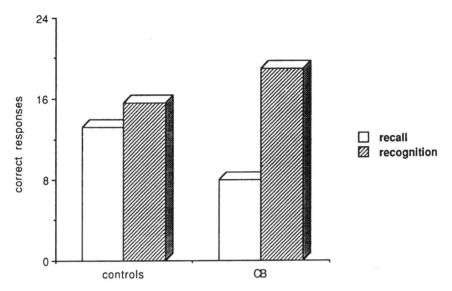

Fig. 6.8. Performance of CB and controls on recall and recognition tasks matched for difficulty. From Parkin et al., (submitted). Reproduced with permission.

The Dysexecutive Syndrome

One recent idea has been to equate the functioning of the central executive with the processing operations associated with the frontal lobes. This research was motivated by observations of patients who have developed memory problems as a result of frontal lobe damage. The deficits suffered by these patients are not as severe as those shown by amnesics such as HM, and they have been brought together under the umbrella term **dysexecutive syndrome**, (Baddeley, 1990), on the grounds that their memory deficit reflects some impairment in the executive control of memory.

Pitchford, Binschaedler, and I (submitted, a) have worked with a patient known as CB, who suffered a form of stroke which damaged part of his frontal lobes. Figure 6.8 shows how CB and controls performed on tests of recall and recognition matched for difficulty (Calev, 1984). On recall CB shows a very substantial deficit, but on recognition his performance is above the control average. This is not the pattern with amnesia, for amnesic patients perform poorly on both recall and recognition. This sparing of recognition compared to recall is perhaps the hallmark feature of the dysexecutive syndrome; but what exactly has gone wrong here?

The frontal lobes are known to play an important role in planning and the execution of response strategies (e.g. Karnath et al., 1991). This aspect of frontal function has been described by Norman and Shallice (1986), and their account assumes that most actions are controlled by **schemata** – well-established routines for dealing with particular situations which, once triggered, allow a sequence of actions to be performed automatically. Additional conscious control, when required, is brought about by a **supervisory attentional system (SAS)**. The SAS is called on in situations where planning, problem solving, or decision making is required; where novel or poorly learned information is being manipulated; in dangerous or technically difficult situations; and in circumstances likely to provoke a strong but inappropriate response.

In chapter 4 we saw that recall is a reconstructive act in which a hypothesis must be devised in order to initiate a search of memory. Recall thus resembles a form of problem-solving activity which would be dependent on the intact functioning of the SAS. In recognition testing, however, the problem-solving aspect is largely side-stepped, in that no hypothesis about what the target might be needs to be generated; hence this type of process is likely to be less disrupted by impairment of the SAS.

The dysexecutive syndrome might be characterized, therefore, as the form of memory deficit arising from damage to the SAS. Thus, on any aspect of memory requiring some form of executive strategy, a deficit appears but when a memory task is not strategy-dependent, deficits are not evident. Further examination of CB's performance emphasizes this point. On the Calev task the normal superiority of recognition over recall is partly avoided because the recall test involves learning words that are taxonomically related to each other. It is assumed that normal subjects make use of these obvious relationships to devise a learning strategy that will promote subsequent recall. Analysis of CB's recall, however, indicated that he made little use of the taxonomic relationships, thus suggesting some deficit in planning either at encoding or retrieval.

If the dysexecutive syndrome is due to some general impairment of the SAS, then these patients should show problems with non-memory tasks that involve SAS-type function. Figure 6.9 shows the 'Tinkertoy test' (Lezak, 1983), which measures the ability of subjects to construct a novel object from various items. CB performed exceptionally badly on this, commenting during his attempts that there was 'no planning going into this at all'.

Patients such as CB, as well as others reported by Baddeley and

 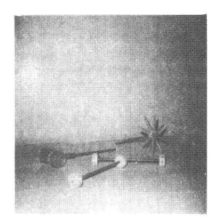

Fig. 6.9. The Tinkertoy Test. On the left is a construction made by a normal adult. On the right one produced by a brain damaged subject. Photo courtesy of Judy Pitchford.

Wilson (1988) and Hanley et al. (in press) show a pattern of memory loss that seems attributable to the inability to plan and execute retrieval processes. For this reason they perform most poorly on tests of recall, because here there is the strongest 'executive' demand. We saw that CB performed normally on tests of recognition, and attributed this to the small demands that recognition makes on executive control. However, we must be careful not to assume that recognition is always normal in the dysexecutive syndrome. Recognition, as chapter 4 showed, is a complex response that can be influenced by a number of factors, some of which might be executive in nature.

CB was given another version of the recognition test, one that differed from the first in a very important way. In the original test he was given a single sheet of paper on which were arranged, in random order, all the targets and distractors. All he had to do was to put a ring around those he recognized. In the second, **single probe** test, he was confronted with each recognition item singly, and had to decide whether or not it was a target. As we know, CB performed above average on the original task, but on this new task he performed very badly (see figure 6.10).

The original task and the single probe task seem relatively similar, and controls do not seem to find one any more difficult than the other. Why, then, does CB find the single probe task so difficult? In chapter 4 we saw that recognition can be based on different types of information elicited by the stimulus. Under one set of conditions it is possible that

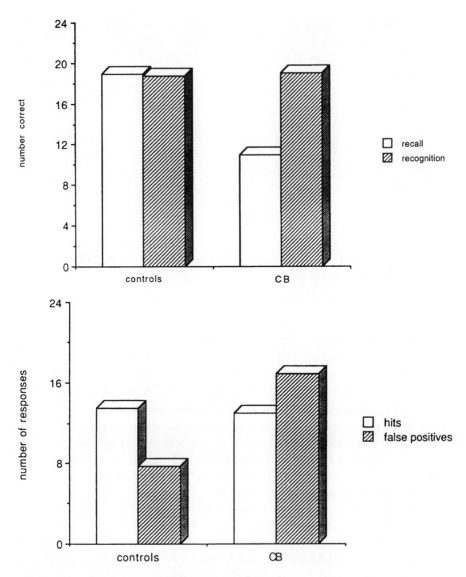

Fig. 6.10. Performance of CB on a single probe recognition test (*top*). Performance of CB on a single probe recognition test with related distractors (*bottom*). From Parkin et al., in press.

the overall familiarity of a stimulus provides a sufficient basis for a correct recognition judgement, whereas under more stringent conditions some context associated with the stimulus must be retrieved before successful recognition can occur.

It is possible that the discrepancy in CB's performance on the two types of recognition test reflects an inability to retrieve (or perhaps to encode) contextual information about the stimuli. On the standard yes–no procedure all targets and distractors are simultaneously available, so it is possible to discriminate targets from distractors by comparing their relative familiarity. However, in single probe recognition, familiarity is less effective because simultaneous comparison with unfamiliar distractors is ruled out.

The above possibility was tested by carrying out a standard yes–no recognition test similar to the Calev test but where the distractors were semantic and rhyming associates of targets (e.g. 'table', 'chair', 'fable'). Under these conditions CB produced a similar number of correct identifications but an abnormally high number of false positives (see figure 6.10). This can be explained on the grounds that the distractors have some familiarity value because of their featural overlap with the target. Normal subjects are not unduly deceived by this, because they have sufficient contextual information to discriminate targets from distractors. CB, however, is deficient in contextual information, and is thus easily led into misidentifying distractors with related features as targets.

The idea of dysexecutive deficit may also help us understand some of the repressive phenomena considered in chapter 4. Evans et al. (1992) examined the autobiographical memory of parasuicidal patients and controls. Subjects were given cue words and were asked to produce a recollection, which was scored in terms of how specific it was. In addition, both groups of subjects were also given a problem-solving test. The results showed that the parasuicidal patients had vaguer memories, thus replicating an earlier study by Williams and Broadbent (1986), and poorer problem-solving abilities. Moreover, correlations revealed that patients with the vaguest memories also had the worst problem-solving scores.

The association between poor memory and poor problem solving strongly suggests that a dysexecutive deficit may be responsible for repressive memory phenomena. The idea that this may be linked specifically to frontal dysfunction comes from a study by Stampfer and myself (Parkin and Stampfer, in press). We studied a patient called CE who, following an extremely traumatic life history, suddenly developed inertness and intellectual impairment, coupled with suicidal tendencies. Interestingly she showed little inability to recall her past up to the point

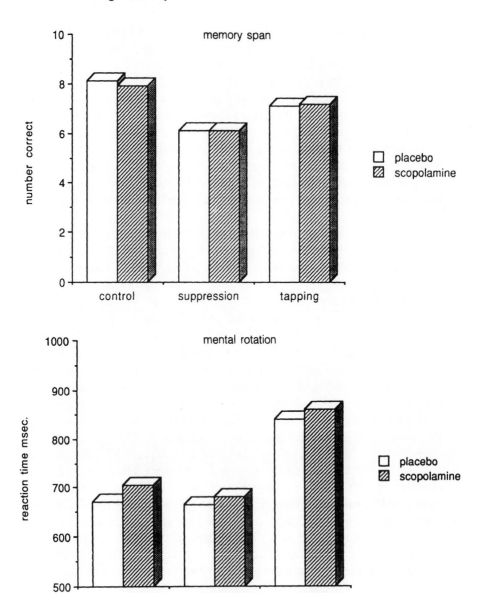

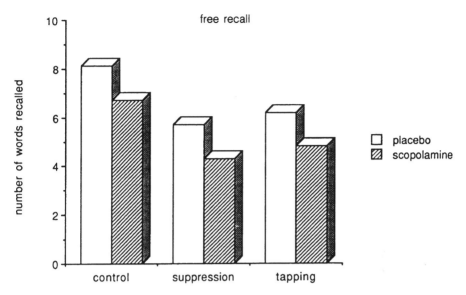

Fig. 6.11. Data from Rusted, 1988, p. 489, showing memory span, mental rotation time, and free recall, with and without scopolamine. See text for explanation.

where, being asked to recall an event that the word 'cut' reminded her of, she failed to remember a suicide attempt in which she had slashed her wrists only 24 hours earlier. Formal examination of CE's memory performance revealed something that very much resembled the dysexecutive syndrome, in that she performed normally on a range of recognition tasks but exhibited levels of recall poorer than those expected in very elderly people. She also showed other signs of frontal lobe disturbance, which lifted as her basic memory and intellectual problems were resolved.

Neuropharmacological Evidence for Working Memory

Rusted (1988) examined the performance of subjects on three memory tasks thought to load primarily on different components of working memory:

Memory span (see above) – articulatory loop
Mental rotation (see chapter 5) – visuo-spatial scratch pad
Free recall (see chapter 1) – central executive

Performance of these tasks was examined under three different perform-ance conditions:

Articulatory suppression – see above
Spatial tapping – subject moves finger continually, making contact with four different locations
Control – no secondary task

Each combination of task and performance condition was examined twice: once under normal conditions and once following administration of scopolamine, which, as we saw in chapter 1, is known to inhibit the cholinergic system.

The aim of Rusted's study was to examine the extent to which cholinergic mechanisms influenced the operation of the different com-ponents of working memory. The results are shown in figure 6.11 and may be summarized as follows. Articulatory suppression gave rise to poorer memory span than the control condition, but had no significant effect on mental rotation. Spatial tapping slowed down mental rotation time relative to control, but articulatory suppression did not. Free recall was impaired in both secondary tasks relative to control. Scopolamine produced a constant decrement in free recall.

Rusted's results provide a nice demonstration of the selective interfer-ence of secondary tasks. Memory span, which is assumed to be mediated by the articulatory loop, is affected by suppression but not be spatial tapping. Mental rotation, which is assumed to depend on the VSSP, is influenced by spatial tapping but not by articulatory suppression. Furthermore, the failure of scopolamine to influence either of these sug-gests that the hypothetical subsystems are not dependent on cholinergic mechanisms. By contrast, free recall is substantially reduced by the administration of scopolamine, but the extent of this deficit is no greater when subjects are required to perform a secondary task during learning. This indicates that scopolamine exerts its influence on the central execu-tive contribution to free recall rather than on any contribution made to this process by other subcomponents of working memory; for, if the latter was the case, one would expect to see a greater difference in performance with and without scopolamine in the two secondary task conditions.

Recently Luciana et al. (1992) have made further neuropharmacological explorations of working memory. They examined performance on a spatial working memory task when subjects were given the drug **bromocriptine**. This drug is known to enhance activity in neural path-ways that depend on the neurotransmitter **dopamine**. The spatial task

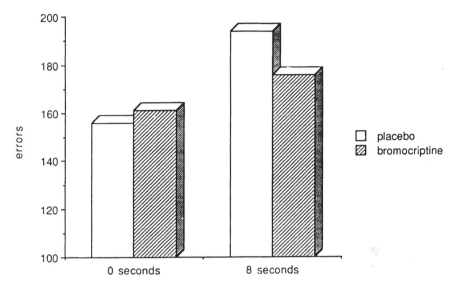

Fig. 6.12. Data from Luciana et al., 1992, p. 61, showing the facilitation of spatial working memory by bromocriptine.

involved the brief (200 msec) presentation of a small circle followed by either no delay or a delay of 8 seconds, after which subjects were asked to indicate where the circle had been presented. Figure 6.12 shows that, with no delay, there was no difference between drug and no-drug conditions, but at 8 seconds, administration of bromocriptine significantly improved performance.

Luciana et al. thus showed that bromocriptine improved performance on a delayed test of spatial working memory. The effect could have been due, however, to a more general drug effect on arousal or attention. To investigate this, they examined how bromocriptine affected performance on a bi-letter cancellation task, in which subjects were asked to put a line through all occurrences of two target letters in a random letter sequence. On this task, subjects administered bromocriptine performed no differently from controls, so it was concluded that the bromocriptine effect on spatial working memory was not due to general factors but to some specific enhancement of spatial working memory ability.

Overview

There is now good evidence that the memory system underlying conscious mental activity is not a single entity but one comprising at least three components. This has been formalized in Baddeley's working memory model, which proposes the separable existence of an articulatory loop, a visuo-spatial scratch pad, and a central executive. Existence of the articulatory loop is supported by memory span experiments showing that performance on this task depends substantially on an articulatory code. This structure is thought to play an important role in language development and to aid the comprehension of more complex linguistic material in adults. The visuo-spatial scratch pad provides a medium for the temporary strorage and manipulation of images; its existence is inferred from studies showing that concurrent spatial tasks interfere with one another. The central executive subsumes the attentional and strategic aspects of working memory, and the effects of its disruption can be seen in the dysexecutive syndrome. Psychological and neuropsychological evidence for the working memory model is now being supplemented by neuropharmacological studies.

7

Growing Up

I like very much people telling me about their childhood. But they'll have to be quick or I'll tell them about mine.

Dylan Thomas

'Never work with children or animals' is an old showbiz maxim which applies quite well to the study of human memory development. Carrying out experiments on young children can be quite problematic and it has been necessary to devise many ingenious ways to try and understand how children's memory works. Young children can be shy; they can decide to be sick or go to the toilet at a critical point in an experiment; and, what's more, they can be devious. Ann Brown (1975) wanted to discover how well children could monitor the contents of their own memory. She used the 'feeling of knowing task' (which we will consider in more detail later), in which a child is shown a picture and, if they are unable to name the object in it, asked to say how likely it was that they would be able to recognize it. Brown wanted to measure how certain any 'feeling of knowing' (see below) might be, so she devised an evens betting procedure: if a child failed to name a picture, they could bet, using sweets, as to how likely they would be to recognize the name. Thus the more certain they were the more sweets they would win. Unfortunately for Brown, the children soon realized that they could maximize the number of sweets they obtained by failing to name every picture and then placing a maximum bet on the recognition test.

Working with animals presents a completely different set of problems. The animal's entire experience can be controlled, and there is no scope for the kind of deviousness shown by Brown's child subjects. The question, however, is whether anything discovered about early memory in young animals has any relevance to humans. Behaviourists certainly saw no difficulty with this (e.g. Keppel, 1964), because they believed in the evolutionary continuity between man and animal. It would certainly be a mistake to think that memory in humans and animals has nothing in common, but, equally, it is misleading to suppose that most important questions about memory development can be addressed by means of animal studies.

A case in point is infantile amnesia (see below), the inability of humans to remember much about their lives before the age of 4. One possible explanation of this is that early memories are forgotten more rapidly. Studies comparing rats of different ages indicate that older rats are better at remembering that a given set of circumstances can give them an electric shock and so is best avoided. Younger rats, however, forget this more rapidly (e.g. Smith and Spear, 1981). This might suggest that old and young rats differ in their ability to remember episodes, but is this a difference in recall as we would understand it in humans? It could be; but because we cannot ask the rats anything, we cannot be sure. However, it is equally plausible that this learning involves the acquisition of conditioned fear responses. We know from the experiments on the unfortunate Little Albert that young children can also be conditioned to fear things (Watson and Rayner, 1920), so the assumption of some continuity between human and animal is justified. This approach is, however, limited and whole aspects of memory development require a different explanatory approach, one that can only be met only by tackling the child head on.

Early Memory

At what point do children start to acquire memories? This is a difficult question to answer because obviously very young children cannot say anything and any memory they have must be inferred in a different way. One approach is to use the **habituation-novelty-preference** procedure (HNP). Infants will naturally tend to gaze more at something they find novel, as compared with something they have seen before. This **novelty preference** can be used as an index of memory, on the basis that if an infant gazes less at a pre-exposed stimulus than a comparable novel stimulus, it must have some memory of the earlier stimulus.

Friedman and his colleagues (e.g. Friedman, 1972; Friedman et al., 1974) used HNP to investigate whether children as young as 1 day old can recognize previously seen objects. Subjects were shown a checkerboard, and the experimenters measured how long the infant looked at it. The checkerboard was re-presented several times, and it was found that the infants spent less and less time looking at it. This was not the case when a different checkerboard was presented on each trial, so the authors concluded that in the first instance the infants must be recognizing the original checkerboard rather than reducing their gaze times because they were becoming tired or bored.

DeCasper and Fifer (1980) trained newborn infants to suck on a nipple that activated a tape recorder. A contingency was then introduced in that if the infant sucked more rapidly, a tape of its mother's voice would play, whereas if the child sucked more slowly, the tape of an unfamiliar woman's voice would be heard. Most infants adjusted their sucking in order to hear their mother's voice, and when the contingency was reversed (i.e. slower sucking produced the mother's voice), the infants readjusted. This experiment is all the more remarkable in that the infants were only 12 hours old, thereby suggesting that the mother's voice had already been learned in those first few hours of life.

The child's very early ability to recognize the sound of its mother's voice was partly explained by a subsequent study. DeCasper and Spence (1986) asked 33 pregnant women to recite a passage out loud during the last 6 weeks of their pregnancy. Newborns were then tested on a learning task for which the reward was either the sound of the passage their mother had recited during pregnancy or a control passage. It was found that the previously exposed passage was more reinforcing. These data indicate that foetuses can learn from their mother's voice. This suggests that DeCasper and Fifer's children may have learned a substantial amount about their mother's voice while still in the womb.

An intriguing study by Cernoch and Porter (1985) required mothers of newborn children to wear a gauze pads in their armpits overnight. Next day one pad was placed alongside one cheek of the infant, and a pad collected from another woman was placed next to the other cheek. Breast-fed babies consistently turned to the gauze pad with their mother's odour, but bottle-fed babies showed no preference. Thus, given the opportunity, babies also remember their mother's odour.

Research on older infants using HNP has charted the development of recognition memory. Martin (1975) tested a range of young infants (aged 2, 3.5, and 5 months) on two successive days. On day 1 the infants were shown six 30-second exposures of a geometric figure (see figure 7.1). On day 2 the figure was again shown six times, again for

Fig. 7.1. Figures used by Martin, 1975, p. 180, in the novelty preference task. Reproduced with the permission of the American Psychological Association.

30 seconds. It was found that, compared with a novel picture, all infants looked at the picture less on day 2, but that this effect was most marked in the older group, thus suggesting that recognition, in some sense at least, was more developed in the older infants.

Rovee-Collier and her associates (e.g. Rovee-Collier, 1989; Rovee-Collier and Hayne, 1987) devised the **conjugate reinforcement** (CR) procedure (see figure 7.2) to explore memory in infants aged between 2 and 4 months. This involves placing a mobile above the baby's cot and connecting it, via string, to the baby's ankle, so that when the baby kicks its leg, the mobile moves. When the baby's ankle is linked to the mobile, its baseline kicking rate doubles, thereby indicating that it understands the relationship between kicking and making the mobile move. Memory for the contingency is assumed if the kicking rate at the start of a subsequent session with the mobile is comparable to that at the end of the initial session.

An additional phenomenon that can be demonstrated with the CR procedure is **reinstatement**, in which a brief encounter with an apparently forgotten stimulus can fully reactivate memory. Sullivan (1982) trained 3-month-old infants on the CR procedure. One group was re-tested 14 days later, and showed little retention. A second group was

Fig. 7.2. Conjugate reinforcement procedure used by Rovee-Collier and colleagues. Photograph courtesy of Carolyn Rovee-Collier.

given a reminder session on day 13 which involved them watching the experimenter pull the ribbon attached to the mobile at approximately the same rate as the baby had activated the mobile by its kicking. When tested the next day, these infants showed clear evidence of retention; watching the ribbon being pulled had somehow reinstated their own memory of the mobile. Interestingly, this reinstatement effect was not instant, and could only be shown if a few hours were allowed to elapse between the reinstating experience and the test.

Using the CR procedure, it has been possible to explore a number of aspects of infant memory. Rovee-Collier et al. (1980), for example, showed that memory for the kicking contingency can last up to a week, although it depends on the age of the infant (Greco et al., 1990), older infants retaining the contingency longer. This age effect appears to be due to older infants retaining more details about the mobile, so that even if they forget a great deal about it, there may still be some aspect they recognize which then results in kicking.

Several studies using the CR procedure have revealed that changes in the training context can disrupt memory for the mobile. In these studies (e.g. Borovsky and Rovee-Collier, 1990; Rovee-Collier and Shyi, in press) the training context was created by draping a colourful cloth around the infant's cot or playpen while learning was in progress. Retention was then tested by seeing whether the infant remembered the mobile in a different context (see figure 7.2). Three-month-old infants showed excellent retention in a different context after 1 day, but not after several days. Infants of 6 months, however, showed no memory what-soever for the mobile when tested in a different context. Subsequent studies have shown that infants' memory for the mobile can be disrupted if re-testing takes place in a new location (Hayne et al., 1991) and that under conditions where the learning context remains constant, a novel mobile can reinstate the kicking contingency (Shields and Rovee-Collier, 1992).

The above studies show that the ability to recognize and learn stimulus – response contingencies appears to be present at a very early age, whereas the ability to recall things emerges only later. Infants of 7 months will look for an object that is placed out of sight or covered up, but younger infants fail to do this (e.g. Fox et al., 1979). However, the time over which young children can recall the location of hidden objects is very limited, with even 18-month-old infants failing to remember after only 30 seconds (Daehler et al., 1976). On the other hand, this may be a rather conservative estimate, in that Baillargeon et al. (1990) found that much younger infants could find a hidden object after 70 seconds. In addition, when more distinctive objects and locations were used, infants appeared to be able to recall where something was placed several hours later (e.g. DeLoache and Brown, 1983).

Around the age of 8–10 months, infants exhibit an interesting memory phenomenon known as the $A\overline{B}$ error. Piaget (1954) observed that infants of this age can find an object at an initial location, A. If the infants successfully locate an object at A on several successive occasions, they will continue to search there even if the object is visibly located in a different place, B (G. E. Butterworth, 1977). This finding has intrigued researchers, and many different explanations have been offered (see Harris, 1989), the most compelling, and perhaps the simplest, being that the $A\overline{B}$ error is due to the rapid forgetting characteristic of infants of this age. Fox et al. (1979), found no evidence of the $A\overline{B}$ error in 9-month-old infants when the delay between hide and test was 3 seconds, but the error did arise when longer hide–test intervals were used. Ten-month-old infants, however, did not show the $A\overline{B}$ error, even at a hide–test interval of 7 seconds.

Schacter and Moscovitch (1984) cite a number of developmental studies in support of their rapid forgetting explanation of the $A\overline{B}$ error. In addition, they present converging evidence from a study of adult amnesic patients. In phase 1, each patient watched as the experimenter placed an object behind some books (location A) in a room, and was then asked to indicate the object's location. After 2.5 minutes the patient was asked to locate the object again. This was repeated until the patients were correct on three successive trials. The process was then repeated, except that a different location, B, was used. In phase 2, location A was made directly visible to the patient and the object was relocated there as in phase 1, but after two successful retrievals by the patient, the object was then placed in location C, which was in full view of the subject.

In phase 1, all the patients located the object at A, even after a delay. When the object was switched to location B, all the amnesic patients located it successfully with immediate testing, but after a delay, the patients committed the $A\overline{B}$ error by searching incorrectly at A. When confronted with their error, none of the patients could remember the object being hidden at B. More surprising results were obtained when the object was 'hidden' at location C. Retrieval of the object from location A was again normal, but when the object was placed in location C, five of the six amnesic patients failed to search at the correct location after delay, and instead looked for the object in location A. Discussing their data, Schacter and Moscovitch suggest that the results are best interpreted as a **mnemonic precedence** effect in which interference from a well-established response pattern prevents the formation of a new permanent memory. Furthermore, they argue that the close parallel between the infant data and the amnesic data (i.e. in both cases the $A\overline{B}$ error arises only when a delay is interpolated) reinforces the idea that the $A\overline{B}$ error is most plausibly explained in terms mnemonic precedence.

Memory Strategies and Development

One influential view of why memory improves with age is that older children are able to employ increasingly more complex strategies for remembering information (see Kail, 1990, and Schneider and Pressley, 1989, for reviews). In chapter 1 we saw that rehearsal is an important determinant of remembering, and many studies have investigated whether memory development is related to increased use of rehearsal. Flavell et al. (1966) showed children of varying ages seven pictures, and told them to try and remember two of them. The experimenter was trained in lip reading and could therefore count the number of times each child rehearsed each target picture. The results showed a very clear developmental trend with only 10 per cent of 5-year-olds employing rehearsal, but 60 per cent of 7-year-olds and 85 per cent of 10-year-olds.

Two studies by Cuvo (1974, 1975) demonstrate that this increase in the use of rehearsal is not simply quantitative; for increased age brings with it a more sophisticated approach to the use of repetition in remembering. In one experiment, Cuvo (1974) presented words that were associated with either high or low incentives to remember (specifically, recall of words was rewarded with either 1 cent or 10 cents). College students allocated substantially more rehearsal to high-incentive words, and eighth-graders showed a similar tendency. Fifth-graders, however, showed no differential rehearsal of high and low-incentive words. In a second study (Cuvo, 1975) found that fifth- and eighth-graders tended to rehearse items immediately they were presented, but not to incorporate these items into subsequent rehearsals. By contrast, college students tended to rehearse items repeatedly and to rehearse larger numbers of items at any one time.

The emergence of rehearsal as a strategy is strongly suggested in a study that I and some colleagues made (Parkin et al., submitted, b) which examined the influence of spacing (see chapter 4) on recall and recognition at different stages of development. The experiment was derived from an experiment by Greene (1989) which examined spacing effects on recall and recognition in adults. Greene found spacing effects, as measured by free recall, whether or not subjects knew that their memory would be tested. By contrast, only intentional learning instructions produced better recognition of spaced versus immediately repeated targets.

Greene argued that spacing effects in free recall arose from an automatic process, but that recognition depended on the application of some intentional learning strategy which, given the stimulus materials, might very likely be some form of rehearsal. I and my colleagues reasoned that, if correct, this theory would predict that spacing effects measured by recall and recognition should show different trends and, more specifically, that a spacing effect should emerge later in recognition than recall. Our data showed that even 5-year-old children produce greater recall of spaced pictures but that a spacing effect in recognition does not emerge until the age of 10. The idea that spacing effects in recognition but not recall might depend on intentional strategies like rehearsal is supported by a further finding that only spacing effects in recognition are abolished if adult subjects perform an attention – demanding secondary task during learning (but see Toppino et al., 1991).

Studies of rehearsal thus provide us with some indication of how and why memory changes with age. But, as we noted in chapter 1, rehearsal is a rather limited way of exploring the relationship between learning and memory, because so much of what we remember is not suited to even sophisticated rehearsal strategies.

More Complex Strategies

Bousfield (1953) introduced an important methodology for studying how **subjective organization** influences remembering. In a prototypical experiment subjects are presented with a random sequence of words or pictures for subsequent free recall. Inherent in this sequence there may be an organizational factor (e.g. items being drawn from four distinct taxonomic categories) or scope for the subject to impose his or her own organization on the material. At recall the experimenter assesses not only the amount recalled, but the extent to which the organizational features (e.g. categorical information) of the list influenced the pattern of recall. This is most commonly done by taking a measure of **clustering**, which, in terms of our examples, would be the extent to which subjects recalled target items from the same category adjacent to one another at recall or, across successive recalls, tended to recall the same items together.

Moely et al. (1969) presented children of varying ages with a series of pictures to remember. The pictures were drawn from a number of obvious categories, but, at recall, only the oldest group (11-year-olds), showed evidence of significant clustering. This study suggests that the use of categorially based learning strategies emerges later than rehearsal, which, as we saw above, begins to be evident in the learning processes of 7-year-olds. However, this developmental disparity may reflect the degree of association present in the material, because when lists of highly associated items are used, even young children show evidence of organization during recall (e.g. Schneider, 1986).

Clustering experiments thus show that older children are more likely to use category information present in a list in their attempts to remember it. But why? A simple solution is that younger children are unable to impose organizational frameworks on material they are trying to learn. To test this hypothesis, Lange and Griffith (1977) examined the influence of subjective organization on the recall of first-grade children through to adults. Subjects were initially required to recall a series of unrelated pictures, after which they were asked to sort these pictures into categories. A final free recall test was then given, and it was found that even the youngest children showed strong evidence of clustering related to the categories they had devised during sorting. This and other similar studies (e.g. Worden, 1975) suggest that younger children fail to initiate categorial organization, rather than being incapable of utilizing it.

A study by Melkman et al. (1981) sheds some light on why younger children might not spontaneously use category membership or other forms of conceptual knowledge when attempting to learn. Two tasks were administered to children aged 4, 5, and 9 years. In a 'grouping task' subjects were shown an 'anchor' picture along with two comparison pictures, and were asked 'which of these goes with it' (the anchor picture). One of these two pictures matched the anchor picture along the dimension of colour, form, or category. The grouping task revealed a clear chronological progression: colour and form determined 4-year-olds' grouping behaviour about equally; 5-year-olds sorted primarily in terms of form, and 9-year-olds relied primarily on categorial attributes.

Melkman et al. then examined the extent to which this age difference in grouping behaviour might influence memory. Three lists were designed: one organized by colour, one by form, and one by category. Clustering reflected the developmental trend in grouping behaviour, with the youngest group showing the greatest clustering for the colour-organized list, 5-year-olds the greatest clustering on the form-related listed, and the 9-year-olds maximal clustering for the categorially organized list. These data suggest that the absence of category-based clustering in younger children may arise because they organize the world differently from older children and adults. This is borne out by an earlier study by Denney and Ziobrowski (1972), in which it was found that young children tended to link items in terms of functional attributes (e.g. cake and knife) rather than conceptual categories (e.g. cake and carrot). In addition, studies by Rosch (1973) suggest that poor categorial organization in younger children stems from their lack of knowledge about non-prototypical members of categories.

Strategies can also influence the retrieval process. Kobasigawa (1974) showed children 24 'small' pictures (three from each of eight common categories). It was ensured that all children knew that the various pictures came from the designated categories. The pictures from each category subset were placed with a 'large' picture which linked them together in some way (e.g. three zoo-animal pictures might be linked to a picture of a zoo with three empty cages). Subjects were told that the large pictures went with the small pictures but that they should try to remember only the latter. When provided with the large pictures as retrieval cues,

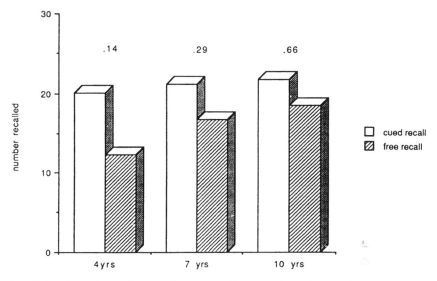

Fig. 7.3. Data from Ceci and Howe, 1978, p. 436. The numbers indicate the 'switching index' for the three ages. Reproduced with permission.

some interesting age differences emerged. Use of the large pictures as cues increased from 33 per cent in the 6-year-olds to 90 per cent in the 11-year-olds. There was also a tendency for older subjects to make more extensive use of the cues. Eight-year-olds, for example, might use each cue to recall only one item, whereas older children used the cue for an average of 2.5 words. This and more recent studies (e.g. Ackerman, 1988) suggest that older children make more use of cues *per se*, and, when doing so, use them far more extensively.

One problem in demonstrating apparent differences in retrieval strategies across age is that younger children may simply not learn the original information as effectively. To get around this problem, Ceci and Howe (1978) presented children of 4, 7, and 10 years with a picture sequence that could be sorted in terms of either categories or a theme (a horse, for example, could be part of an 'animals' category or a 'western' theme). At learning, it was ensured that children could sort the pictures completely accurately in terms of both categories and themes. Next there was a cued recall test in which half the children were cued with category cues and half with theme cues. Finally, 24 hours later, subjects undertook a free recall test for the items.

Figure 7.3 shows that there was no significant difference between age-groups on the cued recall measure; this indicated that the number of items available in memory was constant across the different age-groups.

On free recall a clear age-related improvement was evident. In addition, the authors examined the extent to which the children's retrieval strategy reflected that the list was organized in two ways (e.g. following recall of an item from a category with recall of an item linked to it by theme – 'horse', 'cowboy'). The extent to which children showed this flexibility in retrieval was calculated as a 'switching index', and it was clear that older children did this far more often.

Metamemory

If we are to use our memory effectively, it is essential that we employ the correct strategy and are able to monitor progress. These diagnostic and memory skills are typically referred to as **metamemory** (Kail, 1990; Flavell and Wellman, 1977; Paris and Cross, 1983). The development of metamemory has been examined in questionnaire studies in which children have been asked questions about how memory works. Best known is the study of Kreutzer et al. (1975) in which children were examined on a whole range of different questions.

One question tapped children's ability to appreciate that some people might have better memories than them and that their own memory abilities might vary depending on the situation. Both 9- and 11-year-olds understood this, but kindergarten subjects always thought they had better memories than their friends, and 30 per cent thought that they never forgot anything (see also Wellman, 1977) – a point worth bearing in mind when dealing with recalcitrant 3-year-olds!

This developmental trend in understanding the limitations of one's own memory was neatly illustrated in a study by Yussen and Levy (1975) in which children of different ages were asked to predict their memory span. As figure 7.4 shows, young children's predictions are wildly over-optimistic, and do not become accurate until about fourth grade.

The Kreutzer et al. study also provided evidence consistent with the developmental trend we considered in the previous section, in which it was shown that younger children made less use of organizational factors when learning. The subjects were asked to explain how they would learn nine pictures (three from each of three categories) in a few minutes. There was a marked age trend, with only one kindergartner suggesting a categorization strategy, but 80 per cent of the fifth-graders indicating some grasp of the relation between categorization and learning. In a more practical vein, participants were asked to say how they would ensure that they remembered to take their ice skates to school the next

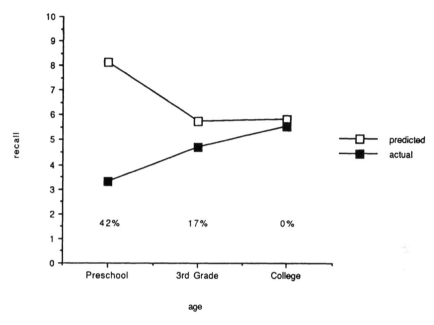

Fig. 7.4. Data from Yussen and Levy, 1975, p. 506, showing developmental improvement in the ability to predict recall. Percentages indicate the number of subjects who thought they could recall all the items from a list.

day. There were four main categories of answer. Three were **external**: manipulating the skates (e.g. putting them by the front door), using cues (e.g. writing a note to oneself), and relying on other people (e.g. asking one's mother to remind one). The fourth was **internal**, and made use of strategies like rehearsal. With increasing age, the number of solutions thought up increased substantially, particularly internal strategies.

Wellman (1978) was interested in how well children understood that different factors might interact in determining memory performance. Five- and 10-olds were presented with three cards at a time, each of which depicted a 'memory scenario' of varying difficulty. A 'simple' triple might involve a single child confronted with remembering either 3, 9, or 18 pictures. Here a correct rating of difficulty would be 3<9<18. An 'interactive' triple might show (a) a child being asked to remember 18 pictures by just looking at them, (b) a child who just looked at three pictures, and (c) a child who wrote down the names of the three pictures. On this triple the correct response was considered to be c<b<a. No age differences were found on the simple problems, but 10-year-olds performed much better on the interactive problems.

Wellman's finding seems to be that young children cannot understand the joint influence of two factors on memory performance. However, a subsequent study (Wellman et al., 1981) produced a contradictory result. Subjects ranging in age from 5 to 18 were asked to predict how well a person would perform in a situation in which the amount to be remembered and the amount of effort were varied at the same time. All children were aware of the combined influence of the two variables (e.g. that eight items would be recalled better with effort than without). But young children tended to rate effort more important than amount; and although older children rightly emphasized the importance of amount, appropriate responses were apparent only in the oldest age-group.

Our earlier conclusions about the relative lack of flexibility in the retrieval strategies of younger children were also confirmed by the Kreutzer et al. questionnaire. In one question children were asked to suggest ways of helping a friend to remember how old his or her dog was. About half the kindergartners had no idea how to help, but older children were quite good at suggesting strategies – for example, by asking how many Christmas presents the dog has had.

So far, we have used the term 'metamemory' to describe what children know about how their memory works and how best to use it. However, we can extend it to cover the ability to know whether or not we possess a specific memory. One way of measuring this is the **feeling of knowing** (FOK) task (Hart, 1965), in which subjects are asked to make a decision about the current state of an item in memory. Most commonly this technique is applied in situations in which a subject fails to recall an item and is then asked to estimate how likely it is that they would be able to recognize that item if it were shown to them. Using this technique, Wellman (1977) showed first- and third-graders pictures and, if they failed to name the objects in them, asked them whether they would recognize the name from a list. A clear developmental trend was found with younger children making less accurate judgements. However, a more recent study by Butterfield et al. (1988) has criticized earlier studies such as Wellman's on various grounds, including the possibility that younger children may not properly understand how to make FOK judgements. To get around this, Butterfield et al. included extensive training on how to make FOK judgements before critical testing; they found a developmental *decrease* in FOK accuracy, a finding for which they did not offer any strong theoretical explanation. It is also notable that, using this training technique, Butterfield et al. found no decline in FOK accuracy between 18 and 80 years, a finding that runs contrary to the ageing literature (see next chapter). The developmental aspect of FOK thus remains problematic.

Memory Strategies and Metamemory: An Overview

In this chapter so far, we have seen that, as children develop, they become more successful at employing various strategies at encoding and retrieval. This applies to both relatively simple learning strategies, such as rehearsal, and more complex ones involving categorial organization. In parallel with this, there is a development of metamemory, in that children become increasingly competent at understanding how memory works and how its functions can be affected under different circumstances. The question that follows inevitably from this is: What is this memory development the development of? We will consider this question in due course, but first, another body of findings will be considered.

Implicit Memory in Children

Given the extensive investigation of implicit memory in adults, it is somewhat surprising that so few studies have examined children on implicit tests of memory. Indeed, only four studies of this kind have been carried out so far (see Naito and Komatsu, in press). Carroll et al. (1985) presented children of different ages (5, 7, and 10) with pictures to name, and measured the time taken to do this. The pictures were then re-presented, and naming time was measured again. The subjects were also asked whether they recognized a picture as one from the previous naming session. Within this paradigm, recognition served as the explicit measure, and a significant decrease in naming the picture when re-presented indicated implicit memory. In addition, encoding was also manipulated, with some subjects processing each picture in a shallow manner (noting whether there is a cross in the picture) and others performing a deeper orienting task (noting how heavy the depicted object is).

Recognition showed an age-related improvement, and was also better following deep, as opposed to shallow, encoding operations. There was also a reliable priming effect in all age-groups, and the extent of this, in relation to baseline naming at first presentation, was constant. An effect of encoding condition, with deeply processed pictures producing greater priming, was also observed. This runs contrary to the normal finding that implicit memory is insensitive to encoding manipulations (see chapter 3), and it is important to note that Carroll et al. found no effect of encoding manipulation in a comparable study of adult implicit

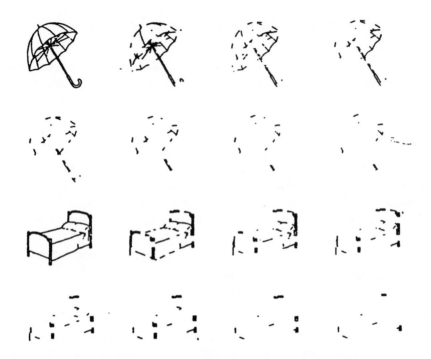

Fig. 7.5. Picture completion paradigm of Snodgrass et al., 1987. Figure taken from Parkin and Streete, 1988. Reproduced with permission.

memory and that in a subsequent study of children the effect of encoding manipulations on picture priming was not found.

Streete and I (Parkin and Streete, 1988) used the picture completion paradigm devised by Snodgrass et al. (1987) to examine implicit memory in children (3, 5, and 7 years) and adults . This involves the presentation of increasingly informative picture sequences until the subject can identify the depicted item (see figure 7.5). After the training phase, a retention interval is arranged, followed by a test phase in which the old sequences are re-presented along with new sequences. Two indices of implicit learning can be gathered, which, following the terminology introduced by Snodgrass et al. (1987), are **perceptual learning**, which is calculated as the difference between the average point at which subjects can identify old pictures compared with new pictures, and **skill learning**, which represents any improvement in identifying new pictures relative to performance on the old pictures in the initial training phase. Both measures meet the definition of implicit memory, because no overt reference to the initial phase is made at any point. However, as we shall see, it is evident that explicit recollection plays an important role in performing this task.

Streete and I found clear evidence of perceptual learning in even the youngest age-group, and, when calculated in proportional terms to allow for baseline differences, the extent of implicit memory appeared to be constant across age-groups. We were somewhat cautious in interpreting these data, but Graf (1990) felt confident that they were good evidence for invariant implicit memory in different age-groups. I (Parkin, 1992) have subsequently re-examined these initial findings, and produced a new analysis which uses a correction for differences in baseline performance rather than a simple proportion. With this new analysis, a marked age-related increase in implicit memory is found. However, interpretation of these data is ambiguous, because Streete and I also found age-related increases in explicit memory, as measured by improved ability to recognize which pictures had been seen before. Furthermore, perceptual learning was greater in items that were also recognized, except in the younger children in whom recognition memory was at chance levels. The apparent age-related improvement in implicit memory may therefore be entirely due to increased explicit influence on perceptual learning performance. Our data thus show that implicit memory is operating in very young children, but are ambiguous as to whether or not there is an age-related improvement.

Greenbaum and Graf (1989) showed young children (3, 4, and 5 years) line drawings of familiar things usually seen in one particular place (e.g. a zoo or a park) and asked the children to both name and memorize them. Immediately after this, the children were told a brief story about going to one of the places and were asked to describe what would typically be found there. Implicit memory was measured in terms of the difference between children using items from the memorization phase in their descriptions, compared with a baseline measure in which no priming was involved. Although there was an age effect, in that older children produced more items in their descriptions, all age-groups showed a priming effect; moreover, the extent of the effect was constant. This contrasted with a measure of recall for the pictures in which a marked age-related improvement was observed.

A final study is reported by Naito (1990), who examined fragment completion priming and recall in schoolchildren (first- to sixth-graders) and adults. During the study phase, subjects performed either a semantic or a non-semantic orienting task on the stimuli. After the retention interval, subjects undertook either fragment completion or free recall. Regardless of age, there was a strong repetition priming effect that was uninfluenced by encoding manipulation. Furthermore, the extent of this priming effect again appeared independent of age. By contrast, recall increased with age, and was significantly influenced by encoding instructions. A further experiment replicated the priming finding, and showed that the extent of priming did not vary across a 6-day interval.

Although few in number, studies comparing implicit and explicit memory in children show consistent findings. All four studies show that children exhibit strong priming effects, even children as young as 3. In addition, all four studies indicated that the implicit memory component in memory performance is the same across all age-groups (although we must note the ambiguity surrounding the Parkin and Streete data). We thus have the strong suggestion that the memory system(s) responsible for implicit learning, at least as measured in these four studies, are intact by the age of 3. Moreover, as we shall see below, there are grounds for believing that implicit memory is operative at much earlier times in development.

What is Implicit Memory For?

There seems little doubt that implicit memory is intact in even quite young children, but what, if anything, does this form of memory do? Could it, for example, be a vestige of our animal ancestry, with no functional role to play? This seems unlikely. In the section on early memory, we saw that young infants show a range of recognition responses and other forms of learning. These data were gathered in preverbal children, so there is no obvious way of knowing whether the children performing these tasks were, or were not, consciously recollecting previous learning episodes. In chapter 3 we concluded that recognition was a dual-component process, comprising both an explicit recollective component and one based on implicit familiarity information. Given that performance on implicit tasks appears to predate the development of explicit memory, it does not seem unreasonable to suppose that early recognition memory may be more dependent on the implicit memory responsible for familiarity-based responding.

Although not extensive, there is some support for the above idea. Rovee-Collier and her colleagues (see above) found that context changes influenced only older infants' performance on the CR procedure, thus suggesting that the familiarity of the mobile might be the only basis on which younger infants recognize a previously exposed mobile, whereas older infants are also beginning to find context important. Using the HNP procedure, a number of studies have examined infants' novelty preferences involving a **cross-modal shift**, where the mode of presentation is changed between learning and test (e.g. familiarize in tactile mode, test for preference in visual mode) or under conditions of **intermodal shift** (familiarize visually, but test for preference in both visual and tactile modes). These studies (e.g. Gottfried et al., 1977; Mackay-Soroka et al., 1982) have consistently demonstrated that infants between 6 and 9 months do not show novelty preference under either cross-modal or intermodal conditions, whereas older infants do. In chapter 3 it was emphasized that one feature of implicit memory was that it is often sensitive to changes in the perceptual features of a stimulus between learning and test. The fact that younger infants do not appear to recognize a previously exposed stimulus (i.e. show a preference for a concurrently presented novel object) when some change in modality occurs suggests that implicit memory may be making a critical contribution to their recognition memory.

In a different vein, Durkin (1989) has suggested that implicit memory may play an important role in language acquisition. He draws attention to the phenomenon of **fast mapping** (Carey, 1978). This is a rapid process in which the child is able to incorporate a new word, including partial information about its syntactic and semantic properties, after only a brief exposure. In an examination of fast mapping, Dockrell and Campbell (1986) exposed children to non-words which were each given a specific meaning, and then tested the children's retention of the meaning in two ways. When given an implicit test – 'Does the word make sense in this sentence?' – the children were successful, but when asked to give an explicit definition, the children performed randomly. Implicit memory may, therefore, provide the memory substrate for the fast-mapping component of language acquisition (see Durkin for a more extensive discussion of how implicit memory and language acquisition might interact).

What is Memory Development the Development Of?

The preceding discussion suggests that at least some aspects of memory development, particularly in the very early stages of life, reflect the early function of implicit memory. However, the bulk of memory development we have considered involves how children improve on tests of explicit memory such as recall and recognition and how children become increasingly aware of what their memories contain and how they may be used.

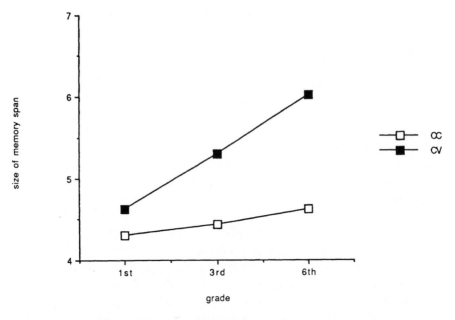

Fig. 7.6. Data from Dempster, 1978, showing that memory span for syllables increases significantly as children get older, but that span for strings of consonants changes little.

Perhaps the simplest hypothesis of memory development is that it is due to an increase in **processing capacity**. In recent research this hypothesis has been framed within the working memory model (chapter 6), in which memory is seen to be determined, in part at least, by the amount of processing resource available in the central executive. Much of this research has focused on trying to explain developmental increases in memory span in terms of increased rehearsal. We saw earlier that rehearsal does not show a simple quantitative increase with age; as children get older, their rehearsal pattern changes qualitatively as well. A theory of memory span development based solely on increased rehearsal rate has unsurprisingly, failed (Frank and Rabinovitch, 1974).

A more sophisticated hypothesis is that memory span evolves because subjects develop the ability to process larger chunks of information at a time. Dempster (1981) investigated this **chunking hypothesis** by comparing age differences in memory span for pairs of consonant letters (e.g. MK) and consonant–vowel pairs (e.g. IS). The assumption was that pairs of consonant letters would be less amenable to chunking than consonant–vowel pairs because the latter could more easily be placed in groups. Figure 7.6 shows Dempster's results. For the pairs of consonant letters, there is a small, non-significant increase in recall with age; but for the consonant–vowel pairs, span increases substantially with age.

Although Dempster's study suggests that changes in the amount of chunking accompany increased memory span, it does not explain why the increase occurs. The most plausible explanation, of course, is that more sophisticated chunking arises because older children can bring greater knowledge to bear on the task; in the case of Dempster's study, this knowledge would relate to the structure of the letter patterns. We thus come to the idea that memory development is primarily determined by **knowledge**.

Schank (1982) has proposed that one aspect of knowledge is the acquisition of **scripts** or **schemata** – general knowledge frameworks representing what typically comprises a given event (e.g. eating in a restaurant, going to school). K. Nelson (1986) has proposed that scripts are one of the earliest forms of knowledge to develop. In theories concerning the role of schemata in adult memory, it is contended that information consistent with the schemata is absorbed, while aspects that deviate from them may be retained as distinct episodes. Thus, on remembering a visit to a restaurant, only the fact that the people at the next table started arguing might be remembered specifically (Schank, 1982).

Developmental psychologists have proposed that children's memory for events depends on the current state of their internal schemata. More specifically, it has been argued that younger children are likely to have less specific schemata, which, in turn, means that they are less likely to regard any given event as a deviation (Goodman, 1980). To test this idea, Farrar and Goodman (1992) examined 4- and 7-year-olds' recall of events that were either repeated exactly or included a deviation from the norm. This was achieved by asking childen to visit an activity room, where they were greeted by an adult dressed as an animal and invited to play animal games which included dressing up as an animal. A fixed set of play activities then followed (e.g. a frog and a rabbit jumping over a fence). This visit was designated a 'standard' visit, and some children made three such visits. There was then a 'deviation' visit, in which the adult appeared dressed as a different animal and different activities took place. The children were later questioned about these two types of event, using the adults' costume as a cue. Younger children were found to have more difficulty distinguishing the two types of event, a finding that was attributed to their lesser ability to construct distinctive schemata for the two.

The role of knowledge in memory is aptly illustrated in a classic study by Chi (1978). She examined the ability of child chess experts and adult chess novices on a conventional memory span task and a task involving memory for chessboard positions. The conventional memory span task showed the usual advantage for adults, but on memory for chessboard positions the children performed better. This study illustrates that knowledge, rather than absolute age, can be the critical factor in determining memory. In a related study, Weinert (1986) examined fourth-, sixth-, and eighth-graders who were either experts or novices at football. Not surprisingly, experts were able to remember more about a passage of text describing football than novices. More impressive, however, was that the youngest experts outperformed the oldest novices.

In an unusual study, Chi and Koeske (1983) discovered a $4\frac{1}{2}$-year-old boy who was an expert on dinosaurs. In the first phase of their investigation, they discovered that the child knew the names of 40 different kinds of dinosaurs. Following this, the experimenters played a game with him which provided information about the properties he associated with each known dinosaur and the extent to which different known dinosaurs shared those properties. The dinosaurs were then divided into familiar and unfamiliar on the basis of their occurrence in dinosaur books and observations of the mother. The boy's recall for the familiar and unfamiliar dinosaurs was examined, and performance was found to be consistently better for those judged familiar. Finally, a year later, during which the boy had shown little interest in dinosaurs, he was asked to name all 40 dinosaurs again. At this point, he named 11 of the familiar dinosaurs correctly, but only three of the unfamiliar ones. The authors then examined the properties of the familiar and the unfamiliar dinosaurs, as produced by the child, and it was clear that the familiar ones shared more links. Chi and Koeske concluded that the greater recall and long-term retention of the familiar dinosaurs arose because these had a more extensive and integrated knowledge base.

The influence of knowledge on memory is not restricted to experts. In an earlier section, for example, we saw how encoding strategies can be dependent on children's understanding of general category relationships. Bjorklund and his colleagues (e.g. Bjorklund, 1987; Bjorklund and Harnishfeger, 1990) asked children of different ages (7, 9, and 11 years) to recall the names of children in their class and memorize and try to recall a list of taxonomically related items. On the list learning task the older children performed better, showing a greater degree of clustering, but on recall of their classmates, children of all ages performed similarly. The implication is that when knowledge is matched across age, as it is assumed to be for classmates, developmental differences are not found. However, where the task is dependent on the development of conceptual knowledge, such as the nature of categories, age differences do emerge.

However, not everyone is convinced that knowledge is the sole determinant of memory performance. DeMarie-Dreblow (1991) has drawn attention to a number of problems in studies attempting to relate memory development to knowledge. One point she raises is that much of the evidence is based on a comparison of child experts with adults, data which may represent a special case rather than the normal relationship between knowledge and memory. Another difficulty is that most studies are purely **correlational**; that is, they show that subjects with different levels of knowledge also have different levels of memory performance. Evidence showing that increased knowledge **causes** better memory is not presented. To make this direct test, DeMarie-Dreblow tested children's memory of birds, after which they watched a video about birds. This knowledge acquisition phase was then followed by another memory test. The videotape session was successful in increasing knowledge about birds, but did not lead to any improvement in memory performance. She concluded that although knowledge may be important in determining memory development, it is not the only factor.

Our question regarding what memory development is the development of therefore has an incomplete answer. Knowledge clearly plays an important role, because it determines, among other things, what information a child might extract from material in order to try and remember it. What other factors might be relevant? In chapter 6 we considered evidence that there might be a link between defective problem solving and loss of more complex forms of memory function. Extrapolating from this, it is not unreasonable to suppose that the later emergence of more complex aspects of memory might also have some direct relation to children's problem-solving ability. Many of the findings from metamemory studies, for example, indicate that what children develop is an understanding of how to use their memory most effectively in different situations. In addition, the fact that younger children often possess knowledge that could help them remember better but do not use it (e.g. DeMarie-Dreblow, 1991) suggests that the development of problem-solving skills may be an essential component of normal memory development.

The idea that problem-solving skills might have some direct bearing on memory development is suggested in a study by W. J. Friedman (1991). Children of 4, 6, and 8 years experienced two events (a videotaping talk and a demonstration of how to clean their teeth properly) separated by 7 weeks. They were then asked to decide which of the two was most recent and, for the earlier of the events, to specify when it happened. All children recalled the events. The two older groups had no difficulty deciding which of the two events was most recent, but some of the youngest ones got this wrong. On dating, however, only the older children were successful.

It is inconceivable that the brain has a 'date-stamp' which provides temporal information about events; rather, we reconstruct temporal information about an event from what is available in our memories. Thus a particular event may be successfully placed on the grounds that a specific feature is present. For example, I can always remember the year John Lennon died because I heard the news at Goldsmiths' College, where I taught only during 1980. Memory for temporal information thus depends, in part at least, on the ability to appreciate which aspects of an event might be salient in determining when it occurred. The development of temporal memory may therefore be a good case for illustrating the relation between problem solving and memory.

Infantile Amnesia

In the section on infant memory, we saw that children as young as 1 day old can remember in various ways. It is a curious fact, however, that, as adults, we can recall little of what happened to us prior to the age of about 4. This inability to recall early memories has been termed **infantile amnesia,** and was demonstrated empirically in a study by Waldfogel (1948) in which students were required to recall memories from before their eighth birthday and state how old they were at the time (see figure 7.7). This finding was confirmed by Crovitz et al. (1980), who used a cue-word technique as a means of eliciting early memories. Some cues were known to be very good at helping subjects remember specific experiences, but even these failed to evoke much in the way of memories from the earliest years.

Infantile amnesia is thus a genuine phenomenon; but what causes it? Perhaps the simplest explanation is that children younger than 4 cannot form memories of episodes, and so, when asked to retrieve early experiences, they lack the relevant memories. But this theory cannot be correct. Consider the following conversation described by Fivush and Hamond (1990, p. 223):

Child: Once on Halloween the kids was over and I had a princess dress on me.

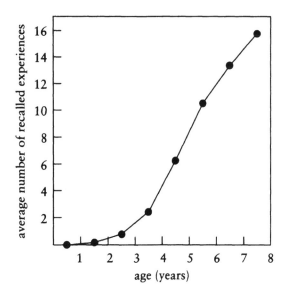

Fig. 7.7. Average number of experiences recalled by adults as a function of age at the time of experience. Data from Waldfogel, 1948 adapted by Kail 1990. Reproduced with permission.

Adult: You had a princess dress on? Did you get any candy? Did you go door to door? What happened?

Child: We went treating.

Adult: You went treating! And who took you?

Child: Andrea's mother took us. And my mom . . . and we brought a pumpkin too.

Adult: What did you do with the pumpkin?

Child: We lighted it.

Adult: What did it look like? Was it scary?

Child: Uh-huh. Dad made cuts in it with a razor. He made a face too. That was funny.

The child was just under 3 years old, and her comments suggest very good recall of events during the years which infantile amnesia will subsequently wipe out. Experimental studies also confirm this. For example, Hamond and Fivush (1991) asked 4-year-old children to recall trips to Disneyworld when they were 2 years old, and found that recall was remarkably good.

Freud (1915, 1943) was perhaps the first psychologist to describe infantile amnesia, which he portrayed as that 'which veils our earliest childhood from us and estranges us from it' (p. 335). In chapter 4 we briefly reviewed Freud's psychosexual theory of development, and you will recall that a key point was the oedipal phase, in which the male child resolves his conflict between sexual desire towards the mother and fear of the father. This was held to happen around 3–5 years of age. Freud held that children would suppress memories of this disturbing, phase and replace them with 'screen memories' – emotionally neutral memories with some superficial similarity to the disturbing memories which somehow block the emotionally laden ones.

There is little value in Freud's theory. If correct, it would predict that any memories recalled from the infantile amnesia period would be rather banal; but research shows that what little we do recall from this period is usually emotionally intense (Waldfogel, 1948; Crovitz et al., 1980). In addition, it is hard to believe that the young child's life is entirely taken up with psychosexual matters, so one would expect memories from other aspects of experience to be accessible. Furthermore, using a technique that attempts to measure the evocation of screen memories by adults recalling their past, Kihlstrom and Harackiewicz (1982) found that very few subjects ever produced any.

While repression may not be the cause of infantile amnesia, a more general retrieval deficit account based on inappropriate contextual cues may be more plausible. One could argue, for instance, that early memories are not retrieved because the environmental contexts (e.g. cots and play-pens) are absent from the adult retrieval environment. This theory seems, on intuitive grounds, unlikely, but it would none the less be interesting to bring back some of Rovee-Collier's mobile-kicking children when they are teenagers and see what they remember when again confronted with the mobiles and context patterns that were once so salient.

Recently Perner (1992) has put forward an interesting alternative explanation of infantile amnesia, based on the child's development of a 'theory of mind' (Perner, 1991a). To understand this, consider the following experiment. Children of 3 or 4 of age either observe an object being put in a box and are told what the object in the box is or are given no information at all. The children are then asked if they know what is in the box, and all of them answer correctly. However, only the older children can explain the source of their knowledge (i.e. that they had seen it being placed in the box or been told it was in there). Thus, at around the time when memories of our past first become reasonably accessible, children begin to understand the relationship between what they have seen and what they know.

According to Perner, the 4-year-olds succeed because they have developed what Tulving has termed 'autonoetic awareness' – the awareness of having experienced a situation or event before (see chapter 3).

Infantile amnesia is thus explained in terms of the inability of younger children to encode experience in such a way that they can subsequently be aware that they experienced it before. So memories of early experience may well exist, but in a form that no longer allows the individual to realize that they are memories of specific experiences.

Perner (1993) backs up his claim with an experiment which examined the relationship between children's performance on 'theory of mind' tasks, such as that described above, and memory ability. Children of different ages were given tests of free recall and cued recall, the former being assumed to depend more heavily on autonoetic awareness. The results showed that free recall ability and performance on the 'theory of mind' tasks were related, but that this was not the case for cued recall. Perner's approach is an interesting attempt to relate aspects of memory development to more general theories of cognitive development, and it will be interesting to see how far it succeeds.

Overview

Even the youngest children appear capable of recognition, and rudimentary recall ability is present by around 5 months of age. Memory development can be described as the gradual emergence of more complex strategies for encoding and retrieving memories, along with a parallel development of metamemory skills. Studies of implicit memory indicate that priming appears intact in children as young as 3 years, and, intriguingly, this implicit memory appears to show no developmental improvement. The question of what underlies memory development has yet to be answered. The child's state of knowledge plays a central role, but other factors, as yet unidentified, must be implicated. One of these may be problem-solving ability. But infantile amnesia remains a puzzle.

8

Getting Old

The distant past, when I was acting my solo version of Hamlet before the blind eyes of my father, duelling with myself and drinking my own poisoned chalice or, further back, when I was starting an English education, with huge balloons of boxing gloves lashed to the end of white, matchstick arms, grunting, stifled with the sour smell of hot plimsolls which is, to me, always the smell of fear, seems as clear as yesterday. What are lost in the mists of vanishing memory are the events of ten years ago.

John Mortimer

Everyone is aware that memory gets poorer as we get older, but even a moment's thought tells us that this decline is not even; some aspects of memory fail badly, while others remain largely intact. Recruiting subjects for our studies of ageing, we discovered a lady of 100 years old who could still play (and win) Scrabble in three languages, even though she had marked difficulty remembering what she had just had for lunch. Older people retain and enjoy motor skills acquired in their youth (e.g. ballroom dancing), even though they may have increasing difficulty remembering the names of new people they meet at their club. Dissociations like these bear a marked similarity to those we encounter in amnesic patients, and suggest that normal, age-related memory loss may be understood within the same conceptual framework we have developed in preceding chapters. However, it is important to be aware of certain methodological problems that affect the interpretation of research on ageing.

Methodological Issues in Research on Ageing

The commonest form of ageing study uses the **cross-sectional** or **cohort design,** in which an experimenter compares samples of people assumed to be representative of different age-groups. This may seem a straightforward enough approach, but cross-sectional designs present the researcher with some interesting methodological problems. Most obvious, perhaps, is the inclusion within the elderly sample of subjects presenting the early stages of dementing illnesses such as Alzheimer's disease and multi-infarct dementia. In order to tackle this problem, psychologists have tried to devise tests sensitive to the early stages of dementia. One example is the Anomalous Sentences Repetition Test (Weeks, 1988), in which an inability to repeat back syntactically correct but meaningless sentences such as 'Colourless green dreams sleep furiously' is considered indicative of dementia.

The longer you have been alive, the more exposed your brain has been to various factors that could damage it. This has led to the view that many differences that appear to be related to age may be exaggerated, because older subject groups contain a higher proportion of 'non-optimum performers' – the more likely presence of people who perform poorly not because of age, but because of some other 'risk factor', such as alcoholic brain injury, late-onset diabetes, minor head injury, depression, or the residual effects of earlier psychiatric treatment (e.g. a course of electroconvulsive therapy).

The importance of risk factors is illustrated in a study of memory scanning by Houx et al. (1991). In this task, old and young subjects were asked to memorize a set of numbers and then decide as quickly as possible whether individually presented probe numbers were part of the memory set. As one might expect, older subjects took longer to respond, but when the presence of risk factors was taken into account, the effect of age on response time was relatively small. Thus, as well as excluding people with dementing illness, a good study of ageing and memory must also rule out the contaminating influence of increased risk factors in the elderly.

Even if you are satisfied that an elderly cohort has been properly screened, there are problems ahead. Young people growing up today experience different living conditions from those experienced by the current elderly population during their youth. Most obvious, perhaps, is educational level, with older subjects far more likely to have left school early, as compared with their younger counterparts. Educational level, as measured by tests such as Verbal IQ (Wechsler, 1981), is known to be correlated with memory ability. In making age-related comparisons of memory performance, it is therefore essential to include some control for educational level; but this control itself raises a different interpretive problem.

Matching young and old for educational level in a cross-sectional study assumes that without that matching, any age-group comparison would be confounded because the older group would have a poorer educational standard. This is not a problem if all we are concerned with is the **internal validity** of our experiment – that is, if all we wish to be able to say is that the age differences we find are not due to educational differences. It is a different matter if we want to argue that our experiment has **external validity** – i.e. that our findings can be generalized to all young and old subjects of comparable age, because these populations are characterized by differences in memory ability *and* educational level. A proper explanation of all age-related memory differences must therefore take educational level into account.

Problems with cohort design have led researchers to consider an alternative, **longitudinal** design, in which age-related changes are examined by testing the same individuals at different points in their lives. Unfortunately this type of design also has major problems. First, there is the obvious difficulty of keeping track of the same subject group across a span of 50 years or more. Second, there is the 'drop-out' problem, in that successive test sessions will comprise fewer subjects, and those who continue to be tested will tend to be good performers – poorer performers deciding that one or two demonstrations that they have poor memories is enough! As a result, the group average at the end of the study will be based on better performing subjects than that at the start.

One answer to this 'selective attrition' problem is to analyse data only from non-drop-outs. This rules out the above difficulty, but introduces a more subtle contamination, which is illustrated in a famous study by Owens (1959, 1966). Owens began by testing 363 college freshmen in 1919 on an army intelligence test. Testing was carried out twice more, in 1950 and 1961, by which time the sample had been reduced to 96. Surprisingly, Owens found a tendency for performance to *improve* with age; however, as one would expect with selective attrition, the surviving group had much higher average ability at the start, so their age-related improvement might just be because they were good performers from the outset. At present, we do not understand the relation between initial ability and rate of change across the lifespan, so data from longitudinal studies which only consider subjects who complete the study are difficult to interpret.

Longitudinal designs also create other problems. Carrying out the same task a number of times, even separated by years, introduces the possibility of **practice effects**, which may be enhanced by cultural changes allowing the subject to adopt a more sophisticated approach to the task. Changes in the precise characteristics of the test situation (e.g. the experimenter, the testing environment) might also have a significant and confounding influence on performance. More sophisticated investigative methods, known as **cohort-sequential** designs (Schaie, 1965) attempt to rule out the confounding elements present in both cross-sectional and longitudinal designs. However, these more complex designs still involve longitudinal testing, with its inherent difficulties of time to completion and subject contact.

Finally, there is the simple problem of confidence. In his book *A Good Age* Alex Comfort (1976, cited by Kausler, 1990) points out that 'although perfectly able to learn . . . older people get upset and anxious because of fear of failure. They may in fact appear not to learn because they would rather risk not answering than to give a wrong answer which confirms their own fears and other people's prejudices' (Comfort, 1976, p. 120). This observation reflects the distinction between **competence**, a subject's real ability, and **performance**, factors affecting the subject's expression of that ability. Self-doubt is one factor that can adversely affect memory performance in the elderly. Another is task interest. Young subjects may, for various reasons, be more willing than the elderly to engage in the often meaningless and seemingly trivial memory tasks produced by experimental psychologists. Age-related studies of memory must therefore ensure that the elderly are not under-performing because of poor confidence or lack of motivation.

The study of ageing and memory is therefore methodologically complex; but within these limitations, investigations of age-related memory loss have produced many interesting findings, as well as genuine progress towards understanding a problem that is of relevance to us all (see Kausler, 1990, for an excellent overview of these issues). We will now examine some of these findings.

Experimental Findings

Short-term storage, as measured by tasks such as digit span, generally survives in people who suffer drastic impairments to other aspects of their memory (see figure 1.3). Immediate memory, when measured by digit span, is similarly preserved in later life, with performance declining by around only 8 per cent (e.g. Botwinick and Storandt, 1974). Interestingly, this is one effect that cannot be due to uncontrolled cohort differences, because age-based comparisons of digit span have been conducted for many years, and the results are remarkably consistent (Kausler, 1990).

However, the elderly do not do well on all tests of immediate memory. Wingfield et al. (1988) compared young and elderly people on three tests of short-term storage: digit span, word span, and **loaded word span**. In the last of these, subjects read sentences and had to decide whether each one made sense, and at various points had to repeat back the last word of each sentence they had read. Age differences on the two simple span tasks were minimal, but the elderly showed much poorer performance on the loaded span task. This task is very much like the working memory task used by Daneman and Carpenter (1980; see chapter 6); the results therefore suggest that there is an age-related decline in what we have termed 'working memory', a conclusion supported by a number of other studies conducted within the working memory framework (e.g. Morris et al., 1988; Gick et al., 1988).

The elderly also show reliable deficits on the **Brown–Peterson task**. In this task the subject is presented with some stimuli to learn, and is then distracted for a short period of time – usually by asking him or her to count backwards in threes from a three-figure number. After various intervals the distracting activity is stopped, and the subject is asked to recall the stimuli. Figure 8.1 shows the results of a study by Walter and myself (Parkin and Walter, 1991). It can be seen that longer distracting intervals produce poorer performance and that older subjects remember less overall. What is also noticeable is that the effect of age is a constant and that age differences do not increase with longer distraction intervals. This finding rules out an interpretation of age differences as due to more rapid forgetting of stimuli, because, if this were so, age difference would be expected to become greater at longer distracting intervals. Poor Brown–Peterson performance must therefore be explained in some other way, and we return to this later in the chapter.

As we discussed earlier, longer-term memory performance can be assessed in various ways, but a typical comparison is between free recall and recognition. This contrast reveals something very interesting about the nature of age-related memory loss because, despite showing very large declines in free recall ability, elderly subjects show relatively little change in recognition memory (e.g. White and Cunningham, 1982).

Recently Micco and Masson (1992) have provided interesting evidence

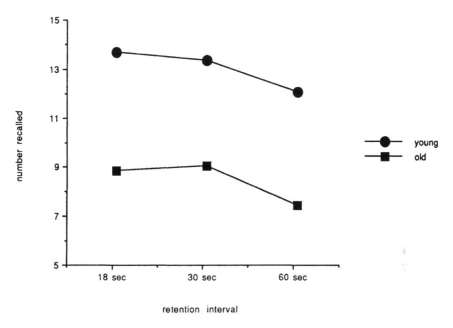

Fig. 8.1. Data from Parkin and Walter, 1991, p. 177. Reproduced with permission.

concerning the poor ability of older subjects on recall. Young and old subjects were presented with a target word and a context cue word that was either a strong or a weak associate (e.g. 'crowd' – 'people'; 'crowd' – 'riot') and were required to generate a set of one-word clues that would enable another person to produce the target. A second group of young and old subjects were then given the clues in the presence of either the strong or the weak associate and were asked to try and generate the target word. Clues generated by older people were less effective in facilitating target production, particularly in the presence of a weak associate. In addition, older subjects also found it more difficult to work out what the target word was, especially when clues were presented alongside weak associates. The authors interpreted these data as indicating an age-related decline in the ability to encode and retrieve context-specific information; they found this deficit to be particularly in evidence when the context does not reflect information typically associated with the stimulus. Given that generative strategies may play an important role in retrieval (see chapter 4), one can see from these data that the elderly might show recall impairments because they are less efficient at using cues to specify potential targets.

Recognition, of course, is a much easier task, so the absence of any

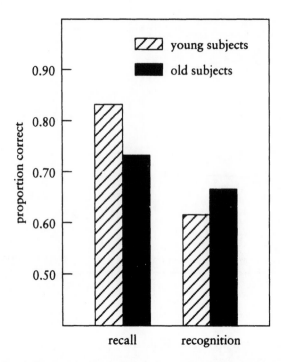

Fig. 8.2. Data from Craik and McDowd, 1987, p. 476, showing that disproportionate impairment of recall versus recognition in older subjects remains, even when the recognition task is more difficult than the recall task. Reproduced with the permission of the American Psychological Association.

great age effect could simply reflect insensitivity of the test procedure, with subjects generally performing too well to pick up an effect. This point is nicely countered in a study by Craik and McDowd (1987), who devised a recognition test that was more difficult than a recall test. As figure 8.2 shows, age-related differences were still not found on the recognition test, even though the easier recall test did elicit better performance by the young. This selective preservation of recognition memory in older subjects is not, therefore, a test-sensitivity artefact, but a true reflection of a selective age-related decline in some aspect of memory performance.

The above findings, taken at face value, suggest that the mechanisms of recognition memory do not deteriorate significantly with age. More refined analysis of recognition memory does indicate some worsening of performance, however. In an experimental task known as **multiple-item recognition memory** (MIRM) subjects are shown an array of items in which one is designated as the target word that they should try to

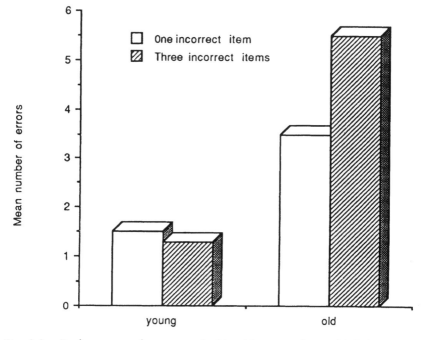

Fig. 8.3. Performance of young and old subjects on the multiple-item recognition test. Data from Kausler and Kleim, 1978.

remember and the others as irrelevant items (e.g. *parrot*, fern, pliers, tissue). At a later point the array is re-presented minus the target indicator, and the subject tries to identify the target item. Figure 8.3 shows data obtained by Kausler and Kleim (1978), who compared the performance of young and old under conditions where the array contained either one or three irrelevant items. Young subjects made far fewer errors overall, and were not influenced by the number of irrelevant items in the array. Older subjects performed more poorly, and made substantially more errors when three irrelevant items were present.

To understand why the elderly do so poorly on MIRM compared with other tests of recognition memory, we must first examine the recognition tasks more closely. The Craik and McDowd study used a yes–no recognition task in which target items had to be distinguished from distractors that had not been pre-exposed. In chapter 3 we noted that recognition memory is not a single process, but the joint product of two processes: a context-free assessment of familiarity and a context-dependent explicit recollection. The standard yes–no recognition task maximizes the possibility of familiarity-based responding, because the

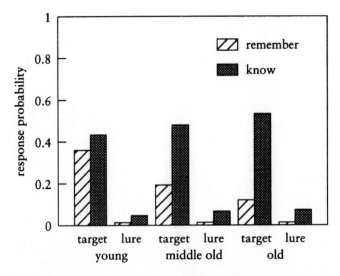

Fig. 8.4. The effects of age on the experiential nature of recognition memory. Target refers to words subjects were instructed to try and learn. Lures are items subjects did not study that are present in the recognition test. Data from Parkin and Walter, 1992, p. 295. Reproduced with the permission of the American Psychological Association.

distractors, unlike the targets, have not been exposed prior to the recognition test and do not have any enhanced familiarity. MIRM is different, because both targets and distractors have been pre-exposed, and correct recognition of targets depends critically on the retrieval of explicit contextual information (e.g. in that array it was 'parrot' that was the target). Given the poorer encoding of context implied by the study of Micco and Masson (1992), the age deficit on MIRM is perhaps to be expected.

Our interim conclusions about ageing and recognition memory can therefore be revised by stating that ageing interferes little with the use of familiarity as a basis for recognition, but has a substantial effect on any recognition task that demands the retrieval of context. This account of ageing and recognition memory gains further support from a study conducted by Walter and myself (Parkin and Walter, 1992) in which age differences in recognition memory were explored using the recognition and conscious awareness paradigm (described in chapter 4). Two groups of older subjects (one of average age 67 years, the other 81 years) were compared with a group of young subjects, and the results are shown in figure 8.4. As you can see, there is a dramatic change in the subjective nature of recognition memory as we get older, with the number of 'remember' (R) responses declining and the number of 'know' (K) responses increasing. K responses are an indication that the subject's recognition response is based on familiarity rather than any contextual recollection, so the age-related increase in K responses supports our contention that older subjects rely more on familiarity information when recognizing something.

Earlier we saw that a possible confounding factor in age and memory studies is that older subjects underperform because they are less confident, rather than genuinely less able for a task. Walter and I considered the possibility that increased K responses in the elderly might be due simply to reduced confidence, rather than a change in the subjective nature of their recognition memory. This possibility was examined using the method that Gardiner used to rule out a confidence judgement explanation of his data using the R and K paradigm. When 'sure' and 'not sure' are substituted for R and K, the resulting pattern is very different, with both age-groups' responses characterized by primarily 'sure' responses. The age-related increase in K responses is not, therefore, due to declining confidence, but to some real change in the nature of recognition memory itself.

Chapter 4 showed that the memory processes underlying K responses appear to have properties similar to those that selectively affect implicit memory performance. A plausible interpretation of increased K responding in the elderly is that it arises from greater reliance on implicit familiarity information. Support for this view can be found in a recent study of age effects in facial recognition memory. Bartlett and Fulton (1991) found that older subjects made more false positive responses on a yes–no recognition test and that these false responses occurred most frequently for faces that physically resembled the target faces they were looking for. Implicit memory performance is considered to be more data-driven (i.e. dependent on the perceptual features of stimuli), so, if implicit memory contributes to recognition performance, there should be more errors on distractors that share physical features with targets. The age-related deficit on facial memory can thus be attributed to increased reliance on implicit, familiarity-based responding, which, because of its data-driven qualities, makes the subject more susceptible to distracting information that bears a physical similarity to the target.

The substantial age-related impairments on episodic memory tasks are not found in tests of semantic memory. Comparison of young and old subjects on standardized vocabulary tests such as the *Wechsler Adult Intelligence Scale* (Wechsler, 1981) indicates little effect of age (e.g. Berkowitz, 1953; Salthouse, 1982). Indeed, it is not unusual ageing research to find that older subjects have a slightly higher vocabulary score than younger subjects. However, reliance on vocabulary scores alone may be misleading. Botwinick and Storandt (1974), for example, found that younger subjects produced qualitatively better definitions of words than older subjects, even though vocabulary scores in the two age-groups did not differ. Also, in a study by Bowles and Poon (1985), older subjects performed more poorly in a 'reverse' vocabulary test which required them to give a word in response to a definition – a finding that probably taps the same kind of deficit as that revealed in the Micco and Masson study discussed above.

Vocabulary test data thus suggest a small age-related loss of semantic memory. An alternative approach is to consider whether age leads to a slowing down of semantic memory processes, as opposed to a loss of information. Charness (1979, 1983), for example, examined the effects of age on bidding strategy in bridge, and found that older expert players performed as well as younger players, although the older subjects needed more time to respond. In a laboratory setting, Howard et al. (1986) examined the nature of **associative priming** in young and elderly subjects. In their study, subjects were presented with single words known as **primes**, followed by a string of letters (target) which varied randomly as to whether it was a real English word or not. Further, when it was a word, it could either be related to the prime (e.g. 'bird' – 'eagle') or unrelated (e.g. 'bird' – 'sock'). Subjects were required to decide as quickly as possible whether each string of letters was or was not a word, a task known as **lexical decision**. Under these conditions, a **priming effect** is typically found, in that lexical decision for real words is faster when the prime is related to the target. Howard et al. found that young subjects showed a priming effect even when the time elapsing between the prime and the target was as little as 150 milliseconds. Older subjects also showed priming effects, but these occurred only when the time between prime and target was increased to around half a second or more. Associative priming effects enable us to measure the speed at which one part of semantic memory, that corresponding to the prime, can activate another, that represented by the target. The fact that old subjects showed priming, but not at the shortest inter-stimulus intervals, indicates that the semantic network is intact, but that the mechanism of activation across it is slower.

Metamemory

There has been increasing interest in how age affects people's ability to monitor the contents of their own memories. Butterfield et al. (1988)

compared 18- and 70-year-olds on the feeling of knowing task (FOK), and found no age difference; but a subsequent study by Anooshian et al. (1989) found a reliable decrease in the FOK accuracy of older people. Bruce et al. (1982) compared old and young subjects on their ability to predict how well they would recall a word list. The age-groups did not differ in their predictions, but, as one might expect, the older subjects recalled less. Older subjects thus seem over-optimistic about their memory ability. This phenomenon is further illustrated in a study by Lovelace and Marsh (1985), in which old and young subjects were presented with individual word pairs and asked to rate how easily they would be able recall each of them later. Both groups were accurate in their predictions, in that more pairs rated as easy to recall were recalled successfully, but there was a big age difference in performance, in that, even for the word pairs that subjects thought they would certainly remember, the younger subjects recalled substantially more. However, older subjects do not always overrate their memory. Hertzog et al. (1990), for example, asked old and young subjects to predict their performance on recall of a categorized list and a narrative text. Older subjects were found to recall less on both tasks, but accurately predicted this.

Memory questionnaires have also been used to evaluate the extent to which older subjects' self-rating of their memories provides a valid basis for predicting actual memory performance. Rabbit and Abson (1991) gave older subjects four laboratory memory tasks (recognition, memory span, recall, and cumulative learning) and two questionnaires probing their subjective knowledge of their mental efficiency in everyday life. Memory performance was found to be uncorrelated with subjects' own estimates of their memory ability. However, significant relationships were found between memory ability and the extent of self-rated depression, age, and intelligence. Other studies of the relation between answers on memory self-assessment questionnaires and objective memory ability are inconsistent, with some showing positive relationships (e.g. Dixon and Hultsch, 1983) and others negative relationships (West et al., 1984).

Loewen et al. (1990) asked young and old subjects to answer questions about their memory capacity, their knowledge of the demands that different tasks make on memory, and the extent to which they employed strategies. Older subjects reported having poorer memories, and were less likely to employ encoding strategies. However, no age differences were found in the subjects' knowledge about memory task demands.

Metamemory studies of ageing thus present a confusing picture, with some experiments indicating an age-related decline and others not (see

Kausler, 1990, for an extensive review). The reasons for these inconsistencies are not clear, although one obvious possibility concerns the age and neurological status of the elderly samples. Deficits in metamemory function are known to be linked with disturbance of the frontal lobes (e.g. Janowsky et al., 1989), and, as we shall see in a subsequent section, frontal dysfunction is also evident in older subjects. Part of the discrepancy between the various studies might therefore reflect variations in the degree of frontal involvement in the older subjects. However, methodological issues may also be important (cf. differences in the studies by Anooshian et al., 1989, and Butterfield et al., 1988).

Implicit Memory and Ageing

Motor skills acquired early in life certainly remain intact as we get older. In an intriguing single case study involving himself, Hill (1957), at the age of 30, made detailed records of how quickly he learned to type. His measure was how well he could type a specific 100-word passage. Without any intervening practice, he then retested himself on this passage when aged 55 and 80 years. At the age of 80 his performance was the same as that attained after eight days of learning when he was 30, and after only 30 days, he reached the same level of typing ability as he had acquired following 126 days of his original training.

Salthouse (1984) examined Hill's claim more formally, by comparing typing speeds of typists of different ages. The subjects copy-typed a passage displayed on a screen, and the time between each successive key stroke was recorded. Somewhat surprisingly, there was no age difference in the average time between key strokes. This did not reflect a general absence of response slowing in the older group, however, because on a simple reaction time task, the older subjects were much slower. Further investigations by Salthouse showed that the absence of any slowing down in typing with age arose because older subjects had evolved sophisticated strategies to compensate for their general slowness. In particular, it was found that older typists appeared to look further ahead, thus allowing greater response preparation.

Light and Singh (1987) examined possible age differences in cued recall and stem completion tasks. The results showed a marked age effect on cued recall, but only a small, non-significant age difference on stem completion. This finding mirrors an earlier study by Light et al. (1986) in which fragment completion priming also failed to elicit a significant age difference, even though young subjects again showed a

small advantage. Other studies, however, have found poorer performance by elderly subjects on implicit memory tasks (e.g. Chiarello and
Hoyer, 1988), and it has been suggested that sample size may be the
critical factor, with smaller studies being insensitive to difference.

A recent study offers an alternative explanation of why age deficits
in implicit memory might emerge. Implicit memory refers to the measurement of memory when no direct reference to a prior learning episode
is *required* by the experimenter. This does not mean, however, that the
subject may not use explicit recollection to aid performance, and when
age differences are found in implicit memory, they may actually be
caused by differences in the use of explicit recollection as an aid to
performance. Russo and I (in press) made age-based comparisons of
implicit memory using the **picture completion paradigm** (see chapter 7).
Subjects were first shown degraded picture sequences, which then
became systematically more informative until the subject identified
the depicted object. Twenty-four hours later, subjects were reshown
the original sequences plus an equal number of new sequences, and the
critical variable was whether the subjects would show perceptual learning. Initial analysis indicated a strong perceptual learning effect in both
groups of subjects, with previously exposed sequences being identified
much more easily than novel pictures. However, the extent of this effect
was much greater in the young, thus showing an apparent age difference in implicit memory.

Further analysis by Russo and myself suggested an alternative interpretation of the results. At the testing phase, subjects were also asked
to recall the names of the objects depicted in the sequences used in the
original learning episode. As you would expect, the elderly performed
more poorly on this explicit measure. But, more interestingly, this measure
also allowed the picture completion data to be reanalysed in terms of
the extent of perceptual learning for pictures that were also recalled and
those that were not. Confirming earlier studies (Parkin and Streete,
1988; Parkin and Russo, 1990), young subjects showed much greater
priming for pictures they were able to recall. However, the elderly
showed no such difference. Furthermore, when analysis was restricted
to non-recalled sequences, no significant age differences in picture
completion priming were found. These results suggest that the poorer
implicit memory performance of the elderly arose simply because they
had less explicit memory available to help them with the task.

Why did the elderly show no advantage for picture sequences they
were able to recall? One possibility is that the level of explicit memory
available to the older subjects was insufficient to influence performance
significantly. Alternatively, the elderly may have lacked the ability to

utilize their explicit memory. These two possibilities were teased apart by investigating a second group of young subjects who undertook the learning task while also doing a secondary, tone-monitoring task (see chapter 6). The latter had the effect of reducing their explicit recollection of the learning phase to a level indistinguishable from that of the elderly; yet these subjects still showed significantly greater savings for picture sequences they could also recall. The elderly deficit was not, therefore, due to the absolute amount of explicit memory available, but to an inability to use available explicit memory effectively.

Recently Howard and Howard (1992) have demonstrated another interesting age difference in memory, using an implicit learning task. Subjects watched for an asterisk to be shown in one of four boxes, and when it appeared, pushed the key underneath the box as quickly as possible. Subjects were given blocks of trials in which a particular sequence was repeated ten times. Implicit learning is measured in terms of the increased speed with which subjects can press the buttons indicated by the asterisks in repeated trials by comparison with random sequences. Explicit memory is assessed by asking subjects to try to predict which box the next asterisk will appear in. Howard and Howard found no difference between young and old on the implicit test, but that older subjects were significantly poorer on the prediction task.

Reviews of recent work on ageing and implicit memory can be found in Howard (1991) and Mitchell (in press).

Ageing and Memory: A Summary

Our next task is to try and explain why age-related memory impairments take the form they do; but before doing this, it will be useful to summarize the principal findings of ageing and memory studies.

Performance on tests of short-term storage is largely unaffected by age unless the task has a working memory component (e.g. loaded memory span).

Age produces a marked impairment in recall ability, as shown on the free recall and Brown–Peterson tasks.

Recognition memory undergoes an age-related decline, but the extent of it depends on the type of recognition task employed. On tests requiring discrimination of targets from novel distractors, the elderly perform well; but where recognition depends on more than just an assessment of familiarity (e.g. MIRM), elderly subjects show substantial impairments.

Age produces a change in the subjective nature of recognition memory, with responses being judged far more as familiarity-based.

There is little evidence of a decline in semantic memory, although the speed at which older people can access their knowledge declines notably.

There is some evidence of a decline in metamemory performance.

Implicit memory ability is largely intact, and where deficits are found, they may be due to older people making less use of explicit memory.

Explaining Age-Related Memory Deficits

There have been many attempts to explain age-related memory loss. One influential idea has been that older subjects have a **processing capacity deficit**; that is, they simply have fewer processing resources available to help them learn new information (e.g. Craik and Simon, 1980). A number of studies are consistent with this hypothesis. Mitchell and Perlmutter (1986) presented old and young subjects with target words and required them to make either a semantic or a non-semantic decision about each one. Each target word was accompanied by a 'flanker' word which subjects were told to ignore. For half of each age-group the learning instructions were intentional, while for the others they were incidental. Measurements taken during the initial learning phase indicated that the orienting tasks evoked similar processing strategies in both age-groups, and this was reflected in the incidental learning results, which showed no age difference. However, intentional learning instructions produced better learning in the young and also greater recall of the flanker words.

Light and Zelinski (1983) asked young and old subjects to remember a tourist map specifying a number of different structures (e.g. a church). Half of each age-group were told to remember just the structures, while the other half were told to remember the structures and their location. However, at recall, all subjects were asked to recall both the structures and their locations. Subjects given instructions to learn both types of information did better, but this difference was most marked in the older group.

Older people are poorer at recalling stories, and Zelinski et al. (1984) hypothesized that this was because they make less use of story structure as a retrieval aid. Yet their data showed no difference in the ability of young and old to use story structure as an aid to recall. A study by Hess (1984) provided a rather different result, however. Young and old subjects read passages describing everyday activities such as eating in a restaurant. Most of the events described were typical (e.g. paying the bill), but some were atypical (e.g. picking a napkin off the floor). Old and young subjects did not differ in their memory for typical actions, but the young showed superior memory for atypical actions. This finding suggests that older people may have less flexible schemata available to help them remember.

Stanhope (1989) examined the pattern of **source forgetting** in young and older subjects. Subjects watched a monitor on which one of two people spoke fictitious facts. Retention was then tested for both the fact and the source (i.e. speaker) of that fact. Old subjects showed some decline in recalling facts, but their source memory was extremely poor (see also McIntyre and Craik, 1987; Hashstroudi et al., 1989). In a subsequent study, Stanhope asked young subjects to perform a secondary task while learning, and under these conditions their performance was indistinguishable from that of older subjects.

The above studies suggest that older subjects' memory is poorer when they are asked to remember peripheral and unpredictable aspects of an event and that young subjects' memory performance can be made to resemble older people's by the imposition of a secondary task during learning (see also the study by Russo and myself described earlier). If we accept the idea of processing resources, it is easy to see how all these types of finding could be predicted if the effect of age is to reduce the amount of resource available.

Ageing, Memory, and Frontal Lobe Dysfunction

The term 'processing resource' is rather vague, and if it is to have any real explanatory value, we must be more specific as to what sort of resources we are talking about. One approach to this problem begins with figure 8.5, which shows the level of neuron density in normal brains of different ages in the frontal lobes. It is clear that loss from the frontal region is substantial. This frontal deterioration is mirrored in neuropsychological test performance, which shows that the elderly increasingly develop problems on various tasks assessing frontal lobe functions, such as planning and response flexibility (Mittenberg et al., 1989; Parkin and Walter, 1992; see also figure 8.6).

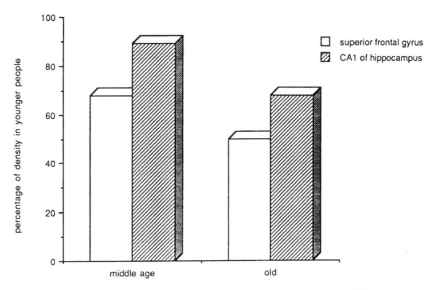

Fig. 8.5. Neuron density in two regions of the brain in two different age groups. Data from Flood and Coleman, 1988, pp. 457–8.

In chapter 6 we encountered the dysexecutive syndrome, and concluded that this deficit was attributable to frontal lobe disturbance. The frontal lobes have been implicated in memory function in other ways. Damage to the frontal lobes produces marked problems in remembering the temporal order of events, and can also cause source forgetting (Petrides, 1989; Janowsky et al., 1989). Given that ageing is associated with loss of frontal lobe function and memory loss, it is not a difficult step to suggest that these two might be causally related.

Evidence implicating frontal disturbance as a causative factor in age-related memory loss is growing. The much greater decline in recall relative to recognition is, as we have seen, a 'hallmark' feature of the dysexecutive syndrome. The finding that older people's recognition memory breaks down when familiarity is insufficient for performance is also characteristic of a dysexecutive impairment. Still other evidence points to some relationship between frontal disturbance and age-related memory deficits. Craik et al. (1990) examined young and old subjects on a source-forgetting task, and found that the extent of source forgetting in the elderly was predicted by the deficits they showed on tests of frontal lobe function.

Walter and I (Parkin and Walter, 1991) explored the relationship

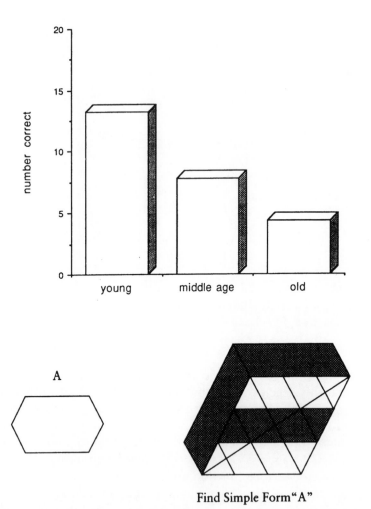

Find Simple Form"A"

Fig. 8.6. The effect of age on measures of frontal lobe function. Figure a shows the number of correct responses on the Embedded Figures Test in the three age-groups. In this test the subject must identify the simple shape hidden in the complex figure. Figure b shows that ageing produces increased errors and increased perseverative errors on the Wisconsin Card Sorting Test (WCST). In this test the subject must discover a rule by which to sort

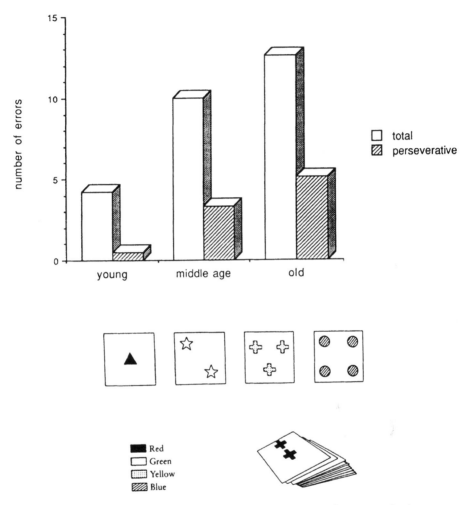

sequence of cards (e.g. placing all cards with the same shape together). When the subject has established a rule, he or she is asked to find another rule (e.g. placing all cards with the same number of symbols together). When the subject fails to do this, an error occurs. If the subject continues to sort with the rule he or she had been using prior to being asked to change, this is called a perseverative error. Data from Parkin and Walter, 1992, p. 295. Reproduced with the permission of Oxford University Press.

between frontal lobe function and age deficit on the Brown–Peterson task (see figure 8.1). We found that older subjects with poorer frontal lobe function also showed the biggest deficit on the recall task. We also investigated whether frontal dysfunction was related to the elderly's tendency to make familiarity, rather than contextually based recognition, responses (see figure 8.4). Correlations showed that familiarity-based responding was significantly greater in subjects with poor performance on frontal lobe tests. Finally, we (Parkin and Walter, 1993) showed that age produces a substantial impairment in memory for temporal order, despite little change in recognition memory, and, furthermore, that this decline is related to evidence of impaired frontal lobe function.

We therefore have reasonable grounds for proposing that, with advancing age, the frontal cortex declines more rapidly than many other parts of the brain, and that this decline may be responsible for at least some of the memory deficits we observe. More specifically, it can be argued that ageing undermines the executive functions of memory: those processes that are responsible for initiating the encoding of context (hence the poorer generation of context-specific cues, poorer recall of peripheral information, poor recognition on tasks such as MIRM, and impaired memory for source and temporal order), initiating recall (hence the failure to retrieve explicit information to facilitate implicit performance), and inflexibility during learning (hence poorer recall of unexpected events and lesser ability to use encoding strategies).

While the above conclusions seem reasonable, we must be cautious. Although we have taken the notion of what we mean by processing capacity deficit a little further, we have not explained how these mechanisms become impaired. This will come about only when we can explain the nature of these various memory failures more precisely – a task that might be facilitated by a greater understanding of the precise relationship between correlated failure on memory tasks and certain non-memory measures of frontal function such as problem-solving ability.

We should also be wary of explaining all age-related memory loss in terms of frontal lobe dysfunction. The temporal lobes also play a major part in memory, and one substructure in particular, the hippocampus, has been directly implicated in consolidation. Figure 8.5 also illustrates changes in the number of neurons present in field CA1 of the hippocampus, and again one sees a substantial reduction. There is now considerable evidence that the hippocampus is critically involved in consolidation; and, given the age-related decline in hippocampal neurons, there is every reason to believe that deficits in consolidation may also play a substantial role in explaining memory loss.

Memory Loss, Ageing, and Mental Activity

There are two competing theories concerning the relationship between ageing and neural decline. One suggests that neural decline is simply a function of use: the more that neurons are used, the quicker they decline. The other is that continuing activity leads to a slowing down in the rate of neuronal decline. So, is it a good idea to encourage your grandmother to do the crossword everyday or not?

Animal studies come down heavily against the 'wear and tear' hypothesis, favouring the idea that mental activity reduces the effects of ageing on neural decline (Swaab, 1991). They have shown that animals allowed to age in a stimulating and challenging environment show less neurological decline than animals denied this stimulation (e.g. Cohen, 1990). The prevailing view is that the brain retains a degree of functional growth and a repair capacity throughout the lifespan that can be induced by stimulating activity.

Our society provides a sad analogue of animal experiments in the effects of rich versus impoverished environments. Many old people remain active until they die; others spend the last part of their lives in institutions, even though many of them do not have any neurological abnormalities when they are admitted. The relationship between a residential environment and the development of memory impairment has begun to receive some attention. Winocur (1982) has provided a number of demonstrations that institutionalized elderly perform more poorly on memory tests compared with elderly people living at home. Craik et al. (1987) examined memory performance in elderly subjects who were either living actively in the community, living in a residential facility that encouraged activities, or living in a standard institution in which activity was minimal. The results showed no differences between the first two groups but poorer memory performance for those living in the standard institution.

Cockburn and Smith (in press) examined the prospective memory (remembering to do things) in people admitted to care at different points in their lives. Interestingly, they found poorer prospective memory in people admitted to care earlier in their lives. Institutions rely heavily on routines, so perhaps it is not surprising that longer-serving inmates should have the poorest prospective memory. The idea that institutionalization stops the use of certain memory functions is backed up by Holland and Rabbitt (1991), who found that institutionalized old people tended to spend much more of their time dwelling on the past. So, encourage granny to do the crossword!

Ageing and Memory: An Evolutionary Perspective

From what we have learned in chapters 7 and 8, it is clear that memory functions develop and decline unevenly. Performance on implicit memory tasks appears to be operational at a very early stage, and continues largely intact in later life. By contrast, the more explicit aspects of memory, such as those concerned with recall, emerge later in life, and start to decline earlier. The parallel between memory development and age-related decline is quite striking. Consider, for example, the fact that both young children and older adults are over-optimistic about their memory performance, less flexible in their use of encoding strategies, and poorer at temporal discrimination.

Why does memory exhibit this 'last in, first out' pattern of change across the lifespan? One possible answer could lie in the different evolutionary history of the two types of memory (Parkin, in press; Reber, 1992, but see Parker, 1992). It can be argued that the various memory mechanisms responsible for implicit memory in humans may be developments of 'simpler' mechanisms that carry out comparable tasks in lower animals. It is not difficult to imagine, for example, that the perceptual representation system proposed by Schacter as an account of perceptual priming (see chapter 3) might also be present in many other animals, allowing them similar kinds of learning ability. By contrast, the more complex function of explicit memory may be unique to humans, since we have no way of knowing whether any other animal possesses consciousness. Explicit memory may therefore be a much more recent development.

There is good reason to suppose that parts of the brain underlying the older, simpler memory systems responsible for implicit memory may develop at an earlier stage than structures essential for explicit memory, a fact that may be directly attributable to the earlier emergence of these implicit memory structures in the phylogenetic sequence. The visual areas of the brain, which are assumed to be the locus of the perceptual representational system, are fully developed long before the frontal cortex, which does not become fully differentiated until much later. Furthermore, as we have seen in this chapter, the frontal cortex also has a tendency to decline at a faster rate than other parts of the brain, thereby explaining the more rapid decline of higher explicit memory abilities.

Overview

Research into ageing and memory presents a considerable methodological challenge, but certain consistent findings have emerged. Memory does not decline evenly with age; short-term storage remains normal, although tasks with a working memory element are affected. Performance on explicit memory declines markedly, especially on measures of free recall. Recognition *per se* holds up well with age, but when recognition demands contextual memory, deficits emerge. Implicit memory declines little with age, and where deficits are found, these seem largely due to older people's inability to use explicit memory as an aid to implicit performance. The cause of age-related memory loss has yet to be explained fully, but there is considerable evidence that it arises, in part at least, from frontal lobe dysfunction that occurs naturally as we get older.

References

Ackerman, B. P. (1988) Search set access problems in retrieving episodic information from memory in children and adults. *Journal of Experimental Child Psychology*, 45, 234–261.

Allen, R. and Reber, A. (1980) Very long-term memory for tacit knowledge. *Cognition*, 8, 175–185.

Allport, G. W. (1924) Eidetic imagery. *British Journal of Psychology*, 15, 100–120.

Anderson, C. M. B. and Craik, F. I. M. (1974) The effect of a concurrent task on recall from primary memory. *Journal of Verbal Learning and Verbal Behavior*, 13, 107–113.

Anderson, J. R. and Bower, G. H. (1972) *Human Associative Memory*. Washington, DC: Winston.

Anooshian, L. J., Mammarella, S. L. and Hertel, P. T. (1989) Adult age differences in knowledge of retrieval processes. *International Journal of Aging and Human Development*, 29, 39–52.

Armstrong, A. C. (1894) The imagery of American students. *Psychological Review*, 1, 496–505.

Atkinson, R. C. and Juola, J. F. (1974) Search and decision processes in recognition memory. In D. H. Krantz, R. C. Atkinson, R. D. Luce and P. Suppes (eds), *Contemporary Developments in Mathematical Psychology*. Vol. 1: *Learning, Memory and Thinking*. San Francisco: Academic Press.

Atkinson, R. C. and Shiffrin, R. M. (1968) Human memory: a proposed system and its control processes. In K. W. Spence (ed.), *The Psychology of Learning and Motivation: advances in research and theory*, 2, 89–195. New York: Academic Press.

Attneave, F. (1974) How do you know? *American Psychologist*, 29, 493–499.

Baddeley, A. D. (1966a) Short term memory for word sequences as a function of acoustic, semantic and formal similarity. *Quarterly Journal of Experimental Psychology*, 18, 362–365.

Baddeley, A. D. (1966b) The influence of acoustic and semantic similarity on long-term memory for word sequences. *Quarterly Journal of Experimental Psychology*, 18, 302–309.

Baddeley, A. D. (1976) *The Psychology of Memory*. New York: Basic Books.

Baddeley, A. D. (1978) The trouble with levels: a re-examination of Craik and Lockhart's framework for memory research. *Psychological Review*, 85, 139–152.

Baddeley, A. D. (1986) *Working Memory*. Oxford: Oxford University Press.

Baddeley, A. D. (1990) *Human Memory: theory and practice*. Hove: Erlbaum Associates.

Baddeley, A. D. (1992) Working memory. *Science*, 255, 556–559.

Baddeley, A. D. and Hitch, G. (1977) Working memory. In G. A. Bower (ed.), *Recent Advances in Learning and Motivation*, 8, 647–667. New York: Academic Press.

Baddeley, A. D. and Lewis, V. J. (1981) Inner active processes in reading: the inner voice, the inner ear and the inner eye. In A. M. Lesgold and C. A. Perfetti, (eds), *Interactive Processes in Reading*, 107–129. Hillsdale, NJ: Erlbaum.

Baddeley, A. D. and Warrington, E. K. (1970) Amnesia and the distinction between long and short-term memory. *Journal of Verbal Learning and Verbal Behavior*, 9, 176–189.

Baddeley, A. D. and Wilson, B. (1988) Comprehension and working memory: a single case neuropsychological study. *Journal of Memory and Language*, 27, 479–498.

Baddeley, A. D., Thomson, N. and Buchanan, M. (1975) Word length and the structure of short-term memory. *Journal of Verbal Learning and Verbal Behavior*, 14, (1990), 575–589.

Baddeley, A. D., Logie, R. H., Nimmo-Smith, M. I. and Brereton, N. (1985) Components of fluent reading. *Journal of Memory and Language*, 24, 119–131.

Bahrick, H. P. (1970) Two-phase model for prompted recall. *Psychological Review*, 77, 215–222.

Baillargeon, R., DeVros, J. and Graber, M. (1990) Location memory in 8-month old infants in a non-search AB task. *Cognitive Development*, 4, 345–367.

Bartlett, F. C. (1932) *Remembering*. Cambridge: Cambridge University Press.

Bartlett, J. C. and Fulton, A. (1991) Familiarity and recognition of faces. *Memory and Cognition*, 19, 229–238.

Bassili, J., Smith, M. and MacLeod, C. (1989) Auditory and visual word stem completion: separating data drive and conceptually driven processes. *Quarterly Journal of Experimental Psychology*, 41, 439–453.

Berkowitz, B. (1953) The Wechsler–Bellevue performance of white males past 50. *Journal of Gerontology*, 8, 76–80.

Berry, D. C. and Broadbent, D. E. (1984) On the relationship between task performance and associated verbalisable knowledge. *Quarterly Journal of Experimental Psychology*, 36A, 209–231.

Berry, D. C. and Broadbent, D. E. (1988) Interactive tasks and the implicit-explicit distinction. *British Journal of Psychology*, 79, 251–272.

Berry, D. C. and Dienes, Z. (in press) *Implicit and Explicit Learning in Human Performance*. Hillsdale, NJ: Erlbaum.

Besner, D., Davies, J. and Daniels, S. (1981) Reading for meaning: the effects of concurrent articulation. *Quarterly Journal of Experimental Psychology*, 33A, 415–437.

Bjork, R. A. and Whitten, W. B. (1974) Recency-sensitive retrieval processes. *Cognitive Psychology*, 6, 173–189.

Bjorklund, D. F. (1987) How age changes in knowledge base contribute to the development of children's memory. *Developmental Review*, 7, 93–130.

Bjorklund, D. F. and Harnishfeger, K. K. (1990) The resources construct in cognitive development: diverse sources of evidence and a theory of inefficient inhibition. *Developmental Review*, 10, 48–71.

Blakemore, C. (1977) *Mechanics of the Mind*. Cambridge: Cambridge University Press.

Blaxton, T. A. (1985) Investigating dissociation among memory measures: support for a transfer appropriate processing framework. *Journal of Experimental Psychology: learning, memory, and cognition*, 15, 657–668.

Block, R. I. and Wittenborn, J. R. (1985) Marijuana effects on associative processes. *Psychopharmacology*, 85, 426–430.

Borovsky, D. and Rovee-Collier, C. (1990) Attention-gating of memory retrieval by context at 6 months. *Child Development*, 61, 1569–1583.

Botwinick, J. and Storandt, M. (1974) *Memory, Related Functions, and Age*. Springfield, IL: C. C. Thomas.

Bousfield, W. A. (1953) The occurrence of clustering in the recall of randomly arranged associates. *Journal of Genetic Psychology*, 49, 229–240.

Bower, G. H. (1970) Imagery as a relational organizer in associative learning. *Journal of Verbal Learning and Verbal Behavior*, 9, 529–533.

Bower, G. H. (1981) Mood and memory. *American Psychologist*, 36, 129–148.

Bower, G. H. and Mayer, J. D. (1985) Failure to replicate mood-dependent retrieval. *Bulletin of the Psychonomic Society*, 23, 39–42.

Bower, G. H., Gilligan, S. G. and Monteiro, K. P. (1981) Selectivity of learning caused by affective states. *Journal of Experimental Psychology: general*, 110, 451–473.

Bowles, N. L. and Poon, L. W. (1985) Aging and retrieval of words in semantic memory. *Journal of Gerontology*, 40, 71–77.

Bradley, B. P. and Baddeley, A. D. (1990) Emotional factors in forgetting. *Psychological Medicine*, 20, 351–355.

Broadbent, D. E. (1958) *Perception and Communication*. London: Pergamon Press.

Brooks, L. R. (1968) The suppression of visualization by reading. *Quarterly Journal of Experimental Psychology*, 19, 289–299.

Brown, A. L. (1975) The development of memory: knowing, knowing about knowing, and knowing how to know. In H. W. Reese (ed.), *Advances in Child Development and Behavior*, 10, 103–152. New York: Academic Press.

Brown, A. L. (1978) Knowing when, where, and how to remember: a problem of metacognition. In R. Glaser (ed.), *Advances in Instructional Psychology*. Hillsdale, NJ: Erlbaum.

Brown, A. S. and Murphy, D. R. (1989) Cryptomnesia: delineating inadvertent plagiarism. *Journal of Experimental Psychology*, 15, 432–442.

Bruce, P. R., Coyne, A. C. and Botwinick, J. (1982) Adult age differences in metamemory. *Journal of Gerontology*, 37, 354–357.

Burke, M. and Mathews, A. (1992) Autobiographical memory and clinical anxiety. *Cognition and Emotion*, 6, 23–36.

Butterfield, E. C., Nelson, T. O. and Peck, V. (1988) Developmental aspects of feeling of knowing. *Developmental Psychology*, 24, 654–663.

Butters, N. and Brandt, J. (1985) The continuity hypothesis: the relationship of long-term alcoholism to the Wernicke–Korsakoff syndrome. In M. Galanter (ed.), *Recent Developments in Alcoholism*, 3, 207–226.

Butterworth, B., Campbell, R. and Howard, D. (1986) The uses of short-term memory: a case study. *Quarterly Journal of Experimental Psychology*, 38A, 705–738.

Butterworth, G. E. (1977) Object disappearance and error in Piaget's Stage IV task. *Journal of Experimental Child Psychology*, 23, 391–401.

Calev, A. (1984) Recall and recognition in chronic and non-dementing schizophrenics: use of matched tasks. *Journal of Abnormal Psychology*, 93, 172–177.

Calev, A., Ben-Tzvi, E., Shapira, B., Drexler, H. et al. (1989) Distinct memory impairments following electroconvulsive therapy and imipramine. *Psychological Medicine*, 19, 111–119.

Carey, S. (1978) The child as word learner. In M. Halle, J. Bresnan and G. A. Miller (eds), *Linguistic Theory and Psychological Reality*, 264–293. Cambridge, MA: MIT Press.

Carroll, M., Byrne, B. and Kirsner, K. (1985) Autobiographical memory and perceptual learning: a developmental study using picture recognition, naming latency, and perceptual identification. *Memory and Cognition*, 13, 273–279.

Ceci, S. J. and Howe, M. J. A. (1978) Age related differences in recall as a function of retrieval flexibility. *Journal of Experimental Child Psychology*, 26, 432–442.

Cernoch, J. M. and Porter, R. H. (1985) Recognition of maternal axillary odors by infants. *Child Development*, 56, 1593–1598.

Chance, J. E. and Goldstein, A. G. (1976) Recognition of faces and verbal labels. *Bulletin of the Psychonomic Society*, 14, 115–117.

Charlot, V., Tzourio, N., Zilbovicius, M., Mazoyer, B. and Denis, M. (1992) Different mental imagery abilities result in different regional cerebral blood flow activation patterns during cognitive tasks. *Neuropsychologia*, 30, 565–580.

Charness, N. (1979) Components of skill in bridge. *Canadian Journal of Psychology*, 33, 1–16.

Charness, N. (1983) Age, skill, and bridge bidding: a chronometric analysis. *Journal of Verbal Learning and Verbal Behavior*, 22, 406–416.

Chi, M. T. H. (1978) Knowledge structures and memory development. In R. Siegler (ed.), *Children's Thinking: what develops?* Hillsdale, NJ: Erlbaum.

Chi, M. T. H. and Koeske, R. D. (1983) Network representation of a child's dinosaur knowledge. *Developmental Psychology*, 19, 29–39.

Chiarello, C. and Hoyer, W. J. (1988) Adult age differences in implicit and explicit memory: time course and encoding effects. *Psychology and Aging*, 3, 359–366.

Chomsky, N. (1959) Review of Skinner's 'Verbal Behavior'. *Language*, 35, 26–58.

Claparede, E. (1951) Recognition and 'me-ness'. In D. Rapaport (ed.), *Organization and Pathology of Thought*. New York: Columbia University Press. Reprinted from *Archives de psychologie*, 11, (1911), 79–90.

Clark, D. M. and Teasdale, J. D. (1981) Diurnal variation in clinical depression and accessibility of positive and negative experiences. *Journal of Abnormal Psychology*, 91, 87–95.

Cockburn, J. and Smith, P. T. (in press) Correlates of everyday memory among residents of Part 111 homes. *British Journal of Clinical Psychology*.

Cohen, G. D. (1990) Psychopathology and mental health in the mature and elderly adult. In J. E. Birren and K. W. Schaie (eds), *Handbook of the Psychology of Aging*, 359–371. New York: Academic Press.

Cohen, N. J. and Squire, L. R. (1980) Preserved learning and retention of pattern analyzing skill in amnesia: dissociation of knowing how and knowing that. *Science*, 210, 207–210.

Comfort, A. (1976) *A Good Age*. New York: Simon and Schuster.

Conrad, R. (1964) Acoustic confusion in immediate memory. *British Journal of Psychology*, 55, 75–84.

Conrad, R. (1971) The chronology of the development of covert speech in children. *Developmental Psychology*, 5, 398–405.

Contini, L. and Whissell, C. (1992) Memory disadvantages for CVC associates of emotional words. *Perceptual and Motor Skills*, 75, 427–431.

Conway, M. A. (1990) *Autobiographical Memory: an introduction*. Milton Keynes: Open University Press.

Coons, P. M., Milstein, V. and Marley, C. (1982) EEG studies of two multiple personalities. *Archives of General Psychiatry*, 39, 823–825.

Cooper, L. A. and Shepard, R. N. (1973) Chronometric studies of the rotation of mental images. In W. G. Chase (ed.), *Visual Information Processing*. New York: Academic Press.

Cooper, E. C. and Pantle, A. J. (1967) The total time hypothesis in verbal learning. *Psychological Bulletin*, 68, 221–234.

Corkin, S. (1968) Acquisition of motor skill after bilateral medial temporal lobe-excision. *Neuropsychologia*, 6, 255–265.

Corkin, S., Cohen, N. J., Sullivan, E. V., Clegg, R. A., Rosen, T. J. and Ackerman, R. H. (1985) Analyses of global memory impairments of different aetiologies. *Annals of the New York Academy of Sciences*, 444, 10–40.

Craik, F. I. M. (1970) The fate of primary memory items in free recall. *Journal of Verbal Learning and Verbal Behavior*, 9, 143–148.

Craik, F. I. M. (1977) 'A level of analysis' view of memory. In P. Pliner, L. Krames and T. M. Allaway (eds), *Communication and Affect*, Vol. 2: *Language and Thought*. New York: Academic Press.

Craik, F. I. M. and Jacoby, L. L. (1976) A process view of short-term retention. In F. Restle (ed.), *Cognitive Theory*, 1, 173–192. Hillsdale, NJ: Erlbaum.

Craik, F. I. M. and Lockhart, R. S. (1972) Levels of processing: a framework for memory research. *Journal of Verbal Learning and Verbal Behavior*, 11, 671–684.

Craik, F. I. M. and McDowd, J. M. (1987) Age differences in recall and recognition. *Journal of Experimental Psychology: learning, memory, and cognition*, 13, 474–479.

Craik, F. I. M. and Simon, E. (1980) Age differences in memory: the roles of attention and depth of processing. In L. W. Poon, J. L. Fozard, L. S. Cermak, D. Arenberg and L. W. Thompson (eds), *New Directions in Memory and Aging: proceedings of the George Talland Memorial Conference*. Hillsdale, NJ: Erlbaum.

Craik, F. I. M. and Tulving, E. (1975) Depth of processing and the retention of words in episodic memory. *Journal of Experimental Psychology: general*, 104, 268–294.

Craik, F. I. M., Byrd, M. and Swanson, J. M. (1987) Patterns of memory loss in three elderly samples. *Psychology and Aging*, 2, 79–86.

Craik, K. (1943) *The Nature of Explanation*. Cambridge: Cambridge University Press.

Crovitz, H. F., Harvey, M. T. and McKee, D. C. (1980) Selecting retrieval cues for early childhood amnesia: implications for the study of shrinking retrograde amnesia. *Cortex*, 16, 305–310.

Curran, H. V., Gardiner, J. M., Java, R. I. and Allen, D. (in press) Effect of lorazepam on recollective experience in word recognition. *Psychopharmacology*.

Cuvo, A. J. (1974) Incentive level influence on overt rehearsal and free recall as a function of age. *Journal of Experimental Child Psychology*, 19, 265–278.

Cuvo, A. J. (1975) Developmental differences in rehearsal and free recall. *Journal of Experimental Child Psychology*, 19, 265–278.

Daehler, M., Bukatko, D., Benson, K. and Myers, N. (1976) The effects of size and color cues on the delayed response of very young children. *Bulletin of the Psychonomic Society*, 7, 65–68.

Daneman, M. and Carpenter, P. A. (1980) Individual differences in working memory and reading. *Journal of Verbal Learning and Verbal Behavior*, 19, 450–466.

Darwin, C. J., Turvey, M. T. and Crowder, R. G. (1972) An auditory analogue of the Sperling partial report procedure: evidence for brief auditory storage. *Cognitive Psychology*, 3, 255–267.

Davidson, R. J. and Schwartz, G. E. (1977) Brain mechanisms subserving self-generated imagery: electrophysiological specificity and patterning. *Psychophysiology*, 14, 598–601.

DeCasper, A. J. and Fifer, W. P. (1980) Of human bonding: Newborns prefer their mothers' voices. *Science*, 208, 1174–1176.

DeCasper, A. J. and Spence, M. J. (1986) Prenatal maternal speech influences newborns' perception of speech sounds. *Infant Behavior and Development*, 9, 133–150.

DeLoache, J. S. and Brown, A. L. (1983) Very young children's memory for the location of objects in a large-scale environment. *Child Development*, 54, 888–897.

DeMarie-Dreblow, D. (1991) Relation between knowledge and memory: a reminder that correlation does not imply causality. *Child Development*, 62, 484–498.

Dempster, F. N. (1981) Memory span: sources of individual and developmental differences. *Psychological Bulletin*, 89, 63–100.

Denney, N. and Ziobrowski, M. (1972) Developmental changes in clustering behavior. *Journal of Experimental Child Psychology*, 13, 275–282.

Descartes, R. (1649/1941) *Discours de la Methode*, (ed.), G. Gadoffre. Manchester: Manchester University Press.

De Vreese, L. P. (1991) Two systems for colour-naming defects: verbal disconnection vs colour imagery disorder. *Neuropsychologia*, 29, 1–18.

Dittuno, P. L. and Mann, V. A. (1990) Right hemisphere specialization for mental rotation in normals and brain damaged subjects. *Cortex*, 26, 177–188.

Dixon, R. A. and Hultsch, D. F. (1983) Structure and development of metamemory in adulthood. *Journal of Gerontology*, 38, 682–688.

Dockrell, J. and Campbell, R. (1986) Lexical acquisition strategies in the preschool child. In S. A. Kuczaj II and M. D. Barrett (eds), *The Development of Word Meaning: progress in cognitive development research*, 121–154. New York: Springer Verlag.

Drachman, D. A. and Sahakian, B. J. (1979) Effects of cholinergic agents on human learning and memory. In R. Barbeau et al. (Eds.) *Nutrition and the Brain*. 5, New York: Raven Press. 351–66.

Durkin, K. (1989) Implicit memory and language acquisition. In S. Lewandowsky, J. C. Dunn and K. Kirsner (eds), *Implicit Memory: theoretical issues*, 241–258. Hillsdale, NJ; Erlbaum.

Ebbinghaus, H. (1885) *Über das Gedachtnis*. Leipzig: Dunker.

Eich, J. E. (1980) The cue-dependent nature of state-dependent retrieval. *Memory and Cognition*, 8, 157–173.

Eich, J. E. and Metcalfe, J. (1989) Mood-dependent memory for internal versus external events. *Journal of Experimental Psychology: Learning, memory, and cognition*, 15, 443–455.

Ellis, A. W. and Young, A. W. (1988) *Human Cognitive Neuropsychology*. Hove: Erlbaum Associates.

Evans, J., Williams, J. M. G., O'Loughlin, S. and Howells, K. (1992) Autobiographical memory and problem-solving strategies of parasuicide patients. *Psychological Medicine*, 22, 399–405.

Eysenck, M. W. (1982) *Attention and Arousal: cognition and performance*. Berlin: Springer.

Eysenck, M. W. (1978) Levels of processing: A critique. *British Journal of Psychology*, 69, 157–169.

Farah, M. J. (1988) Is visual imagery really visual? Overlooked evidence from neuropsychology. *Psychological Review*, 95, 307–317.

Farah, M. J., Peronnet, F., Gonon, M. A. and Giard, M. H. (in press) Electrophysiological evidence for a shared representational medium for visual images and percepts. *Journal of Experimental Psychology: general*.

Farrar, M. J. and Goodman, G. S. (1992) Developmental changes in event memory. *Child Development*, 63, 173–187.

Fivush, R. and Hamond, N. R. (1990) Autobiographical memory across the preschool years: toward reconceptualising childhood amnesia. In R. Fivush and J. A. Hudson (eds), *Knowing and Remembering in Young Children*. New York: Cambridge University Press.

Flavell, J. H. and Wellman, H. M. (1977) Metamemory. In R. V. Kail and W. J. Hagen (eds), *Perspectives on the Development of Memory and Cognition*, Hillsdale, NJ: Erlbaum.

Flavell, J. H., Beach, D. R. and Chinsky, J. M. (1966) Spontaneous verbal rehearsal in a memory task as a function of age. *Child Development*, 37, 283–299.

Flexser, A. J. (1991) The implications of item differences: Commentary on Hintzman and Hartry. *Journal of Experimental Psychology: Learning, Memory, and Cognition*, 17, 338–40.

Flexser, A. J. and Tulving, E. (1978) Retrieval independence in recognition and recall. *Psychological Review*, 85, 153–171.

Flood, D. G. and Coleman, P. D. (1988) Neuron numbers and sizes in aging brain: comparisons of human, monkey, and rodent data. *Neurobiology of Aging*, 9, 453–463.

Fox, N., Kagan, J. and Weiskopf, S. (1979) The growth of memory during infancy. *Genetic Psychology Monographs*, 99, 91–130.

Frank, H. S. and Rabinovitch, M. S. (1974) Auditory short-term memory: developmental changes in rehearsal. *Child Development*, 45, 397–407.

Freud, S. (1915) Repression. In Freud, *Collected Papers*, 6. London: Hogarth Press.

Freud, S. (1943) *A General Introduction to Psychoanalysis*. Garden City, N.Y.

Friedman, S. (1972) Newborn visual attention to repeated exposure of redundant vs 'novel' targets. *Perception and Psychophysics*, 12, 291–294.

Friedman, S., Bruno, L. A. and Vietze, P. (1974) Newborn habituation to visual stimuli: a sex difference in novelty detection. *Journal of Experimental Child Psychology*, 18, 242–251.

Friedman, W. J. (1991) The development of children's memory for the time of past events. *Child Development*, 62, 139–155.

Gardiner, J. M. (1988) Functional aspects of recollective experience. *Memory and Cognition*, 16, 309–313.

Gardiner, J. M. (1991) Contingency relations between successive tests: Accidents do not happen. *Journal of Experimental Psychology: Learning, Memory and Cognition*, 17, 341–5.

Gardiner, J. M. and Java, R. I. (in press) Recognition memory and awareness: an experiential approach. *European Journal of Cognitive Psychology.*

Gardiner, J. M. and Parkin, A. J. (1990) Attention and recollective experience in recognition memory. *Memory and Cognition*, 18, 579–583.

Gardner, H., Boller, F., Moreines, J. and Butters, N. (1974) Retrieving information from Korsakoff patients: effects of categorical cues and reference to task. *Cortex*, 12, 163–175.

Geiselman, R. and Machlovitz, H. (1987) Hypnosis memory recall: Implications for forensic use. *American Journal of Forensic Psychology*, 5, 37–47.

Gick, M., Craik, F. I. M. and Morris, R. G. (1988) Task complexity and age differences in working memory. *Memory and Cognition*, 16, 353–361.

Glanzer, M. and Cunitz, A. R. (1966) Two storage mechanisms in free recall. *Journal of Verbal Learning and Verbal Behavior*, 5, 351–360.

Glanzer, M. and Razel, M. (1974) The size of the unit in short-term storage. *Journal of Verbal Learning and Verbal Behavior*, 13, 114–131.

Glenberg, A. M., Bradley, M. M., Stevenson, J. A. et al. (1980) A two process account of long-term serial position effects. *Journal of Experimental Psychology: Human Learning and Memory*, 6, 692–704.

Glisky, E. L. and Schacter, D. L. (1989) Extending the limits of complex learning in organic amnesia: computer training in a vocational domain. *Neuropsychologia*, 27, 107–120.

Glisky, E. L., Schacter, D. L. and Tulving, E. (1987) Learning and retention of computer-related vocabulary in memory-impaired patients: method of vanishing cues. *Journal of Clinical and Experimental Neuropsychology*, 8, 292–312.

Godden, D. and Baddeley, A. D. (1975) Context-dependent memory in two natural environments: on land and under water. *British Journal of Psychology*, 66, 325–331.

Godden, D. and Baddeley, A. D. (1980) When does context influence recognition memory? *British Journal of Psychology*, 71, 90–104.

Goldenberg, G., Steiner, M., Podreka, I. and Deeke, L. (1992) Regional cerebral blood flow patterns related to verification of low- and high-imagery sentences. *Neuropsychologia*, 30, 581–586.

Goodman, G. S. (1980) Picture memory: how the action schema affects retention. *Cognitive Psychology*, 12, 473–495.

Goodwin, D. W., Powell, B., Bremer, D., Hoine, H. and Stern, J. (1969) Alcohol and recall: state-dependent effects. *Science*, 163, 1358–1360.

Gottfried, A. W., Rose, S. A. and Bridger, W. H. (1977) Cross modal transfer in human infants. *Child Development*, 48, 118–123.

Graf, P. (1990) Life-span changes in implicit and explicit memory. *Bulletin of the Psychonomic Society*, 28, 353–358.

Graf, P. and Mandler, G. (1984) Activation makes words more accessible, but not necessarily more retrievable. *Journal of Verbal Learning and Verbal Behavior*, 23, 553–568.

Graf, P. and Schacter, D. L. (1985) Implicit and explicit memory for new associations in normal and amnesic subjects. *Journal of Experimental Psychology: learning, memory, and cognition*, 13, 45–53.

Graf, P., Squire, L. R. and Mandler, G. (1984) The information that amnesic patients do not forget. *Journal of Experimental Psychology: learning, memory, and cognition,* 9, 164–178.

Greco, C., Hayne, H. and Rovee-Collier, C. (1990) Roles of function, reminding, and variability in categorization by 3-month-old infants. *Journal of Experimental Psychology: learning, memory, and cognition,* 16, 617–633.

Greenbaum, J. L. and Graf, P. (1989) Preschool period development of implicit and explicit remembering. *Bulletin of the Psychonomic Society,* 27, 417–420.

Greene, R. L. (1989) Spacing effects in memory: evidence for a two-process account. *Journal of Experimental Psychology: learning, memory, and cognition,* 15, 371–377.

Gregy, V. H. (1986) *Introduction to Human Memory,* London: RKP.

Grinker, R. R. and Spiegel, J. P. (1945) *Men under Stress.* New York: McGraw-Hill.

Haber, R. N. (1979) Twenty years of haunting eidetic imagery: where's the ghost? *The Behavioural and Brain Sciences,* 2, 583–629.

Hamond, N. R. and Fivush, R. (1991) Memories of Mickey Mouse: young children recount their trip to Disneyworld. *Cognitive Development,* 6, 443–8.

Hanley, J. R., Davies, A. D. M. and Downes, J. (in press) Impaired recall of verbal material following an anterior communicating ortery aneurysm.

Hardyk, C. D. and Petrinovich, L. R. (1970) Subvocal speech and comprehension level as a function of the difficulty level of reading material. *Journal of Verbal Learning and Verbal Behavior,* 9, 647–652.

Harris, P. (1989) Object permanence in infancy. In A. Slater and G. Bremner (eds), *Infant Development.* Hove: Erlbaum.

Hart, J. T. (1965) Memory and the feeling of knowing experience. *Journal of Educational Psychology,* 56, 208–216.

Hasher, L., Rose, K. C., Zacks, R. T., Sanft, H. and Doren, B. (1985) Mood, recall, and selectivity effects in college students. *Journal of Experimental Psychology: general,* 114, 104–118.

Hashstroudi, S., Johnson, M. K. and Chrosniak, L. D. (1989) Aging and source monitoring. *Psychology and Aging,* 4, 106–112.

Hayman, C. A. G. and Tulving, E. (1989a) Contingent dissociation between recognition and fragment completion: the method of triangulation. *Journal of Experimental Psychology: learning, memory, and cognition,* 15, 228–240.

Hayman, C. A. G. and Tulving, E. (1989b) Is priming in fragment completion based on a 'traceless' memory system? *Journal of Experimental Psychology: learning, memory, and cognition,* 15, 941–956.

Hayne, H., Rovee-Collier, C. and Perris, E. (1987) Categorization and memory retrieval by three-month olds. *Child Development,* 58, 750–767.

Hayne, H., Rovee-Collier, C. and Borza, M. A. (1991) Infant memory for place information. *Memory and Cognition,* 19, 378–386.

Hebb, D. O. (1949) *Organization of Behavior.* New York: Wiley.

Hertzog, C., Dixon, R. A. and Hultsch, D. F. (1990) Relationships between metamemory, memory predictions, and memory task performance in adults. *Psychology and Aging*, 5, 215–227.

Hess, T. M. (1984) Effects of semantically related and unrelated contexts on recognition memory of different-aged adults. *Journal of Gerontology*, 39, 444–451.

Hewitt, K. (1973) Context effects in memory: a review. Cambridge University Psychological Laboratory.

Hill, L. B. (1957) A second quarter century of delayed recall or relearning at 80. *Journal of Educational Psychology*, 48, 65–68.

Hintzman, D. L. (1991) Contingency analyses, hypotheses, and artifacts: reply to Flexser and to Gardiner. *Journal of Experimental Psychology: learning, memory, and cognition*, 17, 334–337.

Hintzman, D. L. (1992) Mathematical constraints on the Tulving–Wiseman law. *Psychological Review*, 102, 536–542.

Hintzman, D. L. and Hartry, A. L. (1990) Item effects in recognition and fragment completion: contingency relations vary for different subsets of words. *Journal of Experimental Psychology: learning, memory, and cognition*, 17, 341–345.

Hitch, G., Rejman, M. J. and Turner, N. C. (1980) A new perspective on the recency effect. Paper presented at the July Experimental Psychology Society meeting in Cambridge.

Holland, C. A. and Rabbitt, P. M. A. (1991) Ageing memory: use versus impairment. *British Journal of Psychology*, 82, 29–38.

Houx, P. J., Vreeling, F. W. and Jolles, J. (1991) Rigorous health screening reduces age effect on memory scanning task. *Brain and Cognition*, 15, 246–260.

Howard, D. V. (1991) Implicit memory: an expanding picture of cognitive aging. In K. W. Schaie and M. P. Lawton (eds), *Annual Review of Gerontology and Geriatrics*, 11, 1–22.

Howard, D. and Butterworth, B. (1989) Developmental disorders of verbal short-term memory and their relation to sentence comprehension: a reply to Vallar and Baddeley. *Cognitive Neuropsychology*, 6, 455–463.

Howard, D. and Howard, J. H. (1992) Adult age differences in the rate of learning serial patterns: evidence from direct and indirect tests. *Psychology and Aging*, 7, 232–241.

Howard, D. V., Shaw, R. J. and Heisey, J. G. (1986) Aging and the time course of semantic activation. *Journal of Gerontology*, 41, 195–203.

Howell, P. and Darwin, C. J. (1977) Some properties of auditory memory for rapid formant transitions. *Memory and Cognition*, 5, 700–708.

Huey, E. B. (1908) *The Psychology and Pedagogy of Reading*. New York: Macmillan.

Hulme, C., Thomson, N., Muir, C. and Lawrence, A. (1984) Speech rate and the development of short-term memory span. *Journal of Experimental Child Psychology*, 38, 241–253.

Humphreys, G. W. and Bruce, V. (1989) *Visual Cognition: computational, experimental and neuropsychological perspectives*. Hove: Erlbaum.

Humphreys, G. W. and Riddoch, J. (1987) *To See but Not to See: a case study of visual agnosia.* London: Erlbaum.

Hunkin, N. M. and Parkin, A. J. (in press) Recency judgments in Wernicke-Korsakoff and Post-Encephalitic Amnesia: influences of proactive interference and retention interval. *Cortex.*

Huppert, F. A. and Piercy, M. (1978) The role of trace strength in recency and frequency judgments by amnesic and control subjects. *Quarterly Journal of Experimental Psychology,* 30, 346–354.

Jacoby, L. L. (1983) Remembering the data: analyzing interactive processing in reading. *Journal of Verbal Learning and Verbal Behavior,* 22, 485–508.

Jacoby, L. L. and Dallas, M. (1981) On the relationship between autobiographical memory and perceptual learning. *Journal of Experimental Psychology: general,* 110, 306–340.

James, W. (1890) *Principles of Psychology,* vol. 1. New York: Holt.

James, W. (1899) *Talks to Teachers on Psychology: and to students on some of life's ideals.* New York: Holt.

Janowsky, J. S., Shimamura, A. P. and Squire, L. R. (1989) Source memory impairment in patients with frontal lobe lesions. *Neuropsychologia,* 27, 1043–1056.

Jelic, M., Bonke, B., Wolters, G. and Phaf, H. (1992) Implicit memory for words presented during anaesthesia. *European Journal of Cognitive Psychology,* 4, 71–80.

Johnston, W. A., Dark, V. J. and Jacoby, L. L. (1985) Perceptual fluency and recognition judgments. *Journal of Experimental Psychology: learning, memory, and cognition,* 11, 3–11.

Johnston, W. A., Hawley, K. J. and Elliot, J. M. G. (1991) Contribution of perceptual fluency to recognition judgment. *Journal of Experimental Psychology: learning, memory, and cognition,* 17, 210–233.

Jones, E. B., O'Gorman, J. G. and Byrne, B. (1987) Forgetting of word associates as a function of recall interval. *British Journal of Psychology,* 78, 79–89.

Kail, R. V. (1990) *The Development of Memory in Children,* 3rd edn. New York: Freeman.

Kaminer, H. and Lavie, P. (1991) Sleep and dreaming in Holocaust survivors: dramatic decrease in dream recall in well adjusted survivors. *Journal of Nervous and Mental Disease,* 179, 664–669.

Karnath, H. O., Wallesch, C. W. and Zimmerman, P. (1991) Mental planning and anticipatory processes with acute and chronic frontal lobe lesions: a comparison of maze performance in routine and non-routine situations. *Neuropsychologia,* 29, 271–290.

Kausler, D. H. (1990) *Experimental Psychology, Cognition and Human Aging.* New York: Springer Verlag.

Kausler, D. H. and Kleim, D. M. (1978) Age differences in processing relevant versus irrelevant stimuli in multiple item recognition memory. *Journal of Gerontology,* 33, 87–93.

Keller, R. and Shaywitz, B. A. (1986) Amnesia or fugue state: *Journal of Developmental and Behavioural Pediatrics,* 7, 131–132.

Keppel, G. (1964) Verbal learning in children. *Psychological Bulletin*, 61, 63–80.

Kihlstrom, J. F. (1980) Posthypnotic amnesia for recently learned material: interactions with 'episodic' and 'semantic' memory. *Cognitive Psychology*, 12, 227–251.

Kihlstrom, J. F. and Harackiewicz, J. M. (1982) The earliest recollection: a new survey. *Journal of Personality*, 50, 134–148.

Kihlstrom, J. F., Evans, F. J., Orne, M. T. and Orne, E. C. (1980) Attempting to breach hypnotic amnesia. *Journal of Abnormal Psychology*, 89, 603–626.

Kihlstrom, J. F., Schachter, D. L., Cork, R. C., Hurt, C. A. and Behr, S. E. (1990) Implicit and explicit memory following surgical anesthesia. *Psychological Science*, 1, 303–306.

Kintsch, W. (1970) *Learning, Memory and Conceptual Processes*. New York: Wiley.

Kleiman, G. M. (1975) Speech recoding in reading. *Journal of Verbal Learning and Verbal Behavior*, 24, 323–339.

Kobasigawa, A. (1974) Utilization of retrieval cues by children in recall. *Child Development*, 45, 127–134.

Komatsu, S. and Naito, M. (1992) Repetition priming with Japanese Kana scripts in word fragment completion. *Memory and Cognition*, 20, 160–170.

Kopelman, M. D. (1987) Crime and amnesia: a review. *Behavioral Sciences and the Law*, 5, 323–342.

Kosslyn, S. M. (1980) *Image and Mind*. Cambridge, MA: Harvard University Press.

Kosslyn, S. M., Ball, T. M. and Reiser, B. J. (1978) Visual images preserve metric spatial information: evidence from studies of image scanning. *Journal of Experimental Psychology: human perception and performance*, 4, 47–60.

Kreutzer, M. A., Leonard, C. and Flavell, J. H. (1975) An interview study of children's knowledge about memory. *Monographs of the Society for Research in Child Development*, 40 (1, serial no. 159), 1–58.

Lange, G. and Griffith, S. B. (1977) The locus of organization failures in young children's recall. *Child Development*, 48, 1498–1502.

Leibniz, G. W. (1916) *New Essays concerning Human Understanding*. Chicago: Open Court.

Levinger, G. and Clark, J. (1961) Emotional factors in the forgetting of word associations. *Journal of Abnormal and Social Psychology*, 62, 99–105.

Levy, B. A. (1977) Reading: speech and meaning process. *Journal of Verbal Learning and Verbal Behavior*, 16, 623–628.

Lezak, M. D. (1983) *Neuropsychological Assessment*, 2nd edn. Oxford: Oxford University Press.

Light, L. L. and Carter-Sobell, L. (1970) Effects of changed semantic context on recognition memory. *Journal of Verbal Learning and Verbal Behavior*, 9, 1–11.

Light, L. L. and Singh, A. (1987) Implicit and explicit memory in young and older adults. *Journal of Experimental Psychology: learning, memory, and cognition*, 13, 531–541.

Light, L. L. and Zelinski, E. M. (1983) Memory for spatial information in young and old adults. *Developmental Psychology*, 19, 901–906.

Light, L. L., Singh, A. and Capps, J. L. (1986) The dissociation of memory and awareness in young and older adults. *Journal of Clinical and Experimental Neuropsychology*, 8, 62–74.

Lloyd, G. G. and Lishman, W. A. (1975) Effect of depression on the speed of recall of pleasant and unpleasant experiences. *Psychological Medicine*, 5, 173–180.

Loewen, E. R., Shaw, R. J. and Craik, F. I. M. (1990) Age differences in components of metamemory. *Experimental Aging Research*, 16, 43–48.

Loftus, E. F. and Loftus, G. R. (1980) On the permanence of stored information in the human brain. *American Psychologist*, 35, 409–420.

Loftus, E. F., Greene, E. and Smith, K. H. (1980) How deep is the meaning of life? *Bulletin of the Psychonomic Society*, 15, 282–284.

Lovelace, E. A. and Marsh, G. R. (1985) Prediction and evaluation of memory performance by young and old adults. *Journal of Gerontology*, 37, 432–437.

Luciana, M., Depue, R. A., Arbisi, P. and Leon, A. (1992) Facilitation of working memory in humans by a D2 dopamine receptor agonist. *Journal of Cognitive Neuroscience*, 4, 58–68.

Luria, A. R. (1975) *The Mind of a Mnemonist*. Harmondsworth: Penguin.

MacCurdy, T. J. (1928) *Common Principles in Psychology and Physiology*. Cambridge: Cambridge University Library.

Mackay-Soroka, S., Trehub, S. E., Bull, D. H. and Corter, C. M. (1982) Effects of encoding and retrieval conditions on infants' recognition memory. *Child Development*, 53, 815–818.

Malpass, R. S. and Devine, P. G. (1981) Guided memory in eyewitness identification responses. *Journal of Applied Psychology*, 66, 343–350.

Mandler, G. (1980) Recognising: the judgement of a previous occurrence. *Psychological Review*, 27, 252–271.

Mandler, G. and Boeck, W. (1974) Retrieval processes in recognition. *Memory and Cognition*, 2, 613–615.

Margolin, C. M., Griebel, B. and Wolford, G. (1982) Effect of distraction on reading versus listening. *Journal of Experimental Psychology: learning, memory, and cognition*, 8, 613–618.

Martin, R. M. (1975) Effects of familiar and complex stimuli on infant attention. *Developmental Psychology*, 11, 178–185.

McAndrews, M. P., Glisky, E. L. and Schacter, D. L. (1987) When priming persists: long-lasting implicit memory for a single episode in amnesic patients. *Neuropsychologia*, 25, 497–506.

McCloskey, M. and Santee, J. (1981) Are semantic and episodic memory distinct systems? *Journal of Experimental Psychology: human learning and memory*, 7, 66–71.

McCullough, M. L., Smith, C. D. and Walker, P. (1976) A note on repression. *Bulletin of the British Psychological Society,* 29, 235–237.

McIntyre, J. S. and Craik, F. I. M. (1987) Age differences in memory for item and source information. *Canadian Journal of Psychology,* 41, 175–192.

McKoon, G. and Ratcliff, R. (1979) Priming in episodic and semantic memory. *Journal of Verbal Learning and Verbal Behavior,* 18, 463–480.

Melkman, R., Tversky, B. and Baratz, D. (1981) Developmental trends in the use of perceptual and conceptual attributes in grouping, clustering, and retrieval. *Journal of Experimental Child Psychology,* 31, 470–486.

Micco, A. and Masson, M. E. J. (1991) Implicit memory for new associations: an interactive process approach. *Journal of Experimental Psychology: learning, memory, and cognition,* 17, 1105–1123.

Micco, A. and Masson, M. E. J. (1992) Age-related differences in the specificity of verbal encoding. *Memory and Cognition,* 20, 244–253.

Milberg, W., Alexander, M. P., Charness, N., McGlinchey-Berroth, R. and Barrett, A. (1988) Learning of a complex arithmetic skill in amnesia: evidence for a dissociation between compilation and production. *Brain and Cognition,* 8, 91–104.

Milgram, S. (1963) Behavioral study of obedience. *Journal of Abnormal and Social Psychology,* 67, 371–378.

Miller, G. A. (1956) The magical number seven, plus or minus two: some limits on our capacity for processing information. *Psychological Review,* 63, 81–97.

Mitchell, D. B. (in press) Implicit and explicit memory for pictures: multiple views across the lifespan. In P. Graf and M. E. J. Masson (eds), *Implicit Memory: new directions in cognition, development and neuropsychology.* Hillsdale, NJ: Erlbaum.

Mitchell, D. B. and Perlmutter, M. (1986) Semantic activation and episodic memory: age similarities and differences. *Developmental Psychology,* 22, 86–94.

Mittenberg, W., Seidenberg, M., O'Leary, D. S. and DiGuilio, D. V. (1989) Changes in cerebral functioning associated with normal aging. *Journal of Clinical and Experimental Neuropsychology,* 11, 918–932.

Moely, B. E., Olsen, F. A., Halwes, T. G. and Flavell, J. H. (1969) Production deficiency in young children's clustered recall. *Developmental Psychology,* 1, 26–34.

Morris, C. D., Bransford, J. D. and Franks, J. J. (1977) Levels of processing versus transfer appropriate processing. *Journal of Verbal Learning and Verbal Behavior,* 16, 519–533.

Morris, R. G., Gick, M. L. and Craik, F. I. M. (1988) Processing resources and age differences in working memory. *Memory and Cognition,* 16, 362–366.

Morton, J. (1970) A functional model for memory. In D. A. Norman (ed.), *Models of Human Memory.* New York: Academic Press.

Morton, J. (1979) Facilitation in word recognition: experiments causing change in the logogen model. In P. A. Kolers, M. Wrolstad and H. Bouma (eds), *Processing of Visible Language,* vol. 1. New York: Plenum.

Murray, D. J. (1968) Articulation and acoustic confusability in short-term memory. *Journal of Experimental Psychology,* 78, 679–684.

Naito, M. (1990) Repetition priming in children and adults: age-related dissociation between implicit and explicit memory. *Journal of Experimental Child Psychology*, 50, 462–484.

Naito, M. and Komatsu, S. (in press) Processes involved in childhood development of implicit memory. In P. Graf and M. Masson (eds), *Implicit Memory: new directions in cognition, development and neuropsychology*. Hillsdale, NJ: Erlbaum.

Neisser, U. (1982) John Dean's memory. In U. Neisser (ed.), *Memory Observed*, 139–159. San Francisco: Freeman.

Nelson, K. (1986) *Event Knowledge: structure and function in development*. Hillsdale, NJ: Erlbaum.

Nelson, K. (1990) Remembering, forgetting and childhood amnesia. In R. Fivush and J. A. Hudson (eds), *Knowing and Remembering in Young Children*. New York: Cambridge University Press.

Nelson, T. O. (1977) Repetition and depth of processing. *Journal of Verbal Learning and Verbal Behavior*, 16, 151–172.

Nissen, M. J., Knopman, D. S. and Schacter, D. L. (1987) Neurochemical dissociation of memory systems. *Neurology*, 37, 789–794.

Nissen, M. J., Ross, J. L., Willingham, D. B., Mackenzie, T. B. and Schacter, D. L. (1988) Memory and awareness in a patient with multiple personality disorder. *Brain and Cognition*, 8, 117–134.

Norman, D. A. and Shallice, T. (1986) Attention to action: willed and automatic control of behavior. In R. J. Davidson, G. E. Schwartz and D. Shapiro (eds), *Consciousness and Self-Regulation: advances in research and theory*, 4, New York: Plenum.

Oakhill, J. V. (1984) Inferential and memory skills in children's comprehension of stories. *British Journal of Educational Psychology*, 54, 31–39.

Oakhill, J. V., Yuill, N. and Parkin, A. J. (1986) On the nature of the difference between skilled and less-skilled comprehenders. *Journal of Research in Reading*, 9, 80–91.

Ogden, J. A. and Corkin, S. (1991) Memories of HM. In W. C. Abraham, M. C. Corballis and K. G. White (eds), *Memory Mechanisms: a tribute to G. V. Goddard*. Hillsdale, NJ: Erlbaum.

Orne, M. T. (1962) On the social psychology of the psychological experiment: with particular reference to demand characteristics and their implications. *American Psychologist*, 17, 776–783.

Owens, W. A. (1959) Is age kinder to the initially more able? *Journal of Gerontology*, 14, 334–337.

Owens, W. A. (1966) Age and mental ability: a second follow-up. *Journal of Educational Psychology*, 57, 311–325.

Paivio, A. (1969) Mental imagery in associative learning and memory. *Psychological Review*, 76, 241–263.

Paivio, A. (1971) *Imagery and Verbal Processes*. New York: Holt, Rinehart and Winston.

Paivio, A. (1986) *Mental Representations: a dual coding approach*. Oxford: Oxford University Press.

Paller, K. A. (1990) Recall and stem-completion priming have different electrophysiological correlates and are modified differentially by directed forgetting. *Journal of Experimental Psychology: learning, memory, and cognition*, 16, 1021–1032.

Paris, S. G. and Cross, D. R. (1983) Ordinary learning: pragmatic connections among children's beliefs, motives and actions. In J. Bisanz, G. Bisanz and R. Kail (eds), *Learning in Children: progress in cognitive developmental research.* New York: Springer Verlag.

Parker, S. T. (1992) 'Robustness' of implicit processes: Artifact or evidence of antiquity? *Consciousness and Cognition*, 1, 134–138.

Parkin, A. J. (1979) Specifying levels of processing. *Quarterly Journal of Experimental Psychology*, 31, 175–195.

Parkin, A. J. (1981) Determinants of cued recall. *Current Psychological Research*, 1, 291–300.

Parkin, A. J. (1982) Residual learning capability in organic amnesia. *Cortex*, 18, 417–440.

Parkin, A. J. (1984) Comment on 'Parkin et al. reconsidered by Rossmann'. *Psychological Research*, 45, 389–394.

Parkin, A. J. (1987) *Memory and Amnesia.* Oxford: Basil Blackwell.

Parkin, A. J. (1989) The development and nature of implicit memory. In S. Lewandowsky, J. C. Dunn and K. Kirsner (eds), *Implicit Memory: theoretical issues*, 231–240. Hillsdale, NJ: Erlbaum.

Parkin, A. J. (1991) The relationship between anterograde and retrograde amnesia in alcoholic Wernicke–Korsakoff syndrome. *Psychological Medicine*, 21, 11–14.

Parkin, A. J. (in press) Implicit memory across the lifespan. In P. Graf and M. Masson (eds), *Implicit Memory: new directions in cognition, development and neuropsychology.* Hillsdale, NJ: Erlbaum.

Parkin, A. J. (in press) HM: the medial temporal lobes and memory. In C. Code, C. Wallesch, A.-R. Lecours and Y. Joanette (eds), *Classic Cases in Neuropsychology.* Hove: Erlbaum.

Parkin, A. J. and Gardiner, J. M. (in prep.) Modality effects and recollective experience.

Parkin, A. J. and Leng, N. R. C. (1993) *Neuropsychology of Amnesic Syndromes.* Hove: Erlbaum.

Parkin, A. J., Russo, R. (1990) Implicit and explicit memory and the automatic/effortful distinction. *European Journal of Cognitive Psychology*, 2, 71–80.

Parkin, A. J. and Russo, R. (in press) On the origin of functional differences in recollective experience. *Memory*.

Parkin, A. J. and Stampfer, H. (in press) Memory following atypical psychosis. In R. Campbell and M. Conway (eds), *Broken Lives.* Oxford: Basil Blackwell.

Parkin, A. J. and Streete, S. (1988) Implicit and explicit memory in young children and adults. *British Journal of Psychology*, 79, 362–369.

Parkin, A. J. and Walter, B. M. (1991) Aging, short-term memory and frontal dysfunction. *Psychobiology*, 19, 175–179.

Parkin, A. J. and Walter, B. M. (1992) Recollective experience, normal aging, and frontal dysfunction. *Psychology and Aging*, 7, 290–298.

Parkin, A. J. and Walter, B. M. (in prep.) The influence of age on temporal and spatial discrimination.

Parkin, A. J., Leng, N. R. C. and Hunkin, N. (1990a) Differential sensitivity to contextual information in diencephalic and temporal lobe amnesia. *Cortex*, 26, 373–380.

Parkin, A. J., Lewinsohn, J. and Folkard, S. (1982) The influence of emotion on immediate and delayed retention: Levinger and Clark reconsidered. *British Journal of Psychology*, 73, 389–393.

Parkin, A. J., Montaldi, D., Leng, N. R. C. and Hunkin, N. (1990b) Contextual cueing effects in the remote memory of alcoholic Korsakoff patients. *Quarterly Journal of Experimental Psychology*, 42A, 585–596.

Parkin, A. J., Pitchford, J. and Binschaedler, C. (submitted, a) Analysis of the executive memory impairment.

Parkin, A. J., Reid, T. and Russo, R. (1990c) On the differential nature of implicit and explicit memory. *Memory and Cognition*, 18, 507–514.

Parkin, A. J., Ruffmann, T. and Cox, S. (submitted, b) The influence of spacing on recall and recognition: a developmental study.

Payne, D. G. (1987) Hypermnesia and reminiscence in recall: a historical and empirical review. *Psychological Bulletin*, 101, 5–27.

Penfield, W. (1958) Some mechanisms of consciousness discovered during electrical stimulation of the brain. *Proceedings of the National Academy of Sciences*, 44, 51–66.

Perner, J. (1990) Experiential awareness and children's episodic memory. In W. Schneider and F. E. Weinert (eds), *Interactions Among Aptitudes, Strategies and Knowledge in Cognitive Performance*. New York: Springer Verlag.

Perner, J. (1992) Grasping the concept of representation: its impact on 4-year-olds' theory of mind and beyond. *Human Development*, 35, 146–155.

Perner, J. (submitted) Episodic memory and autonoetic consciousness: developmental evidence and a theory of childhood amnesia.

Perner, J. (1991) *Understanding the Representational Mind*. Cambridge, MA: MIT Press.

Perrig, W. J. and Perrig, P. (1988) Mood and memory: mood congruity effects in the absence of mood. *Memory and Cognition*, 16, 102–109.

Petrides, M. (1989) Frontal lobes and memory. In Boller, F. and Grafman, J. (eds), *Handbook of Neuropsychology*, 3, 75–90. Elsevier.

Piaget, J. (1954) *The Construction of Reality in the Child*. New York: Basic Books.

Pylyshyn, Z. W. (1973) What the mind's eye tells the mind's brain: a critique of mental imagery. *Psychological Bulletin*, 80, 1–24.

Pylyshyn, Z. W. (1979) The rate of 'mental rotation' of images: a test of a holistic analogue hypothesis. *Memory and Cognition*, 7, 19–28.

Pylyshyn, Z. W. (1981) The imagery debate: analogue media versus tacit knowledge. *Psychological Review*, 86, 16–45.

Rabbitt, P. M. A. and Abson, V. (1991) Do older people know how good they are? *British Journal of Psychology*, 82, 137–151.

Rabinowitz, J. C., Mandler, G. and Barsalou, L. W. (1979) Generation-recognition as an auxiliary retrieval strategy. *Journal of Verbal Learning and Verbal Behavior*, 18, 57–72.

Raine, A., Hulme, C., Chadderton, H. and Bailey, P. (1992) Verbal short-term memory span in speech-disordered children: implications for articulatory coding in short-term memory. *Child Development*, 62, 415–423.

Rajaram, S. (in press) The components of recollective experience: Remembering and knowing. *Memory and Cognition*.

Reber, A. S. (1976) Implicit learning of synthetic languages: The role of instructional set. *Journal of Experimental Psychology: human learning and memory*, 2, 88–94.

Reber, A. S. (1989) Implicit learning and tacit knowledge. *Journal of Experimental Psychology: general*, 118, 219–235.

Reber, A. S. (1992) The cognitive unconscious: an evolutionary perspective. *Consciousness and Cognition*, 1, 93–133.

Reber, A. S. and Allen, R. (1978) Analogic and abstraction strategies in synthetic grammar learning. *Cognition*, 6, 189–221.

Reder, L. M., Anderson, J. R. and Bjork, R. A. (1974) A semantic interpretation of encoding specificity. *Journal of Experimental Psychology*, 102, 648–656.

Richardson, J. T. E. (1980) *Mental Imagery and Human Memory*. London: Macmillan.

Richman, C. L. and Mitchell, D. B. (1979) Mental travel: some reservations. *Journal of Experimental Psychology: human perception and cognition*, 5, 13–18.

Rinck, M., Glowalla, U. and Schneider, K. (1992) Mood-congruent and mood-incongruent learning. *Memory and Cognition*, 20, 29–39.

Roediger, H. L. (1990) Implicit memory: a commentary. *Bulletin of the Psychonomic Society*, 28, 378–380.

Roediger, H. L. and Blaxton, T. A. (1987) Retrieval modes produce dissociations in memory for surface information. In D. S. Gorfein and R. S. Hoffman (eds), *Memory and Learning: the Ebbinghaus centennial conference*. Hillsdale, NJ: Erlbaum.

Roediger, H. L. III and McDermott, K. B. (in press) Implicit memory in normal human subjects. In H. Spinnler and F. Boller (Eds.) *Hanbook of Neuropsychology*, 8, Amsterdam, Elserier.

Roediger, H. L. III, Weldon, M. S. and Challis, B. H. (1989) Explaining dissociations between implicit and explicit measures of retention: a processing account. In H. L. Roediger III and F. I. M. Craik (eds), *Varieties of Memory and Consciousness: essays in honour of Endel Tulving*, 3–41. Hillsdale, NJ: Erlbaum.

Roediger, H. L., Rajaram, S. and Srinivas, K. (in press) Specifying criteria for distinguishing memory systems. In A. Diamond (ed.), *Development and Neural Bases of Higher Cognitive Function*. New York: Annals of the New York Academy of Sciences.

Rosch, E. (1973) Natural categories. *Cognitive Psychology*, 4, 328–349.

Rossmann, P. (1984) On the forgetting of word associations: Parkin et al. reconsidered. *Psychological Research*, 45, 389–394.

Rovee-Collier, C. (1989) The joy of kicking: memories, motives, and mobiles. In P. R. Solomon, G. R. Goethals, C. M. Kelley and B. R. Stephens (eds), *Memory: interdisciplinary Approaches*. New York: Springer Verlag.

Rovee-Collier, D. and Hayne, H. (1987) Reactivation of infant memory: implications for cognitive development. In H. W. Reese (ed.), *Advances in Child Development and Behavior*, 20. New York: Academic Press.

Rovee-Collier, C. K. and Shyi, C. W. G. (in press) A functional and cognitive analysis of infant long-term retention. In C. J. Brainerd, M. L. Howe and V. F. Reyna (eds), *The Development of Long-Term Memory*. New York: Springer Verlag.

Rovee-Collier, C. K., Sullivan, M. W., Enright, M., Lucas, D. and Fagen, J. W. (1980) Reactivation of infant memory. *Science*, 208, 1159–1161.

Rugg, M. D. and Doyle, M. C. (1992) Event-related potentials and recognition memory for low- and high-frequency words. *Journal of Cognitive Neuroscience*, 4, 69–79.

Rundus, D. (1971) Analysis of rehearsal processes in free recall. *Journal of Experimental Psychology*, 89, 63–77.

Russo, R. and Parkin, A. J. (in press) Age differences in implicit memory: more apparent than real. *Memory and Cognition*.

Rusted, J. M. (1988) Dissociative effects of scopolamine on working memory in healthy young volunteers. *Psychopharmacology*, 96, 487–492.

Ryle, G. (1949) *The Concept of Mind*. London: Hutchinson.

Salthouse, T. A. (1982) *Adult Cognition*. New York: Springer Verlag.

Salthouse, T. A. (1984) Effects of age and skill in typing. *Journal of Experimental Psychology: general*, 113, 345–371.

Santa, J. L. and Lamwers, L. A. (1974) Encoding specificity: fact or artifact? *Journal of Verbal Learning and Verbal Behavior*, 13, 412–423.

Schacter, D. L. (1987) Implicit memory: history and current status. *Journal of Experimental Psychology: learning, memory, and cognition*, 13, 501–518.

Schacter, D. L. (1992) Understanding implicit memory. *American Psychologist*, 47, 559–569.

Schacter, D. L., Cooper, L. A. and Delaney, S. M. (1990) Implicit memory for unfamiliar objects depends on access to structural descriptions. *Journal of Experimental Psychology: general*, 119, 5–24.

Schacter, D. L. and Moscovitch, M. (1984) Infant amnesics and dissociable memory systems. In M. Moscovitch (ed.), *Infant Memory: its relation to normal and pathological memory in humans and other animals. Advances in the Study of Communication and Affect*, 9, 173–216.

Schacter, D. L., Moscovitch, M., Tulving, E., McLachlan, D. R. and Freedman, M. (1986) Mnemonic precedence in amnesic patients: an analogue of the A$\overline{\text{B}}$ error? *Child Development*, 57, 816–823.

Schaie, K. W. (1965) A general model for the study of developmental problems. *Psychological Bulletin*, 64, 92–107.

Schank, R. C. (1982) *Dynamic Memory: a theory of reminding and learning in computers and people.* New York: Cambridge University Press.

Schneider, W. (1986) The role of conceptual knowledge and metamemory in the development of organizational principles in memory. *Journal of Experimental Child Psychology*, 42, 318–336.

Schneider, W. and Pressley, M. (1989) *Memory Development between 2 and 20.* New York: Springer Verlag.

Schnorr, J. A. and Atkinson, R. C. (1970) Study position and item differences in the short- and long-term retention of paired associates learned by imagery. *Journal of Verbal Learning and Verbal Behavior*, 9, 614–622.

Shankweiler, D. and Liberman, I. Y. (1976) Exploring the relations between reading and speech. In R. M. Knights and D. K. Bakker (eds), *The Neuropsychology of Learning Disorders: theoretical approaches.* Baltimore: University Park Press.

Sheehan, P. W. and Tilder, J. (1983) Effects of suggestibility and hypnosis on accurate and distorted retrieval from memory. *Journal of Experimental Psychology: learning, memory, and cognition*, 9, 283–293.

Shepard, R. N. and Chipman, S. (1970) Second-order isomorphism of internal representations: shapes of states. *Cognitive Psychology*, 1, 1–17.

Shepard, R. N. and Cooper, L. A. (1983) *Mental Images and their Transformations.* Cambridge, MA: MIT Press.

Shepard, R. N. and Metzler, J. (1971) Mental rotation of three-dimensional objects. *Science*, 171, 701–703.

Sherry, D. F. and Schacter, D. L. (1987) The evolution of memory systems. *Psychological Review*, 94, 439–454.

Shields, P. J. and Rovee-Collier, C. (1992) Long-term memory for context-specific category information at six months. *Child Development*, 63, 245–259.

Skinner, B. F. (1957) *Verbal Behavior.* New York: Appleton-Century-Crafts.

Sloman, S. A., Hayman, C. A. G., Ohta, N., Law, J. and Tulving, E. (1988) Forgetting in primed fragment completion. *Journal of Experimental Psychology: learning, memory, and cognition*, 14, 223–239.

Slowiaczek, M. L. and Clifton, C. (1980) Subvocalization and reading for meaning. *Journal of Verbal Learning and Verbal Behavior*, 19, 573–582.

Smith, G. J. and Spear, N. E. (1981) Role of proactive interference in infantile forgetting. *Animal Learning and Behavior*, 9, 371–380.

Smith, S. M. (1986) Environmental context-dependent memory: recognition memory using a short-term memory task for input. *Memory and Cognition*, 14, 347–354.

Smith, S. M. and Vela, E. (1992) Environmental context-dependent eyewitness recognition. *Applied Cognitive Psychology*, 6, 125–139.

Snodgrass, J. G., Bradford, S., Feenan, K. and Corwin, J. (1987) Fragmenting pictures on the Apple Macintosh computer for experimental and clinical applications. *Behavior Research Methods, Instruments and Computers*, 19, 270–274.

Spanos, N. P. (1986) Hypnotic behavior: a social-psychological interpretation of amnesia, analgesia, and 'trance logic'. *Behavioral and Brain Sciences*, 9, 449–502.

Sperling, G. (1960) The information available in brief visual presentations. *Psychological Monographs: general and applied*, 74, 1–29.

Squire, L. R. (1987) *Memory and Brain*. New York: Oxford University Press.

Squire, L. R. and Frambach, M. (1990) Cognitive skill learning in amnesia. *Psychobiology*, 18, 109–117.

Srinivas, K. and Roediger, H. L. (1990) Classifying implicit memory tests: category association and anagram solution. *Journal of Memory and Language*, 29, 389–412.

Stanhope, N. (1989) Source forgetting in young and elderly adults. Unpublished D. Phil. thesis, University of Sussex.

Stein, B. S. (1978) Depth of processing reexamined: the effects of the precision of encoding and test appropriateness. *Journal of Verbal Learning and Verbal Behavior*, 17, 165–174.

Street, R. F. (1931) *A Gestalt Completion Test*. New York: Teachers' College.

Stromeyer, C. F. (1982) An adult eidetiker. In U. Neisser (ed.), *Memory Observed*, 399–404. San Francisco: Freeman.

Stromeyer, C. F. and Psotka, J. (1970) The detailed texture of eidetic images. *Nature*, 225, 347–349.

Stroop, J. R. (1935) Studies of interference in serial verbal reactions. *Journal of Experimental Psychology*, 18, 643–662.

Sullivan, M. W. (1982) Reactivation: priming forgotten memories in human infants. *Child Development*, 57, 100–104.

Sutherland, N. S. (1972) Object recognition. In E. C. Carterette and M. P. Friedman (eds), *Handbook of Perception*, vol. 3. New York: Academic Press.

Swaab, D. F. (1991) Brain aging and Alzheimer's disease: 'wear and tear' versus 'use it or lose it'. *Neurobiology of Aging*, 2, 317–324.

Taylor, F. K. (1965) Cryptomnesia and plagiarism. *British Journal of Psychiatry*, 111, 1111–1118.

Toppino, T. C. (1991) Kasserman, J. E. and Mracek, W. A. The effect of spacing repetitions on the recognition memory of young children and adult. *Journal of Experimental Child Psychology*, 51, 123–38.

Treffert, D. A. (1988) The idiot savant: a review of the syndrome. *American Journal of Psychiatry*, 145, 563–572.

Tulving, E. (1972) Episodic and semantic memory. In E. Tulving and W. Donaldson (eds), *The Organization of Memory*, 382–404. New York: Academic Press.

Tulving, E. (1983) *Elements of Episodic Memory*. Oxford: Oxford University Press.

Tulving, E. (1985) How many memory systems are there? *American Psychologist*, 40, 385–398.

Tulving, E. (1987) Multiple memory systems and consciousness. *Human Neurobiology*, 6, 67–80.

Tulving, E. (1989) Memory, performance, knowledge and experience. *European Journal of Cognitive Psychology*, 1, 3–26.

Tulving, E. and Flexser, A. J. (1992) On the nature of the Tulving–Wiseman function. *Psychological Review*, 99, 543–546.

Tulving, E. and Osler, S. (1968) Effectiveness of retrieval cues in memory for words. *Journal of Experimental Psychology*, 77, 593–601.

Tulving, E. and Schacter, D. L. (1990) Priming and human memory. *Science*, 247, 301–306.

Tulving, E. and Thomson, D. M. (1973) Encoding specificity and retrieval processes in episodic memory. *Psychological Review*, 80, 353–373.

Tulving, E. and Wiseman, S. (1975) Relation between recognition and recognition failure of recallable words. *Bulletin of the Psychonomic Society*, 6, 79–82.

Tulving, E., Hayman, C. A. G. and MacDonald, C. A. (1991) Long-lasting perceptual priming and semantic learning in amnesia: a case experiment. *Journal of Experimental Psychology: learning, memory, and cognition*, 17, 595–617.

Tulving, E., Schacter, D. L. and Stark, H. A. (1982) Priming effects in word-fragment completion are independent of recognition memory. *Journal of Experimental Psychology: learning, memory, and cognition*, 8, 336–342.

Ucros, C. G. (1989) Mood state-dependent memory: a meta-analysis. *Cognition and Emotion*, 3, 139–169.

Vallar, G. and Baddeley, A. D. (1984) Phonological short-term store, phonological processing and sentence comprehension: a neuropsychological case study. *Cognitive Neuropsychology*, 1, 121–141.

Vallar, G. and Baddeley, A. D. (1987) Phonological short-term store and sentence processing. *Cognitive Neuropsychology*, 4, 417–438.

Vallar, G. and Baddeley, A. D. (1989) Developmental disorders of verbal short-term memory and their relation to sentence comprehension: a reply to Howard and Butterworth. *Cognitive Neuropsychology*, 6, 465–473.

Vandenberg, S. G. and Kuse, A. R. (1978) Mental rotations, a group test of three-dimensional spatial visualization. *Perceptual and Motor Skills*, 47, 599–604.

Verfaellie, M., Bauer, R. M. and Bowers, D. (1991) Autonomic and behavioral evidence of implicit memory in amnesia. *Brain and Cognition*, 15, 10–25.

Wagstaff, G. F. (1981) *Hypnosis: compliance and belief*. Brighton: Harvester Press.

Waldfogel, S. (1948) The frequency and affective character of childhood memories. *Psychological Monograph*, 62, no. 291.

Warburton, D. M. and Rusted, J. M. (1991) Cholinergic systems and information processing capacity. In J. Weinman and J. Hunter (eds), *Memory: neurochemical and abnormal perspectives*, 87–104. Chur: Harwood Academic Publishers.

Warrington, E. K. and Ackroyd, C. (1975) The effect of orienting tasks on recognition memory. *Memory and Cognition*, 3, 140–142.

Warrington, E. K. and Rabin, P. (1970) Perceptual matching in patients with cerebral lesions. *Neuropsychologia*, 8, 475–487.

Warrington, E. K. and Shallice, T. (1969) The selective impairment of auditory verbal short-term memory. *Brain*, 92, 885–896.

Warrington, E. K. and Weiskrantz, L. (1970) Amnesia: consolidation or retrieval? *Nature*, 228, 628–630.

Waters, G., Caplan, D. and Hildebrandt, N. (1991) On the structure of verbal short-term memory and its functional role in sentence comprehension: evidence from neuropsychology. *Cognitive Neuropsychology*, 91, 81–126.

Watkins, M. J. and Gardiner, J. M. (1979) An appreciation of generate-recognize theory of recall. *Journal of Verbal Learning and Verbal Behavior*, 18, 687–704.

Watkins, M. J. and Gibson, M. J. (1988) On the relation between perceptual priming and recognition memory. *Journal of Experimental Psychology: learning, memory, and cognition*, 14, 477–483.

Watson, J. B. (1914) *Behavior: an introduction to comparative psychology*. New York: Holt.

Watson, J. B. and Rayner, R. (1920) Conditioned emotional reactions. *Journal of Experimental Psychology*, 3, 1–14.

Waugh, N. C. and Norman, D. A. (1965) Primary memory. *Psychological Review*, 72, 89–104.

Wechsler, D. (1981) *Manual for the Wechsler Adult Intelligence Scale-Revised*. New York: Psychological Corporation.

Weeks, D. J. (1988) *The Anomalous Sentences Repetition Test*. London: National Foundation for Educational Research-Nelson.

Wellman, H. M. (1977) Preschoolers' understanding of memory-relevant variables. *Child Development*, 48, 1720–1723.

Wellman, H. M. (1978) Knowledge of the interaction of memory variables: a developmental study of metamemory. *Developmental Psychology*, 14, 24–29.

Wellman, H. M., Collins, J. and Glieberman, J. (1981) Understanding the combination of memory variables: developing conceptions of memory limitations. *Child Development*, 52, 1313–1317.

Weinert, F. E. (1986) Developmental variations of memory performance and memory related knowledge across the life span. In A. Sorensen, F. E. Weinert and L. R. Sherrod (eds), *Human Development: multidisciplinary perspectives*, 535–554. Hillsdale, NJ: Erlbaum.

West, R. L., Boatwright, L. K. and Schleser, R. (1984) The link between memory performance, self-assessment and affective status. *Experimental Aging Research*, 10, 197–200.

White, N. and Cunningham, W. R. (1982) What is the evidence for retrieval problems in the elderly? *Experimental Aging Research*, 8, 169–171.

Wicklegren, W. A. (1968) Sparing of short-term memory in an amnesic patient: implications for a strength theory of memory. *Neuropsychologia*, 6, 235–244.

Wilkinson, F. B. and Cargill, D. L. (1955) Repression elicited by story material based on the Oedipus complex. *Journal of Social Psychology*, 42, 209–214.

Williams, J. M. G. and Broadbent, D. E. (1986) Autobiographical memory in suicide attempters. *Journal of Abnormal Psychology*, 95, 145–149.

Williams, J. M. G., Watts, F. N., MacLeod, C. and Mathews, A. (1988) *Cognitive Psychology and Emotional Disorders*. Chichester: Wiley.

Wingfield, A., Stine, E. L., Lahar, C. J. and Aberdeen, J. S. (1988) Does the capacity of working memory change with age? *Experimental Aging Research*, 14, 103–107.

Winocur, G. (1982) Learning and memory deficits in institutionalized and noninstitutionalized old people: an analysis of interference effects. In *Aging and Cognitive Processes*, 155–181. New York: Plenum.

Winograd, E. (1976) Recognition memory for faces following nine different judgements. *Bulletin of the Psychonomic Society*, 8, 419–421.

Winograd, E. (1981) Elaboration and distinctiveness in memory for faces. *Journal of Experimental Psychology: human learning and memory*, 7, 181–190.

Witherspoon, D. and Moscovitch, M. (1989) Stochastic independence between two implicit memory tasks. *Journal of Experimental Psychology: learning, memory, and cognition*, 15, 22–30.

Wolf, A. S. (1980) Homicide and blackout in Alaskan natives. *Journal of Studies in Alcohol*, 41, 456–462.

Wollen, K. A., Weber, A. and Lowry, D. H. (1972) Bizarreness versus interaction of mental images as determinants of learning. *Cognitive Psychology*, 3, 518–523.

Worden, P. E. (1975) Effects of sorting on subsequent recall of unrelated items: a developmental study. *Child Development*, 46, 687–695.

Yarnell, P. R. and Lynch, S. (1973) The ding: amnestic states in football trauma. *Neurology*, 23, 196–197.

Young, R. K. (1985) Ebbinghaus: some consequences. *Journal of Experimental Psychology: learning, memory, and cognition*, 11, 491–495.

Yussen, S. R. and Levy, V. M. (1975) Developmental changes in predicting one's own span of short-term memory. *Journal of Experimental Child Psychology*, 19, 502–508.

Zelig, M. and Beidelman, W. B. (1981) The investigative use of hypnosis: a word of caution. *International Journal of Clinical and Experimental Hypnosis*, 29, 401–412.

Zelinski, E. M., Light, L. L. and Gilewski, M. J. (1984) Adult age differences in memory for prose: the question of sensitivity to passage structure. *Developmental Psychology*, 20, 401–412.

Index of Subjects

Index of Authors